More praise for *The Improvised Woman*

"Altogether engaging. . . . You don't have to be single to be charmed by [Clements's] smart take on relationships in the '90s. . . . *The Improvised Woman* doesn't glide over the messy contradictions that accompany being human. . . . Clements gives her interviewees center stage to speak their minds, and appends a series of thoughtful, witty essays."   —Lauren Shapiro, *Newsweek*

"In her brilliant, enticing book, *The Improvised Woman*, journalist Marcelle Clements explores what life is like for the 43 million women over age 18 and unmarried in America today. What she finds is that many are living below the radar of American cultural life."   —Sherryl Connelly, *New York Daily News*

"*The Improvised Woman* challenges almost everything that has been written, said, or thought about the subject. . . . Just as Betty Friedan did in 1963 with *The Feminine Mystique*, Clements has put her finger on an enormous social change which has not yet been fully acknowledged."   —Joan Smith, *Guardian*

"[Clements] is wise, non-judgmental and patient as she gains the trust of these women, who appear to be as interested in this study as the author is—and as readers, especially other single women—will be."   —*Publishers Weekly* (starred review)

"This book gave me the most fabulous weekend. I spent all day yesterday in front of the fireplace with it, savoring it, marveling at Clements's prodigious mind and reach, nodding vociferously in parts, rereading other parts just for the pure pleasure of her voice. *The Improvised Woman* is a gift to single women and their huge invisible revolution. Marcelle Clements not only dispels the odious myths, she also gives us visibility and the confidence to be seen and heard and respected."   —Mary Kay Blakely

"Who is living the well-lived life, and how are they living it? These are the questions Marcelle Clements asks in a book that shows

D0111939

how far most women's lives depart from the one tale—the fairy tale—we've all grown up on. The women Clements speaks with—articulate, truthful, and funny—are telling a whole new story about fulfillment, esteem, relationship, aloneness. It's important that all of us, married or single, with or without children, listen. This book is strong and riveting."   —Dalma Heyn

"It's your life, honey, but I'm telling you—you want this book. Marcelle Clements tunes into the station called Single Women, but instead of static, she finds a whole new song to dance to. And she's just the writer to do this, sharp, fearless, and profound. Here are the women the world used to feel sorry for, but after you read her book, you will never see them—us!—as anything but cool."
              —E. Jean Carroll

THE IMPROVISED WOMAN

Other books by Marcelle Clements

THE DOG IS US

ROCK ME

THE IMPROVISED WOMAN

Single Women
Reinventing
Single Life

MARCELLE CLEMENTS

W · W · NORTON & COMPANY

NEW YORK   LONDON

For information about permission to reproduce selections from this
book, write to Permissions, W. W. Norton & Company, Inc.,
500 Fifth Avenue, New York, NY 10110

The text of this book is composed in 11/13.5 Fairfield LH Light
with the display set in B Peignot Bold and Fairfield LH Bold Italic
Desktop composition by Gina Webster
Manufacturing by the Haddon Craftsmen, Inc.
Book design by Margaret M. Wagner

Portions of this book were previously published in Ms. magazine.

Library of Congress Cataloging-in-Publication Data

Clements, Marcelle.
The improvised woman : single women reinventing single life /
by Marcelle Clements.
p.   cm.
ISBN 0-393-04643-5
1. Single women—United States. I. Title.
HQ800.2.C54   1998
305.48'9652–DC21   97–38923
                              CIP

ISBN 0-393-31953-9 pbk.

W. W. Norton & Company, Inc.,
500 Fifth Avenue, New York, N.Y. 10110
www.wwnorton.com

W. W. Norton & Company Ltd.,
10 Coptic Street, London WC1A 1PU
1 2 3 4 5 6 7 8 9 0

CONTENTS

PREFACE TO THE PAPERBACK EDITION

Some projects are harder to part with than others, of course, especially those left unfinished in one way or another. I had a very hard time letting go of *The Improvised Woman,* not so much because of what was left out but because of what was to come. For months following its publication in the spring of 1998, I kept running into people whose stories I simply had to make note of . . . just in case. With a consistency I stopped finding odd, these stories often came from the women who interviewed me when I was promoting the book. I came to expect, once the microphones were turned off at the end of a radio show, that the M.C. would let me know she had taken a personal interest in the program because she was also single.

Why take notes? Because here was a situation that seemed both new and reassuring. If the host, the guest, and the callers of a radio show were all women improvising their lives, it suddenly felt as if one didn't necessarily have to feel outside the norm because of one's marital status. It was a sense, for the first time, that there might now be a critical mass of unmarried women.

My notes grew to fill several files. Indeed, I began to notice that I was hearing more and more anecdotes, and also that my clips from newspaper and magazine articles were proliferating to such an extent that I felt quite gratified as the author of *The Improvised Woman* but increasingly outwitted in my attempts to clear my desk of evidence that uncoupled women were indeed constructing a new consciousness.

When I first began work on this subject a decade ago, every bit of such evidence seemed hard to come by. Now, no one was even trying to argue the authenticity of the phenomenon. "Marriage Loses Some Sparkle in United States," ran the headline in *USA Today* in January

1999. We were informed that according to the latest census bureau report just over half of all U.S. adults were married and living with their spouses last year. Among 25- to 34-year-olds, about 35 percent had never been married. Among African Americans in this age group, 53 percent had never been married. The Census Bureau report, "Marital Status and Living Arrangements," also found that 10 percent of all U.S. adults were "currently divorced" in 1998 (as opposed to 3.2 percent in 1970). Ten percent! That's like a small country.

By now single women have at last acquired a presence in this culture—though not necessarily always associated with the complexity and respect to which their numbers and experience should have entitled them. Every newspaper in America, it seemed, had to publish an editorial about whether *Ally McBeal* had a good or a bad attitude. *Sex in the City* ran on HBO as a much-noted series on attractive and ambitious single people. *People* magazine repeatedly published cover stories on unmarried female stars who had children on their own. Books like *Bridget Jones' Diary* and *Diary of a Nobody* were lauded or decried on an ongoing basis. Now, everyone, it seemed, had an opinion about the single women phenomenon, and on any given day it would be declared good, bad, immoral, threatening, lamentable, or exciting. To some the increased visibility of single women was eerie. To others it was depressing. Some found all this inevitable; others experienced it as sci-fi.

If only half of all adults in America are living with a spouse, who makes up the "other half" and why? For all the thousands of words printed on the subject, the myriad sound bytes emitted by television and radio shows of every conceivable stripe, the innumerable conclusions we have been treated to, there still remains a mystery at the heart of this subject, a lack of what we lately call "closure." I think this is because the roots of the phenomenon are as deep and as old as marriage itself, and its manifestations are as varied, rich, subtle, and nuanced as the extraordinary spectrum of women who are its actors and witness. Because *The Improvised Woman* is as much about a set of contradictions as it is about some statistical trends, it seems to me that the paperback edition is timely indeed. For all that the numerical evidence is even more substantial than a year ago, the details of how these many women got from there to here seem as endlessly varied—provocative clues to how the "other half" lives.

M.C.
May 1999

INTRODUCTION

At some point, I came to feel that my life had turned out "strangely." I never expected to be quite so on my own or to have a place that belonged only to me and to think of it as my home, making all my own decisions, keeping my own hours, sleeping alone. Sleeping alone! I hadn't imagined that I would ever be setting a professional course (or an aesthetic one, for that matter), without a husband's or lover's interference or that I would be financially responsible for myself and a small child. Growing up, I wasn't sure what I felt about being a mother, and I never expected to be a single mother. I certainly never expected to become the principal point person and liaison between my own mother and the outside world—let alone that I would be that sort of mother and that sort of daughter all at once. If I had imagined the life I now lead, I doubt I would have wanted it, but it also wouldn't have occurred to me that I could handle it, logistically or psychologically, so I'm surprised and pleased to find that I do. I wandered and meandered my way to here, only figuring out afterward what I had done. This book is, in part, an attempt to do just that.

When I came to the United States from France, aged ten, girls of my generation were routinely exhorted to follow models. And that's a good thing because if we had been asked what it meant to be a woman, we wouldn't have had a clue, and even now, casting my mind back, it seems to me there was a problem of too many models. In a way, we collected them—sort of like 45s—a little of this and that, a few of these. I had two complete sets (at least). I came to this country knowing of Brigitte Bardot and Simone de Beauvoir. I soon learned of Sue Barton, R.N., and Hannah Arendt, Ph.D., and of the great Margaret Mead. That year, according to a Gallup poll, Eleanor Roosevelt was the most admired woman in the United States. I had read Françoise Sagan and Georges Sand. I was yet to discover Betty and Veronica, Archie's girlfriends, and the girls in the love comics who always shed a tear when they were kissed, and the girls who did the stroll on *American Bandstand*. I acquired a collection of Ponytail desk accessories. In both blue and pink plastic, they were stamped with the eponymous teenager, lying on her stomach, feet crossed in the air behind her—and I believe there were spinning 45s hovering about her. I had my own collection of 45s too, and had listened a thousand times to The Teddy Bears' "To Know Him Is to Love Him," in soft, close harmony, with plenty of echo on top; "My Boyfriend's Back"; "Happy Birthday, Baby"; and "Leader of the Pack," the latter being an ode to cool boys, with the sound of a motorcycle revving between choruses. Marilyn Monroe had not yet committed suicide, and Natalie Wood had not drowned. But there was a bevy of adolescent blondes such as Tuesday Weld, Carol Lynley, Sandra Dee, and Yvette Mimieux, who were always "getting in trouble" in movies like *A Summer Place* and *Blue Denim*. At the same time, I had found my way to Willa Cather, Dorothy Parker, Carson McCullers, and Harper Lee. And before much more time had elapsed there was Betty Friedan and Aretha, the Queen of Soul, Jacqueline Kennedy, and Charlotte Moorman, who played the cello naked.

I am not sure when girls totally gave up struggling to define themselves, trying to put together something from all of the above. Women who are older or younger than I am will have their own reference points, but what many of us have in common is that we left the various reductive potentials behind—the perky conformism of the pony-tailed teenagers, the stylized, melancholy-tinged sluttiness of the girls who were not virgins, the majesty of the august widows whose public lives began in earnest only when their duties to their husbands ended. None of us could keep the entire equation in her head at any one time. The Civil Rights movement, the Gay Liberation movement, the antiwar movement, the changes in men, advances in reproductive and contraceptive science—all of these altered how we thought of identity, home, gender, how we viewed our bodies, how we envisioned the life of the mind and the life of the spirit. Meanwhile, class became a fuzzy category. Money and social entrée, which once had guaranteed security, were daily devalued. Having a husband—*having* a husband—or not became one of the very few self-contained contexts left, a definition of sorts. We didn't expect that this one tidy category would become more and more hazy as time went on.

"I'm off the grid," a woman in her late thirties told me recently. "Self-supporting, bringing up two kids, divorced two years ago and not one date since."

Many women have stumbled into no grid to replace the matrimonial grid, no definition other than the insufficient "married" and its sole official variation, "unmarried." As a result, we have felt ourselves becoming conclusively undefined, and, as it turned out, this is a rather interesting thing to be.

Feminism did not replace marriage as a source of definition. That was the whole point of the women's movement: to explode definition. Many women could allow themselves the luxury of being single only once they had learned to identify with other women, thereby abandoning many of the antiwomen stigmas that had prevented most from doing anything new guiltlessly, let alone live on their own, make their own money, and choose their friends and lovers. Of course, some may say that single women trade one type of stigma—the age-old one of the inferior second sex—for a new type, that of the oddball loner. But then others point to the negative image that some women feel is attached to taking care of their children full time. But, as always with prejudice, if some of us have a problem with any such stigma, we all do, for one woman's image is a little bit every woman's image, no? At the very least, that would be the feminist position, and it's a good one to live by, in my view, although I'm afraid that single women—for all that it may have enabled their emergence—are not what feminism bargained for. The feminist paradigm had to do with the two-person relationship; everything outside of that frame was a free-for-all.

For myself, I have yet to formally agree to any one identity as a woman—I only know that I am one. Like many of my peers, I have given up for now on the entire subject of identity and the boat it came in on. Too busy. But after most of a decade of living alone, I do have a sense of leading a life that has a certain kind of order and a distinct atmosphere. These aren't always what I would prefer them to be, but I find myself wishing I could improve them rather than ever desiring to leave them behind altogether. It is in this sense that my life has turned out "strangely." At some point there came the very perplexing realization that I was, of all things, the one thing that I would not have expected: I was fine. Alone, I was fine as I had not been earlier in my life. Most surprising of all was my ongoing dearth of tediously enmeshed sentimental (romantic, sexual, whichever you prefer) relationships, a type of attachment I had always had, if anything, an excess of. I had spent nearly all of my adult life in one relationship or another. Some were better than others, of course, but I had never made a determination against the *genre*; I had just assumed that either I sometimes picked the really wrong men or I needed to do more work on myself. One or both may be correct, but I began to consider whether there wasn't an even more generic problem when, at the beginning of the '90s, after the nasty and protracted breakup of an eleven-year relationship, I found myself thinking that I would rather, much rather, be alone than go through anything like that again. Soon I realized that I was not only living without a man, but that I was also living without looking for one or expecting to be found by one. I didn't rule it out. I don't rule it out. But I came to characterize my present way of living as: permanent, at least for now.

It was then that the idea for this book occurred to me, spurred by my own reaction to my circumstances. How was it that solitude didn't feel to me to be a punishment, an unfortunate fate I had to resign myself to? Like many of my subjects, I still haven't gotten completely used to the surprisingly pure pleasure of living alone. On occasion, my very ease in this kind of life feels worrisome to me. And, of course, sometimes I feel lonely. But when I try to decide whether or not I wish it to be an interim solution or a permanent one, even in the safety of my own fantasies I find myself loathe to give up the romance of independence. But then, and this is the thesis of this book, it is when The Plan fails that we notice we've begun a more interesting improvisation.

I certainly had never expected to be anything that I would have been willing to call "single." Had I guessed that I would wind up living without a man on an ongoing basis, I would have envisioned this solitude as interestingly "marginal" or "idiosyncratic." I wouldn't have thought to place myself in as corny a demographic category as "single"—a word from which there has long emanated the odor of crummy wine, crowded bar scenes, and creepy personal ads, and even this is an improvement over the image that preceded it: the erotically desiccated unescorted female.

Rather than noticing a change in society's attitude toward single-ness, I was aware of a change in attitude toward marriage. A little less than ten years after discovering "To Know Him Is to Love Him" and Ponytail pencil cases, I was married, briefly. I still see my for-mer husband sometimes, and his current wife, both of whom I like, so that when I look back at my decision to marry, I don't think that I was wrong. I was only young. Although I did not legally remarry, it would be twenty years before I reached a point where I would think of myself as being neither in a relationship nor recovering from one. Looking back, now it all makes a certain kind of sense.

It's still true that very few women who are my contemporaries would have made staying single their first choice. But, at the very least, it has become an option that seems preferable to others and, at best, it's an opportunity for a life that is in a number of ways rich-er. For older women, too, things have changed. More and more, those who were widowed found that they didn't necessarily want to remarry. For that generation of women now in their sixties, seven-ties, and eighties, marriage has very specific, inexorable responsibil-ities, and remarriage renews them. Many of these women simply don't want to live with a new boss. As for younger women, indepen-dence is no longer a luxury, it's a necessity for self-fulfillment, and attempting to fulfill oneself is a matter of course.

What happened was an essential change in metaphor. The rela-tionships between men and women once were drama in the age-old style, a sort of opera filled with passion, lust, intrigue, artful domi-nance and submission, and painful third-act curtains. Sure there were solos, but it wasn't long before the *tutti* came right back on for the chorus. Now the theatrical old forms seem obsolete, revivals at best. Not only are relationships searching for new forms, but the lack of a central sexual relationship has become a genre all by itself.

Even before I myself became unattached, I had a number of

friends who were, and I knew that the world of these women was as credible and complete a reality as that of the world of couples. I found I was attracted to the atmosphere of their reality. Different qualities are prized in this new group—or, rather, among these people who no longer see themselves as conforming to all the laws of the old group. Independence is very highly valued, for instance, as are a capacity for solidarity and a well-developed sense of humor.

On the downside, some women complain that, as much as they may love being with women, they just don't have enough contact with men and are afraid of being swallowed up in a ghetto of women. And, as always, many women feel that, as single people and/or single parents, they are especially discriminated against because they are women. But, more and more, single women say they feel, of all things, comfortable.

This was already true when I began to live alone, at the end of the 1980s. As time went on, this became even truer. While I was work-ing on this book, the phenomenon I wanted to describe continued to evolve, and what had once seemed eccentric became pretty ordi-nary. Ten years ago, never marrying or staying single after a divorce was seen as maladapted, even by the women themselves. "I just have to do this for myself," a woman would say, to explain what seemed like crazy behavior. Now being single—at least for a time—seems to many women like the most reasonable option. When I first began my interviews, in the early '90s, I would usually have to explain that I was exploring the possibility that being single is really a choice for a woman and that the second-class status of unmarried women is based on an outdated norm. The women I spoke to seemed surprised to find that they often did not at all envy their married friends. By the time I ended, this was deemed unremark-able. The resulting reorganization in the status hierarchy is still in transition, but some of its consequences are already obvious. "I don't even put down 'divorced' when I'm filling out forms," an attractive fifty-one-year-old woman recently told me. She said that she viewed her former married life as "pathological" and that she felt complete-ly identified with single women. She had married in her twenties, a decision that she now describes as "crazy; I don't know what got into me." Divorced five years later, she has since had affairs but rules out remarrying. "If people ask me, I say that I consider myself single but unavailable."

And what about love in all this, old-fashioned love? It's still a big question, and none of the women I talked to seemed to feel she had finessed the problems it poses. When I first began interviewing, women often told me that they would love to "find" a relationship or to construct one with the "right" person. By the time I ended my interviews, these very terms were questioned, usually referred to with an irony that indicated both disappointment and acceptance and, increasingly, the perception that not being in a long-term relationship offers its own advantages. Love has always been puzzling, but the confidence that a solution can be worked out on one's own or with a therapist or in the right relationship with the right person has faded dramatically. I would say it is the biggest problem many of us face. But the solution is not as easy as "finding someone." Perhaps it is more useful to think of finding *something*, some way of being that allows a woman to have some of the best of both lives, just as many men historically have.

In the course of this decade I asked over a hundred women to talk to me about being single, how they got there, whether they're sorry or glad, what the texture of their experience is. To talk about single women in America now means to talk about power, status, money, class, family, sense of home, fears of old age and death, romance, love, sex, and the future of gender. There exists a very wide range of judgments among single women about being single, plus a spectrum of contradictory emotions that any one woman has over a period of time.

Each chapter in this book consists of what I call a mosaic—clusters of excerpts edited down from thousands of pages of interviews with single women—preceded by an introductory essay. In these introductions I attempt less to answer the questions raised by my interviewees than to offer a parallel commentary, one with which I aim to help provide the reader with a sampling of the numerous provocative hypotheses and conclusions that still make this subject incendiary to many people in this country. I hope less to convince the reader of my point of view than to persuade you to consider reshuffling your own conclusions, just as I was obliged to reshuffle mine again and again.

What is a single woman? I define her as the U.S. Census Bureau does, more or less. She is eighteen and up, divorced, widowed, or never married. That is to say, my statistics are conservative, since the census does not list as single those women who live separated from their husbands, even though of the 58,748,000 married women in this country, millions are separated on a long-term basis.

I spoke to women of many ages—the youngest were in their early twenties and the oldest were among the so-called old-old. The doyenne of my subjects recently celebrated her ninety-fourth birthday, and she is not the least enthusiastic supporter of the single woman's life. Widowed several decades ago, she wouldn't consider remarrying, she told me. "If a woman needs money, I can understand it," she explained. "But otherwise I think a mature woman would be mad to consider it."

My subjects were also economically heterogeneous. You will meet very poor women and very rich ones within these pages, inhabitants of many different regions of the United States. Still, I do not offer my sample as necessarily representative of the general population. Some important groups are missing: There are no women currently on welfare; there are no prostitutes; there are no illegal aliens (that I know of). There are no subjects who define themselves as purely lesbians, though there are numerous women who are either bisexual or describe themselves as heterosexual but who have had affairs with women or sex with men and women together. I interviewed no teenagers because if a woman is too young to be married, she is, by my definition, too young to be single. And there are no older women in nursing homes. In the latter category I did try to obtain an interview with a friend's aunt, who was the only person to turn down a request for an interview in these last few years. She had been in a nursing home for some time, and I had hoped she would give me the benefit of her distinctive vantage point. "I think she's embarrassed," her niece explained to me, "that she never got married." I still remember the remark because at the time I thought it would be the first of many such refusals.

On the contrary, the single women I ran into or was referred to were extraordinarily welcoming and eager—relieved, in many instances—to speak. Many of them understood what I was getting at before I said anything to characterize it. "I'm so happy someone is writing this book!" is something I heard more than once. Indeed, at a certain point, I began to notice a predictable dichotomy. Ten years ago, when I told a married woman what sort of book I was working on, I was often treated to a look that implied an assumption that commiseration was in order. One such married woman exclaimed: "Oh, but it's so sad. . . ." by which she meant *the very topic* of single women. Even when I explained myself, I was often met with friendly but distanced reactions. Now, though, married women are much less likely to express consolation or puzzlement, much more likely to be openly curious. One recent bride (a doctor in her late forties) actually tried to persuade me to interview her. "I haven't been married long, and I still remember everything," she pointed out, "And I so enjoyed being single. I love being married, but I had such a great time when I was single." From the start, however, single women often said, "What a great idea." And though my subject was sometimes greeted with moans and groans—or rather, *mock* moans and groans—these were meant to be funny. Or, more precisely, both funny and not funny. As time went on, the moans and groans endured, but I heard two phrases more and more often. The first was, of all things: "What fun!" The second was: "Finally!"

When I began working on this book in the early '90s, there were thirty-eight million single women. Now there are close to forty-three million. Eleven million single women then headed households; now more than twelve million do. Delayed marriage, divorce rates, low remarriage rates, and longer life spans have created a world in which *most* women can expect to be married only half of their adult lives.

The change in the status and psyche of single women from *Cosmo* icon to powerful sociocultural player is one of the most significant trends of the end of the American century. It will be a major contributing factor in defining the future of our politics and economy. It is transforming our cultural ideals, both reflecting and hastening the most important social change in our era: the dramatic shift that has led more and more women, married and unmarried, to feel that emancipation is at least as desirable—and in some cases more important than—a successful marriage.

This phenomenon is due to three cataclysmic transformations: the postwar economy, feminism in its various forms, and more than a century of slow disintegration of gender stereotypes. In turn, the single-women surge is bound to have a domino effect, and the ensu-ing social transfiguration will shatter our most deeply held beliefs, the very way in which we conceptualize the relations between the sexes. Already, the spinster and the tart seem obsolete categories, not relevant to the new thinking. But some even more profound fan-tasies may be about to take a tumble, some of our most categorical archetypes may turn out to be mere artifacts of a quickly receding past. Cinderella and her pal Sleeping Beauty had better watch out, but so should the earth mother, the defeminized career woman, the oversexed bimbo, the desexualized weirdo, the promiscuous, greedy, welfare-abusing teenager, and the many varieties of cast-out misfit.

Just the other day, I noticed for the first time a big ad on the side panel of a bus shelter, of a woman dressed in white panties and a bra. I knew what brand it was because in the lower right hand cor-ner it said, 100% WONDERBRA. The woman's hair was blond and blowing in the wind. She was performing a dancer's kick, wearing a big dazzling smile. There were three lines of print running across her body. The top line read BEING SINGLE and the bottom line read DOESN'T MEAN GRIEVING and the middle line read, in big bright let-ters, CONFIDENCE.

For all that it may be against the will of those who fear change, the reality is here to stay—no matter how disruptive, disorienting, threatening, frightening. Women, married and unmarried, are increasingly conscious of their power and numbers. Most obviously, for all to see, they now hold powerful jobs. They own homes, they own second homes, they take out mortgages, they make invest-ments. They are running for office and winning. They choose their lovers. They decide how to educate their children. They talk back to their mothers. Of course, the whole world is changing, but women are changing faster.

By the time I concluded these talks, it was hard to go anywhere and *not* meet many women of various types who had wound up being single. By the time I finished, I felt as if the wave had turned into a tide and that a social cycle was nearing completion. And not a moment too soon, I might add, because I had long fallen behind every deadline. I had never expected to work on this project long enough to feel as if I were a witness to a complete cycle of any sort. My original intention was only to collect some voices, to talk about the texture of the experience of being single now. It's not surprising that it took me so long to conclude this project. Like many women, my life is rushed, fragmented, and sometimes feels overwhelming. In a way it's superefficient, though that doesn't prevent it from being very difficult to get anything done. My three-year-old son and my ninety-one-year-old mother provide challenges beyond what the human imagination can encompass, I freelance for a living, I work out of my home, I live in a difficult and overexciting urban environment. Perhaps my life has indeed turned out "strangely," as I am reminded mostly when I find that many thorny situations arise in which there is no precedent to turn to. When I fill out my son's preschool applications, I've finally figured out I can write N.A. on the line that asks for the father's name. When I am running interference for my mother in the world of (dis)organized medicine, health insurance companies, and unpleasant building management agents, I've become accustomed to assuming a certain authority that I think I would prefer not to have. My ambivalent relationship to authority is probably one of the factors that led me in this uncharted direction to begin with. But my guess is that authority itself is mutating into a different role in the culture, and the crisis in marriage results from that rather than the other way around.

Straying from tradition makes many people very anxious, and much of what follows is about how single women deal with their own and other people's anxieties. And yet there is a built-in paradox here. The more women have a choice to be unmarried—and, therefore, to divorce—the more marriage itself can be seen as a choice. Indeed, one of the most peculiar aspects of our social reorganization is that where there was once a wall between the fortress of the married and the wilderness of the unmarried, there is now only a thin, permeable membrane. And, increasingly, many women do not exclude the possibility of passing from one state to the other. You can stay single for X amount of time and then remarry. Or live with someone to "see what happens." And then you could go back and forth among your options. People marry, divorce, remarry. They pause between relationships for a month or for a year or for a decade. They cohabit as if they were married. They commute to their marriage from different cities. Someone's ex-wife is friendly with his new wife's ex-husband. Someone's ex-husband is going out with your ex-husband. There's so much mobility now that motion itself seems to have become a way of life. Through it all, people are well, ill, lonely, cheerful, pessimistic, or forward-looking—whether or not they are married. They fall out of love and fall in love again; sometimes they are redeemed by love and sometimes not. And not only does life go on, but it does so at a vertiginous pace. Turn-of-the century consciousness speeds on, whooshes by, roars away with us, digitally diffuses us; married, unmarried, we're in a hurry.

If you need order, if you want everything to be tidy, you're in big trouble. For me—and this is very personal—what may be the most interesting part of living the way I do is my current relationship to randomness, to improvisation of every kind. I used to struggle against it. I loved adventure, which is certainly a form of the unknown, essentially as a kind of play, but ongoing disarray made me anxious. But lately I've begun to think there is a more natural sense of order to be located within oneself, more and more independently of any of the current rules. Living outside of marriage or some equivalent frees one from any number of other attachments— not just to one other person but to so many social and emotional structures. Unexpectedly, we may get, after all, what women have long been saying they want: liberation, at least from others. To a point. What does it really mean, to be liberated? Perhaps only that we get to choose our own commitments or make them up as we go along. And sometimes that works, and sometimes the joke is on us—but, at the very least, we are led to sense a vastness of potential.

THE IMPROVISED WOMAN

HOW I GOT FROM THERE TO HERE

Does It Really Matter Whose Fault It Was?

Of all the tragic and amusing declarations women make regarding being single, surely the oddest is a certain ritual observation usually stated with an air of mock horrified astonishment, as if the speaker still hadn't come to terms with a bizarre reality. "There are no men!" one woman will proclaim to another. The delivery almost makes it sound like a joke.

Many assumptions greet this coded announcement. You know that when a single woman announces, "There are no men!" she doesn't mean there are no men. Or that she has no interest in men. She may be perfectly willing—eager, in some cases—to be living with someone or married or having a pleasant and sweet albeit temporary romance, or even just hitting the hay with someone now and then. It doesn't mean that she is incapable of desire or that there are no men who desire her. Indeed, she may be having a passionate affair with a man (or more than one), though in all likelihood she is not. It's not that there are no men, it's that there are no men she wants to want, or who would want her the way she wants to be wanted.

What the statement "There are no men!" is really announcing is that the speaker refuses to be perceived as available for just any man who comes along. That she'd rather be alone than in a terrible relationship and that even a mediocre relationship can feel terrible. And maybe she'd rather be alone, period. It is her awareness of choices that separates the single woman from the pitiable "single" of '70s and '80s lore, the distressed and appalling love seeker who used to go out looking for Mr. Right and come home with Mr. Goodbar. The female "single" was not merely unmarried, she was assumed to be frantically longing to marry . . . "anyone." She was an icon of despair and crypto-passivity. Descending from an entirely different set of roots, the evolved, purely single woman, on the other hand, can be anything: desperate or hopeful or simply busy with something else. She is extremely unlikely to conceptualize her life so simplistically that she could refer to the "right man" with a straight face.

Of course, as we know all too well, there are still plenty of "singles" around, plenty of distress and appalling love-seeking, cheap wine, personal ads. Perhaps I need not remind you of the horrors brought to us courtesy of the new technology: the innumerable images in television commercials of people with weird hair fervently promoting computerized dating ventures. In many places in America this is deemed to be the norm. At the very least, it's the association that people have with single women. But I propose that this retro consciousness is less prevalent than we are constantly told. That there are still women who would do anything for "a date" (a date?) is certain, but it's absurd to represent their quest as the only game in town. It's too easy to sell them products, and hope, and make fun of them, once the stereotype is implacably set, just as it's easy to identify the poor black teenagers who monopolize our national image of single mothers. The more interesting truth is that these pathetic singles and poor young women may have a kind of personal style and aspiration that hasn't been noticed in the rush to pigeonhole them as pitiful stereotypes—at the very least a doubleness. If they were asked different questions than "Are you desperate?" their decisions might not seem quite as desperate.

In any event, there are millions of women who are different, who are conscious of having made a choice to be single, at least temporarily. What's generally picked up on, especially by people who feel confused by the idea of any real life outside the couple or the traditional family, is either their wishing for relationships or their inability to stay in them. But, again, when asked different questions, these women's consciousness is quickly revealed as much more ambivalent and rich than either of these clichés. And it's not difficult to find them if one has a reason to do so. My sense is that the desperate single belongs to the past. Despair of the future is more complicated than getting a husband, not getting a husband, losing a husband—or a wife. It is both men and women who, in the present, grapple with uncertainties to an extraordinary degree.

For the new single woman, even someone who is the right man for the moment can seem the wrong potential husband. Perhaps, in the parlance of the times, the relationship just doesn't have enough "sparks" or sufficient "commonality," or it suffers from an inability of the parties to "sustain" commitment or "achieve" intimacy. Too many problems "need to be worked out." Or it has just come to feel like it's not worth the trouble. Perhaps she views him as intolerant of her flaws, cold or tyrannical, potentially abusive, a cheat, a deadbeat, a pathological workaholic. Perhaps he's narcissistic, stifling, sexist or sexless, or simply uninterested. Perhaps he's gay. And some of the types that used to appeal are now turnoffs. A once-attractive man may have a problem with the "girls" if he's a go-to-bed-with-your-boots-on alcoholic, a sexual compulsive, relentlessly rejecting, closed and uncommunicative, neurotically elusive. Men who are enigmatically repressed, egomaniacs, relentless Casanovas, or pathological jocks are no longer so much in favor. Of course, most women will fall for one or more of those outdated bad boys of yesteryear one or more times. But if she is unfortunate enough to marry him, such a woman is increasingly likely to eventually come to and divorce him. Once they break up, she'll get herself to a therapist or a support group, and she'll at least try not to remarry him or his ilk.

And then there's the problem of money, work, and unequal contributions. In her book *The Second Shift*, Arlie Hoshschild tells us that there is "an indirect way in which the woman pays at home for economic discrimination outside the home." Women work roughly fifteen hours longer each week than men, amounting to an extra month of twenty-four-hour days a year. And that figure has gone up since Hochschild's 1989 book.

The higher the income of a couple, the more likely it is that the woman is contributing more than half. *Money* magazine reported recently that 75 percent of married female executives at Fortune 1000 companies outearn their husbands. This is not a phenomenon of the underclass. The more educated and prosperous a woman is, we know, the less likely she is to marry or remarry. There is a popular assumption that this is evidence of a feminine failure: These women aren't marrying or remarrying because they can't find husbands. But it might be much more accurate to say that they can't find husbands whose wives they want to be. Indeed, in a story headed "Divorced, Middle-Aged and Happy: Women, Especially, Adjust to the '90s," Jane Gross of the *New York Times* tells us that demographers and sociologists who interpret divorce and remarriage rate "agree that there is an overriding explanation, and it contradicts the mildewed stereotype about women desperate to tie the knot and men itching for adventure. These experts say that increasingly it is women who now look skeptically at marriage, often viewing it as a bad bargain if they have gained financial and sexual independence."

The motivation may be less pragmatic. Perhaps he's boring, which an astonishing number of women now find a sufficient deterrent, unwilling to continue pretending this is a frivolous consideration. Or he may play so hard to get that it's a turnoff. In this category, today's man is baffling, much more so than the previous generation's. Whatever the reasons—and there are doubtless many—men now express their desire, or lack of it, in an oblique and puzzling manner. A number of women have told me they feel a tremendous switch has occurred, and men have become exasperating teases. Of course, no one has statistics on the ratio, but I'd wager that for every unyielding tease, there's another guy who'd ask for nothing better than tenderness, sex, and companionship. What happens between the interstices of desire and consummation and failed union? What went wrong? Who got too angry or too greedy or too tough or too confused? I must tell you that, just as you might expect, many of my subjects thought that men were more to blame. But the topic no longer comes up very frequently. After all, it's been hashed over endlessly, with no acceptable resolution. Does it really matter whose fault it was? It has become so much more complicated than that.

"He's too young for me." "He's married to his work." "He's still hung up over his last relationship." "All the good ones are taken" often succeeds the declaration that there are no men. What some women will assure you is that the right man is somebody else's husband. Then the conversation sometimes meanders over to the subject of affairs with married men, leading to arguments about whether such affairs are incredibly convenient or self-destructive, which can then easily lead to references to painful relationships with abusive lovers before shifting back to what is both the starting point and the inevitable conclusion: There are no men.

However, once this ground has been duly covered between friends (usually new friends, since any woman's old friends already know her beliefs), the conversation then veers—to considerations of problems at work, to closely argued discussions on whether it is too late to take up meditation, to should one allow one's child to play Nintendo, to important queries regarding lipstick colors, or to various speculations as to whether the Republicans will get the presidency back.

In my experience, the tone of these conversations is not sarcastic or bitter. It reflects the humor of people who have learned to live with something difficult and interesting. Nor are these women cavalier or numb. When queried further, they usually seem not uncaring but wistful. A friend who was widowed several years ago recently said to me: "Yes, I could remarry if I found someone I really liked. At one point I was contemplating it, and I thought, *Ohh . . . the idea of going through somebody else's whatever all over again.* And I thought to myself, *Don't shut yourself off because it's too much trouble.* It's difficult to be with someone. It's easier to just stay separate. I can imagine, in a fantasy sort of way, *Yes, if the right person came along I could get married again,* but the reality of it is I don't believe I could go through it all over again. I'm tired of it. But I don't think that's a good thing."

Many single women are "still looking," and, indeed, many eventually find what they are looking for, or some equivalent. Many, on the other hand, describe themselves specifically as "not waiting." They'll say, "If it happens, that's great, but I'm not going to hang around waiting." In this way, all the bets are hedged: Any problematic remaining traces of the old-think are taken care of by the cliché (or myth?) that circulates among women that all the great relationships happen when you're not waiting.

Are there women who can't get husbands? Are there women "too crazy" or "too angry" to get along with a man? No doubt. On the other hand, as it is often pointed out, women who are incredibly mad, mean, neurotic, ridiculous, or whatever can often somehow get into relationships and stay in them. We do know there are many women (single and married) who feel rejected no matter what, and this has little to do with whether anyone desires them.

But increasingly, women seem tired of the search (and of waiting to be found). Your individual single woman is not leaving out the possibility of a "miracle," as it is often characterized, but eventually, unless she is a retro-masochist, at some point she may throw her hands up, saying, "OK, I give up. And now can I get back to my life, please?" Women who have thrown their hands up tend to joke about it. "I've become a nun," they'll say. (Or, in these Zen-oriented, gender-fluid times: "I've become a monk." Or, simply: "I have no life.") Other women will wander from tepid relationship to tepid relationship or stay far too long in wishy-washy romances or sexually ardent but emotionally empty affairs. But there is a new consciousness about these old stories, and a woman with such a perspective will tell her friends, "I'm wasting my time." Some women have wonderful, passionate lives and express their sexuality however and with whomever they want in impetuous love affairs. (Not many women do, but, in theory, it can be done.) Of course, sometimes someone will be taken by surprise and fall in love ("I can't believe it," she'll say. "This wasn't supposed to happen") and end up in a long-term relationship with someone ("a miracle" or, in the words of one now happily married woman, "Hope triumphs over experience"). However, in all the many times I've heard a woman declare to any number of other women that there are no men, I've never heard an argument. Never!

"There are no men," then, is less about men than it is about women. It's not really about looking for a husband or a lover, it's about not having found a role as a wife or as a lover that makes sufficient sense on a long-term basis. It informs the interlocutor not that there are no men, but that there are no relationships that seem workable. It essentially signals a defection from the old school where women were taught that if you can't be with the one you love, you'll love the one you're with. Not only is it an announcement of dissatisfaction, it also, since it makes no assumptions of entitlement and asks for nothing, predicates an entirely new combination of irony and defiance on the single woman's part. It is certainly a way of complaining, but it also declares one's freedom.

Yet women I interviewed could not give a straight answer to the question: Why are you single? They said they didn't know. They said perhaps it was only because they could afford it financially. They said it was one thing after the other. They said they had never meant for it to happen, but life had led them here somehow. Most could not say whether they were going to stay single, for another year or a decade or a lifetime.

The exceptions were the aged and the very young, whose responses were essentially, "Why shouldn't I be?" My oldest subject, a ninety-four-year-old widow and the veteran of a happy marriage, told me she certainly would not remarry, though she has a boyfriend who would be willing. "Why should I give up my independence and my privacy?" she asked with comfortable certitude. Many women say they become more and more independent as they age, while older men become more dependent. According to a piece in the *New York Times* entitled "What? Me Marry? Widows Say No," older widows are especially likely to choose not to remarry. Again, the odds (about five women to every man) are usually cited in this connection—as if four out of five widows can't find anyone willing to marry them. But the remarriage rate goes *down* in proportion to rising income, and a woman who would presumably be one of the "better" catches is more likely *not* to remarry. What's especially striking is that the researchers say it's often the women who had good relationships who prefer to stay alone: "These women, especially the ones who have had successful marriages and careers," one clinical sociologist is quoted in the article as saying, "are whole unto themselves. They don't have anything to prove."

As for the young, whatever their race, economic level, or background, they already take much of the change for granted, even while their befuddled mothers, teachers, and other putative role models are still groping for definition. A CBS–*New York Times* poll of teenagers produced results so startling that they rated front-page coverage. POLL OF TEENAGERS FINDS BOYS HOLD MORE TRADITIONAL VIEWS ON FAMILY, said one headline. According to this study, "The girls surveyed were more likely than the boys to say they could have a happy life even if they do not marry and that they would consider becoming a single parent." Only 61 percent of the boys said they could have a happy life if they didn't get married, while 73 percent of the girls said they could be happy without being married.

Only one quarter of the girls said they had to be married to be happy! This is not just a trend, it's a new order, especially since this is the stage of a girl's life when she is in the thick of romantic fantasy. It is not her need for romance that has changed, it is the direction that it takes. Just a few decades ago, a woman officially became an old maid at twenty-four. Now she expects to work and have fun.

The women in the huge demographic group in between very young and old-old are considerably more disoriented. They do wonder to themselves how they got from there to here—*there* as little girls, carefully taught to assume a "normal" role, to *here* in an era where very few of the old certainties seem relevant. They recall their girlhood fantasies, they remember the vision of the prince on the notorious white horse. And, realistically, they're aware of their grown-up-woman needs for intimate human exchanges and connection. Nearly all at least sometimes wish for a feeling of home, the End of Loneliness, and some wonderful combination of friendship and sex. But finding comfort in marriage has become rare. Your married friends will tell you that they really *work* at their relationship, and those are the ones in the "good" marriages. Married or not, we all know very well that marriage isn't what anyone had expected, let alone hoped for. That some are addressing these problems from within marriage and others from without is not usually recognized, probably because, in the official hierarchy, marriage is still considered to be on a higher rung. But the reality is that while there are a few truly "good" marriages to be seen, even the good-enough marriage is still felt by many married women to be an arrangement that most benefits the man. "Marriage used to be a very straightforward deal," says one three-times-married woman. "The husband provided the money and the security, and the wife provided emotional and intellectual support, a home, children, sex. But now the men aren't even doing their part, so you have to do both. You have to provide support and children and sex *and* a second income? It's a bad deal."

Many formerly married women describe how nothing so specific ever really destroyed their marriages, but time and again they felt the interest and the intensity wane in a relationship, the quality of the dialogue deteriorated to an unacceptably low level. For many people, marriage doesn't end loneliness, it recycles it.

Yet single women have no collective sense of being a pivotal social force. Our society doesn't prepare women to be single, and there is no recognizable subculture, no movement, to provide definition. There is no concert of gestures, no organization, no named social entity. And so for a surprising number, there is no constructed awareness of this new trajectory. There is a startling contradiction in the disparity between the dramatic statistics of the demographic change and the extraordinary vagueness about its place in history.

Even the word is slippery, and very few women actually think of themselves as "single" except when they're filling out forms. They'll say, "I live alone" or "I'm raising children on my own." More and more, they don't even say, "I've never been married" or "I'm divorced" unless you ask. It's as if they had no easily discernible pattern to refer to, except for those that were the paths not taken. Although they often generalized, "Married people think that . . . ," not one single woman I interviewed began a sentence with the words "Single women think that . . ."

Who are these women who take out their own mortgages, who travel on their own, who raise children on their own, who are able to love and leave, or who tolerate being loved and left? While the problems that plague the institution of marriage are endlessly masticated, few mirrors are held up for those outside the institution. Despite the fact that their numbers are quickly increasing, that they are collectively a crucial cog in the workplace, that their different view of the family is both reflecting and contributing to colossal changes in how the entire country lives, there is no sense of a constituency of any sort.

"Was it a choice?" I asked my subjects. It was and it wasn't, they often said, as if they couldn't quite believe that they have actually come to a position that still seems radical: "I would never give up my independence," said a middle-aged widow. "It's become the most important thing in the world to me." Then she paused and looked thoughtful. "I don't really know what happened . . ." she continued, as if her previous statement hadn't been explanation enough.

A friend in her forties who had just gone through a gruesome divorce and began living alone, getting her bearings, said it is both far preferable and anxiety provoking. "I know this is a real choice; this is the best hope for me at this time. It's because I have hope for myself that I can get through whatever I have to go through living alone. But it's just that every now and then I go in and out of it. It's like getting a radio frequency. Sometimes I get it clearly, and sometimes I just lose it entirely. . . ."

In the course of the conversations that follow, I found myself so often steeped in ambiguity that I had to remind myself of all the very real manifestations of this radical shift. For every three married women in America there are two single women. Eleven million are widowed, ten million are divorced, and, most surprising, more than nineteen million are never married. Beyond the 40 percent drop in remarriage, it is this figure that most dramatically shows the scope of social transformation. In 1970, only one in six Americans over eighteen had never married. By 1995, fully one quarter had never been married.

The economic factor alone is inescapable. Single women head more than twelve million households. While we are bombarded with statistics showing how many unmarried welfare recipients we are supporting, one only need turn on the television and watch the ads to get the other side of the story. There's a young single woman explaining she is going to IKEA to furnish her apartment because she may or may not continue to live alone, and this place is only big enough for her, but why wait? There's the black single woman being treated very, very politely by the bank officer who is trying to persuade her to take a mortgage out from his financial institution. Most telling perhaps is the ad for gold jewelry that is specifically targeted to women: "The gift you give yourself."

If their voice is flagrantly missing from the American dialogue, it is because forty-three million single women seem to have no unified vision of themselves as an American type. No ideology induces them not to get married or not to stay married and they therefore invariably characterize their decisions as personal. There was so much variation in my interviews, so much individual history had come into play, that for a long time I found it difficult to specify what they had in common beyond their legal status. Except, I sensed, an undefinable something. . . . Perhaps, precisely, their lack of definition.

But, of course, that was it. Single women in the '90s have left behind the old contexts. They've always been marginal, defined by what they were not. But, along with the certitude that marriage is irrevocable, even the notion of who is an outsider has changed. Divorce and remarriage rates are evidence that the membranes are now permeable. Women are in relationships or not, or they are for a long time and then they're not. They're angry at men or they're not, or they constantly change their minds about whether they are or not. They have lovers or they're chaste. They don't want to have anything to do with men, or they can't get enough of them. They may be feminine in the old sense (inviting, attractively fragile) and/or feminine in the new sense (independent, combative, resilient, masculine), or both.

As a result, taken as a group, single women's most distinguishing characteristic is an extraordinary degree of cultural ambiguity. They're improvising their living arrangements, their financial arrangements, their sexual relationships, their friendships, their sense of social place. Alternately perceived as ridiculous or impressive, pathetic or enviable, possessed of the most unpredictable of futures, they have no common image. The culture has no fix on single women.

It took me a long time to identify it, but there's an atmosphere I now associate intimately with my subject. It is a floaty feeling, an injection of the ineffable into the imperatives of daily life. It emanates even from women who seem to be extremely bound to the literal, by obligations to work or family. Despite the flat conclusiveness of the phrase "there are no men," this new consciousness, strangely combining loss and freedom, is rich with undiscovered meaning.

But more to the point at any one moment in the life of a single woman are all the decisions to be made and problems to be reckoned with. And the days add up, of course, fast, and it all goes by, and so if you have any occasion at all to ponder the question "How did I get from there to here?" it is in a spirit of tremendous puzzlement.

HERE CAME THE BRIDE

Of course, there are powerful images from long ago. I asked:
What fantasies did you have of yourself as a woman when

you were a little girl? Did you imagine a wedding
where you were the bride?

SUSANNNAH W., who is in her late 40s, recently went through
the excruciating breakup of a ten-year relationship.

Growing up I didn't have any fantasy of marriage. No, I clearly
remember thinking, *I'm never going to get married.* The only fantasy
I had started one day when I was walking home from junior high
school. I still remember what street I was on . . . and, oddly enough,
I thought to myself, *I want to be a lawyer.* Why, I don't know. It could
have been Della in the Perry Mason series—I thought she should be
elevated.

SUE M., is 38 years old, a native of Poughkeepsie, twice
divorced.

A wedding fantasy? No. I must have, but I don't remember one.

MARTHA H. occupies a corner office in a big company. Highly
effective in her work, very attractive, never married. Quite foggy
about how she got from there to here.

No. No wedding ceremony, anyway. Once I became aware that
they existed, I had a fantasy of the announcement in the *New York
Times* but never a fantasy of the wedding itself.

I don't remember a fantasy of being a wife, though I did have one
of being a mother. But mostly what I had were extremely strong
romantic fantasies. Along the line of *Green Mansions* or something
like that. How I was going to get to the Amazon jungle, I don't know.

But when you think about it, of course, isn't the man the whole
point of *Green Mansions?* Rima, the bird girl, or whatever she was,
she gets the guy.

MARY ANN B., 45, is a journalist. One long marriage, one long
affair. Alone for the last five years, save for the occasional fling.

Oh, yeah, every time I went to a wedding. But the fantasy was
about the clothes. If you just gave girls the clothes, it would prevent
a lot of marital disasters. But the clothes indicate the role. They're
the uniform. And they're the metaphor for romance. If you look at
all the bride magazines, it's all about domesticity, but the male fig-

ure is virtually a shadow. I think if women could get married without men, the bride, that figure in a gown, would keep the same meaning.

Well, yes, of course I saw myself as a bride. Who else would you see yourself in the role of? You never see yourself in the role of the mother-in-law.

CALLIE S. is a real estate agent in her late 50s, mother of a grown daughter from a former marriage and a young daughter out of wedlock.

Holy cow! Did I ever see myself as a bride? Honest to God, I don't know. Fantasies of bridal gowns? Nah . . . Not me. What I do remember is playing house. I used to play house with Benny Glinn—his father ran the gas station around the corner. We never played doctor, though. We never did any of that kind of stuff. I don't know why. I want to go back!

ANITA S., turning 40, is an academic who plans to adopt a child next year.

My sister and I had Bess Meyerson bride dolls that my mother gave us. But even before that, there was one year when my mother sewed bride dresses for us for Christmas They were sort of loose—they didn't have a waist—and looked more like communion dresses than wedding gowns. They were very long, of course, and they were kind of gathered at the wrist, and then there was a wraparound apron embellished by white ribbon and that material that's like tulle. We tied it around our waist, which gave it a kind of gauzy thing. And then we had plastic high-heel slippers that had glitter in them, silver glitter, and they were held on by two criss-crossed silver elastic bands.

How old? Oh, I must have been six or seven. And my sister was four. She looked totally confused, like, "What am I doing?" Whereas I was smug. Like Winnicott would say, my mother had met my gesture. No, it wasn't like Halloween at all. Halloween was cowgirls and gypsies, and we worked on the costumes together. But these, my mother made them for us in secret and gave them to us at Christmas.

And it's around then that I got my Bess Myerson bride doll. I had seen it on TV and really wanted it. I couldn't believe my mother sent for it. It came in the mail.

ELLEN P. is textiles curator of a museum, unmarried, much loved. Quite clear about how she got from there to here.

My bride doll was my most precious object when I was little, and I had a most pervasive, profound fantasy about marriage and children. Even now, I religiously read the section of the *Times* about weddings. I'm completely haunted by the idea of this configuration. And I keep imagining that I'm secure and clear enough about what I want for myself that I could share a life with somebody else. That does not go away.

REWRITING *LITTLE WOMEN*

Sentimentality isn't what it used to be.

SUSANNAH W., a film critic, is the one who just had the painful breakup. Black T-shirt, black jeans, black high-heeled sandals. She still smokes.

I do remember, when I was ten, rewriting *Little Women*. I rewrote the whole book and illustrated it. What I did was, I eliminated the guy—do you remember?—he was the sort of wuss. I axed him from my version. And how about Jo who had to sell her hair because her father was fighting in the Civil War? In my version, she didn't have to cut it after all; she kept all her hair. And she sold a story. It was so inappropriate that Jo, who I thought was so terrific, should have to pay the price and end up with that much older man who was just unexciting, so I eliminated him, also. And she had some dashing thing happen to her.

Yes, it's true, Jo would have been the single woman. And she was the one who was talented, she was the voice of the book, I think. And where was Meg? Now it fades. Meg, Amy, Beth. Beth who died . . . Good riddance. I wanted her to get a life.

But that's when I was really little. Seven—or eight, maybe. I think I stopped having ambition when I was ten. My desk was taken away from me at that point because I spent too much time in fantasyland,

as my father called it. I grew up in a house where I knew I couldn't
let anybody know what my ambitions might be. I had an extremely
fraught life with my father, trying to establish how to get around him
all the time. My blocking move was to be extremely private and not
tell anyone what I wanted. But he had the power. My little stuffed
animals were taken away. My books were taken away. He thought I
read too much, and this isn't what he had in mind for me. He wanted me to be his secretary and my mother's nurse. He thought he was
being practical, but it was really because he was a pessimist. He was
really ignorant.

MONICA V., 48, divorced, midwestern entrepreneur. She was
the first interview I did for this book. Smart, warm, and
bemused by the course her life had taken.

I was a gawky kid, I was too tall, I was not very pretty. Intelligence
was not particularly given any social weight where I went to school. I
come from a small town in the Midwest, farm country. I had this very
sort of American, low-class American, upbringing, even though we did
very well—my father was the mayor. But it was so important for me
to really fit in, and I didn't. I never, ever fit in. I was too smart or not
smart enough or didn't look right or, you know, didn't have the sense
of humor, wasn't Miss Personality. And I would worry about never
being able to get married. I would really think about that. I never had
a date in junior high school. I didn't have a date in high school. Not
only did I graduate high school a virgin, I don't think I had even
kissed, I never had a boyfriend. And this was a place where everyone
got married out of high school. And when I've gone back to high
school reunions since then, I mean, these people now have grandchildren! And that was how it was going to be. I think the reason I
went to college was because I would meet a better type of husband. I
went to a big school—Kent State—and there I started to date.

Everything was a lot of fun. It was the '60s. And then at that
point, I started to think, *Well, yeah, I will get married, but maybe not
right away.* . . . And then . . . then I had boyfriends, and then I stopped thinking about what the future was going to be, and then I had
a boyfriend for five years, right out of college, and then I had another boyfriend for five years, and then I had another boyfriend . . . you
know. And then I did get married, but when my marriage broke up

six years ago or whenever, all of a sudden I found myself alone, without any prospects of going into another relationship.

JENNIFER B., born in New Jersey, 32 years old, a portfolio manager, is in a relationship that she characterizes as "OK." She is similarly concise about her marital status.

Why am I single? Because I'm not afraid to be by myself. And I intimidate men.

MARY ANN B., the journalist.

I think my parents are still waiting for my sister and me to settle down and get normal. Even though I'm on the cusp of fifty.

But they really do belong to a purely couple generation. And I think that's the last couple generation we're going to see. I really do. Even though the right wing is trying as hard as they can to restigmatize divorce, as long as women have economic independence, divorce will always be with us.

And I think divorce is good for marriages. If you have a society in which there can be no divorce, men who have all the power right now could keep behaving as badly as they want to because women would have no choice, they couldn't leave.

ANTONIA O. lives in a rural environment. She is a secretary in her late 30s, soft-spoken, delicately courteous, and unself-consciously unconventional.

I don't think I ever thought of myself as being married. I had crushes on boys, but I don't think I ever imagined myself being married and being a housewife. I rode horses and imagined myself being a high jumper. I imagined myself going to school and learning a lot. I don't think I clearly imagined any kind of work, except when I was very young: riding in the westerns, riding back and forth over the hills and prairies, in the background of the westerns. I thought that would be a great job.

GOOFY MESSAGES

Starting with Mom's, many of the signals girls receive turn out to be tricky cultural cryptograms.

ANITA S., the one who plans to adopt a child.

Part of it, too, is like, for me, a lot of goofy messages I got really early that were very subliminal, that marriages were very difficult for women and children were difficult and that you would only be yourself late in life. For my mother, marriage was incredibly hard.

RENNIE N., 34, composer and piano teacher. Lives in Cape May, New Jersey, by the sea in the house her parents left her when they retired to Florida.

What I can remember from when I was a little girl was having what I wanted change all the time. Seeing Margaret Mead wearing a cape and carrying a trident made me want to be an anthropologist. Going to a football game made me want to be a cheerleader. Whatever the costume was that I liked, I wanted to be there. And I always imagined being married and having children. I remember once the teacher asked us to write on a piece of paper what we wanted when we grew up, and I wrote two things. I said I want to build a monument with my name on it in bronze, and I want to have a marriage like my parents. And you know, I really do admire my parents' marriage. The kind of love they enjoy and share. But I have thoughts about their marriage now that I didn't then. I do believe that the person who's really made the marriage work is my mother. There was a real ambivalence.

PAM A. hasn't had a sexual relationship in a year, which she claims is a record. She has had three marriages and is the mother of two young children.

I'm coming to realize as I get older and clearer that in every other area of my life I'm pretty successful. But in the area of getting along with men, even though I've been married three times, I'm just a disastrous failure.

I'm crippled in my relationships with men. You could say it's my childhood models, but I think it's partly because nobody ever said to me it's important to get along with a man. They all said to me it's important to *get* a man. And I got men; I got a lot of men people said I couldn't get. But I didn't realize that getting them wasn't any good if you didn't know how to live with them.

Our fairy tales say all you have to do is get them, and I also think it was an idea that was particularly romanticized in the '50s. I was just brought up to think that all I had to do is get them, and that's all I know how to do. And it's a useless skill.

You get to a certain point in your life—which for me was fifty—when you start looking backwards instead of forward. It's really an astonishing change of perspective. And once I started looking backwards, I saw how bad my relationships with men had really been. Now that I see how bad I am at not being single, I'm happy to be single for a while.

CAMILLE O., 37, might once have been described as a patrician beauty, living on a trust fund. She is considering setting up a nonprofit foundation that will provide grants for young women in the sciences.

When I went out with men as a teenager, I was aware very early on that this was a game. I remember going to parties and thinking it was a good party if you'd gone off with a boy you really liked. I remember being about sixteen and going off to some dance, a barn dance in the summer, and afterward lying in the grass, and there were these boys just leering at this one girl called Rosie, saying things like, well, "I'll give you a thousand dollars to sleep with me." And I remember just lying there saying to myself, *I don't think this is what I want, I really don't. . . .* It was really sort of a big epiphany for me. I was thinking, *I don't want to have to worry about 'Do I have the right sized this or the right sized that.'*

And so I pulled away from the idea of boys, while my sisters were going through this frenzy of trying to attract men and get married and have children. And I watched them. Meanwhile my parents were also divorcing. My father was . . . had been in love with a woman for ten years. It was all very complicated.

THERE ARE NO MEN

*An observation usually made with an air of mock
horrified astonishment.*

NINA L., 28 years old and divorced, is an aerobics instructor in Soho.

It's New York. The men are hopeless in New York.

SABRINA F., a producer in Hollywood, where there is a particularly dense cluster of single women, ranging from some of the top stars to college girls getting their first jobs in the mail rooms of agencies.

It's Los Angeles. The ones who aren't hopeless are married. I don't even think of sex anymore. Deals. I think of deals; it's healthier.

PAULINE M. It was just that there wasn't anyone she wanted to sleep with. She kept waiting for the one who'd do it for her.

I don't know what to do about this. They just all seem schleppy to me. Or else they drink or something.

EVELYN B., a mathematician, speaks with a southern accent. She tells me that her divorce was as bad as her marriage, in exactly the same ways.

You know how the story ends. We have a joke, in my circle of friends; we call it "This is the best it's going to be." You meet a guy, there's instant attraction, and there's that one moment when you think, *Aha, that's the best it's gonna be.* Because the next minute you're going to come to your senses and say, *Oh, sure, right. He's married, he probably drinks, he's like my former husband,* and then you don't go out with him. So that moment of attraction never goes anywhere. I mean, those are the guys you're attracted to, but by now we know what's going to happen. He's not going to leave his wife. He's going to turn out to be dependent. He can't make a commitment. We know. We've been married to those guys.

CHRISTINE L., a Washington lobbyist who says she's too busy to ever think about how she got from there to here, is offended by all the clichés about single women. For instance: "They're too picky."

Yeah, it could be that I'm picky, but what does that even mean? It's so complicated. I'm a person with many faults and difficulties, and it's about whom I'm attracted to, and if I were healthier, would I be attracted to somebody else? There's probably something in that, but there's about five billion people on the planet. You shouldn't have to change yourself to find a companion. And it's always the woman who has to change, anyway, more than the man. And I guess also I actually feel that I've been—what's the word people use?—thrown over, or jilted or dropped as often as I've done the other, so my own experience has been one of being the rejected one, I would say. That's how I look at it. Hopefully there are men I've gone out with who think they're the rejected one.

I feel reasonably well-adjusted at this point in my life, at least relatively.

ANITA S., the academic.

It's not the men, it's the roles that are hopeless. And the poor men, there's nothing in the culture helping them to move out.

MEGAN L., 26, describes herself as an optimist.

The difference between being alone compared with being with somebody doesn't have the meaning it had for Gloria Steinem. If feminism linked you as chattel to men, then it would be a choice. But if you're growing up in an age where being single is not even an issue, then there's no choice to be had. In an age of assumed feminism, the choice is connected to the fact that you can be whatever you want, you can be with a man, you can be with a woman, you can be alone or with anybody.

TURNING POINTS AND POINTS OF NO RETURN

When trying to understand how they wound up single, many women recall a moment in their life when a critical mass of pros or cons was reached.

EILEEN Y., in her early 70s, is a well-known watercolorist. She lives in Gloucester, Massachusetts, where she was born. She retired from teaching four years ago. Seemingly frail but a real Yankee, out in every kind of weather, she has a gentle manner but has been independent and self-sufficient all of her adult life.

At a certain point I thought success had ruined my life. Because I thought that if it hadn't been for success, I would have married X, and I wouldn't have gotten involved with Y. But it wasn't like that.

I think it all pivoted when my mother got cancer. My father had really been totally dependent on her. And we simply . . . I mean, my sister did most of it, but we took turns being with him when he needed somebody, which was most of the time. I would come down for vacations or commute to work. That was five years, or six, counting my mother's illness. So I didn't have any kind of a personal life during the early '60s because I was really tied down with these family responsibilities. My father died in '67 just before things started happening for me, which was really sad because it would have meant a lot to him.

After his death I was much freer, and since then my social life has been based much more on my work. I would say that in many ways, the years since I've accepted being on my own are really . . . the most whole years of my life. Even though certain things are left out of them. I feel very good about how my life has turned out, but all along it simply wasn't going to go in certain ways.

HILLARY P., in her late 20s.

I thought I was in love with him for about a week, then it was, *No, this is not about that at all. This is about sex.* And after that I went out with a guy for about three or four months. It was fun, I thought he was cute, he pursued me, which was very appealing, we broke up, and then I went through my promiscuous phase.

Well, it was just . . . I was into sleeping with people and having sex. I was really interested in men who were interested in me and trying to figure out why they were interested in me, and I guess I ended up sleeping with maybe four or five people. There was one guy who liked me a lot, who I ended up having a one-night stand with. And I thought he was kind of cute, but I just wasn't interested. But I thought, *I'll give him what he wants, I'll sleep with him, and then he'll leave me alone.* So we had this one night stand, and I had another one-night stand with someone else the next night, and I woke up feeling absolutely disgusting and sleazy and it was like, *I HATE THIS!*

So I decided I should keep to myself for a while.

AMELIA J., in her late 40s, is a divorced researcher who insists that the more she learns about herself, the more bewildered she is.

Yes, when the marriage broke up, I did assume that I would be with someone else soon.

So, in other words, when I left my husband, it wasn't really leaving the institution of marriage. No, it was a critique of it—although I used to be embarrassed because I was married, as though I wasn't supposed to be. I was embarrassed to be in a couple. I was embarrassed by the loss of identity that implied. For me. And there is this group of women, a generation, for whom emancipation is at least as important as marriage.

How long since my ex-husband and I split up? It's upsetting: sixteen years.

No, there hasn't been a point at which I've decided that it was not an interregnum, that it was something else, more permanent. I haven't realized *yet*.

NINA L., the aerobics instructor.

After the divorce, I didn't have a home, and I didn't have a job, and I didn't have any money. And I didn't want to go back to my father's house. I went to a girlfriend's house, and she allowed me to live there for a whole year. I took care of her. I was like a gal Friday for her for a year. I helped her with her business—she's a realtor—and I cleaned her house, and I did the shopping and the cooking, drove her around. Everything she needed.

Yes, that's exactly what I was. I became her wife. And she certainly was a much more rewarding husband than mine had been.

ROSA M. was born in Mexico but came to this country when she was three years old. She is a bookkeeper. She talks about someone who she says is the only man she was ever completely in love with.

With a lot of fear and sadness, I told him I was pregnant. And he said, "Well, I would really like to get married with you and be responsible about this, but I'm too young, and I really don't feel that I could take that responsibility." And I said, "That's what I thought. I know that."

I was still in college. And from that point on my goals drastically changed. I went from not caring about my future at all into caring about the whole future. And I finished college, and I worked, and I supported my daughter the whole time.

As far as remarrying was concerned, at that time I think I was still more interested in romance. So I just continued having affairs.

CALLIE S., the real estate agent.

Remarry? No, I never even really came close, although I was sometimes tempted. I had three or four really serious, serious, serious relationships, all of which would have spelled disaster. One was a drunk. Adorable, smart as a whip. Best lay in the western world. All sorts of wonderful things. And I was seeing him for about a year before I figured out that he just didn't drink like a Jewish person. Can anybody be that young and stupid? And there was another one—a very serious one—who was and would always be married to medicine before he would be married to me. And I liked and didn't like that.

IDA R., only recently retired from her role as general helper in the family business, is in her early 80s. On a macrobiotic diet, studying reiki (a healing art). Almost blind, she walks with a cane and carries a backpack.

I was single until I was thirty-nine. I had a wonderful but brief marriage of only five years. Then it was another fifteen years before I met my second husband. And that, too, was a short marriage, of only nine years.

Why did I stay single that long? Well, maybe I didn't have the opportunity. No, that's not true. When I wouldn't go out with someone a second time my mother would say—it's a Jewish expression: *Er tit zich oys far der.* It more or less means: "He stretches himself out for you! He's going all out, and you don't give him a tumble." I couldn't tell her. I couldn't tell her that he was reaching out for my breasts, and I didn't know that this was a proper thing for young men to do in those days. Maybe because I was still a child.

I do indeed know the reason I stayed single so long. Yes. Because I saw marriages that failed. People I was close to who were terribly in love and then separated and divorced. And I said, "If this is marriage, I don't need it."

PHILLIPA C. is turning 50 this spring, and is a living advertisement for the fact that turning points can turn back on themselves.

I mean, there are plenty of women who think it's impressive that I've been married three times. But it's only impressive in its futility.

PHILLIPA C., four months later, in May.

I know! I was convinced that it could never, ever have happened anymore, but here I am, in love again.

I'VE ALREADY TRIED IT (AT LEAST ONCE)

There are women who say, "That part of my life is over."
Sometimes, they say, it's because their last relationship was too
awful, sometimes because it was too good.

VALENTINE J., a New Yorker, recently celebrated her 94th birthday. She was widowed more than thirty years ago.

I think if a woman meets someone and she's older—sixty, say—I think she should have an affair. Not tie herself down to marriage. You can't adjust. You can, but you don't want to. Why would you want to? You're living by yourself, you're your own boss, you spend what you want. You've been married, and you know. . . .

MARY ANN B., the person who said that the dresses are the main thing girls want from weddings.

Another pro: You just don't have to argue as much with men when you're single because your life doesn't depend on their seeing your point of view. If there were such a thing as free time—nobody has any free time—but on those occasions when I'm with a couple, having dinner with a couple, I listen to the many mini-negotiations that take place through the dinner, like "Don't you think . . ." and then the little speech that follows. It's like the burden of educating them is always women's. We always talk about the dual-career women who are raising children and earning a living. That's only two-thirds of the picture. I think the hardest role for women who are raising children and working is to educate men on how to be fathers and how to be husbands. And that's a role that a single-again woman doesn't have anymore. And it's huge. We still have to educate friends and colleagues. But at least in our own queendoms, we don't have to educate men.

MARGUERITE M., probably in her later 60s, has always lived in North Carolina. Her husband was a pilot in the navy, whose plane crashed in Vietnam. She speaks with the distinctive accent of the educated southerner.

I had several opportunities to remarry, but when it just boiled down to it there were too many minuses and not enough pluses. Yes, I missed my husband, absolutely. Winston and I were very happy, and I'm not idealizing it. He was just too good to me. Very unusual.

Afterwards, I felt most of the men were not of his caliber. I went out with a very nice man here. He was getting a divorce. And he was very good-looking, much better looking than Winston. But we had too few things in common. And he wanted children, and I thought, *I'm not going to go through that again. My family is complete except for Winston.*

My first thought when I lost Winston was for the children because they had adored their father and had been so much with him. Once they were grown and out of the nest, I was so used to being my own boss and not answering to anyone except my conscience and my Lord that I really wasn't interested. I don't think I actually decided, but I certainly have no regrets.

REGRETS

This was a subject everyone had to be coaxed to talk about. It's as if they had trained themselves not to dwell.

JUNE W., who was the first African-American woman to run for the Senate in her state.

Still, I know I want someone's heart. I want to share my heart with someone. I don't need it all day the way these wives do, but I want to have that sometimes. A friend who is a lover, not a lover who is a friend.

When I ran for office, I ran alone. I came back to this apartment by myself; I walked in and was alone.

The revenge is living well, eating well, dressing well, because the rest of my current socialization doesn't permit enough pleasure.

ELLEN P., the much-loved curator.

The thing that I regret is that I'm really reluctant to go anywhere alone. To the movies, for example, or even to a restaurant. And so I miss a lot because I don't, I simply don't have . . . I don't know what it is. The courage? I think partly because—this may be a feminist perspective—I like experiencing things in relation to others. I don't like being devastated by something beautiful all alone. Or something horrendous for that matter. I want to come out with somebody and have a conversation about it.

PAULINE M., the art director.

The only thing that I'm aware of missing is the adoring sexual relationship, which even though I know it's a fiction, I find that I long for it. It's a powerful fantasy, even if it is a fantasy.

MARTHA H., speaking in her corner office.

If I'm depressed, not being with someone becomes fuel for that depression; it becomes, *Of course you're not with anyone, you're such a loser.*

MARY ANN B., relieved to be rid of the obligation of educating a husband.

The hard part, the hardest parts, of being single are money and paperwork. Especially with two kids. You have to read all those stupid insurance forms and figure them out by yourself, and, obviously, you have to keep the bills coming and going out. And you can't delegate any of that paperwork stuff. My theory is that ninety percent of the people who become homeless have gotten that way because they fell behind on their paperwork.

CLEAN LONELINESS

Preferring the loneliness of real solitude to the murky loneliness of a wrong relationship is something I heard about often.

PHILLIPA C., the one who considers her three marriages not much of an accomplishment.

The other day I was thinking, *Oh, it was so much easier when I arrived somewhere with someone.* If you have a public life, when you arrive by yourself and there are fifty people, it's so much harder. But I also know what's it's like arriving with a husband and being embarrassed by his behavior. I know what it's like to be thinking all the while that if they judge me by his actions, they're wrong—and knowing at the same time that people do judge you by your husband's actions.

An incident that sticks in my mind is a party at the Rainbow Room, and Patti Lupone came and sang. And a lot of people weren't quiet. So Patti Lupone said, "If you want me to sing, please quiet down." And then my husband yelled, "You bitch!" And everyone at the Rainbow Room could hear. I had to tell myself, "Well, he's him and I'm me, and I'm not responsible for his actions. I have to remember that." But that happened over and over and over again with him. I never went out without feeling dread.

TAMMY F. is 27.

When I think about remarrying, it's terrorizing to think I would be giving up my independence. That's become more important to me than almost anything else. I just really do love not having to get somebody's permission. And I can't even imagine organizing my emotional life around a man anymore.

AMELIA J., the researcher who felt embarrassed to be in a couple.

Well . . . the single woman can really pull it off, can really have affairs with younger men and stuff like that. That's cool. But I really miss living with someone. Though I do remember about the obligation to have sex when you don't want to. I do think about the sort of awful things women complain about, but they're way outweighed by the good parts, I now see.

Here's the always lucid SUSANNAH W., the *Little Women* revisionist.

The being single part that's hard. . . . I have the hardest time when I feel that I'm too self-involved. You can be involved with your friends, of course, but I miss a level of intimate involvement with a partner. There are those moments for me . . . of loneliness. I think, *Well, then it would be nice to be a part of a couple.* But then that passes.

CHOICES

Ambivalent or not, women were usually very clear that the direction taken was no accident.

ELLEN P., the curator whose beauty and charm would overwhelmingly qualify her as what used to be called "a good catch."

It's very hard for people to imagine that there is a choice that's been made and that it's not some deep neurotic deficit. There is still a fable that single women have something wrong with them. I find this very painful. The culture at large doesn't value the pleasures of solitude and how precious solitude is in the very demanding, complex world that we're living in. So there's that.

LAURALYNNE A., a schoolteacher in her mid-30s, has hardly ever been out of some kind of relationship, but she has not seriously considered marriage.

I would rather be in a perpetual state of longing than feeling disappointed, and for me it's one or the other. And longing can be very invigorating; it can be a very nice state to be in. If all I see is that it's either the longing or sign on with someone and have a more formal arrangement and the disappointments that go along with that, I'll choose the longing.

I stayed with Quentin because I felt understood by him, even though I knew that it was an abusive relationship. Now I just accept the fact that I'll never be understood, or it'll be a nice surprise if someone comes along and gets it about me. That was always the thing I wanted. I wanted a guy to get it about me.

JOCELYN H., a pediatric nurse, goes out with a man but lives alone with her child. She separated from her husband years ago and has raised her son on her own.

Cornered by my circumstances? I don't feel cornered because I feel about myself that if I really wanted something to happen I think I could. I just don't want to. But I feel that confidence in myself. I feel it's a different day and age than when I was married the first time, and I can handle what is happening now.

VALENTINE J., the 94-year-old New Yorker, has lived in the same apartment building for the last forty years. Everything there—every piece of furniture, every rug, every basket—is arranged just so.

Not remarrying after my husband died, that I was definite about. I had no intention of marrying again because I didn't need any financial help. Never dawned on me to get married again. I'd been married for forty-five years. When your husband dies, you're sort of independent. Now you do as you please. If you want to come home for dinner, you come home for dinner; if not, you stop at a restaurant or you meet a friend. And I was happy. Once I accepted the fact that I lost my husband, of course. There's a mourning period. Even if people are married and do not have happy marriages, I think when they lose a spouse, there's a mourning period. Because no marriage is that bad that you can't think of the good times.

Yes, I do have a lover now. A younger man. He's eighty-four.

No way. I would never live with him. I think any woman who reaches a mature age is very foolish to. I think if the woman has to marry for financial security, I can understand it. But why should I give up my independence? Why should I give up my privacy?

BLANCHE W. is an endocrinologist who recently turned fifty. Willowy, blond, expressive, very feminine, says she doesn't miss being married but wishes she had someone to kiss.

In fact, when I was married, I felt like I had betrayed myself. I didn't enjoy even the concept of being married. I didn't like the idea of every night sharing my bed with the same person. With anybody for that matter. I missed having my books spread out all over my bed. I really hated having anybody tell me, "It's time to go to bed." And I still feel that way. At the same time I feel a little like a freak.

REGINA M. feels the choice is made unconsciously, long before an entirely logical realization emerges.

Was it intended? No, still isn't. But, it *must* have been a choice.

When I decided to move from New York to my house in Pennsylvania and work on this project, I was waiting to meet someone I could live with. And even though I was in sort of a bad long-distance love affair with someone, the truth is, I was not with anybody, and I had sort of taken myself out of circulation in a definitive way. But it took me a long time to acknowledge that I was alone and to really get into it. Then, I sort of made it my business to do it well, to have a real life, to have a real home, to have people in my life. I haven't quite gotten the vacation thing down, but I'm working on it.

MARTHA H., still in her corner office.

What is the choice? If you ask a psychotherapist, she would say an unconscious choice, yes, an accommodation to your struggles. Maybe it's a better accommodation than being married; I don't know, I've never been married. Maybe if I'd been married I would think not being married is a better accommodation.

I'll tell you, I've been sitting here thinking this: It's so difficult to be single in this society that no one in her right mind would choose to be single if she could do otherwise. If you could get married without feeling that you're compromising yourself out of existence, I would.

SUSANNAH W., who rewrote *Little Women.*

I don't think of myself as being oppressed as a woman because I think I've achieved a lot, so I can't say I think everything is due to a cultural or societal oppression. But I think for me there was a clear choice about being happy as a single person and the feeling that I really had enormous freedom as a single person, that I didn't have to be part of a couple, always getting really angry at the oppressor, getting angry at men. For me the key was to realize that I could no longer wait for men to decide anything about my life, couldn't wait anymore. And I don't know if that impatience has something to do with what happens to women when they are my age and they are single, or if this is something that women who are younger have, too. Because I thought, *What am I doing all these years, sleeping, waiting for some man to tell me I can do something?*

CHRISTINE L., the Washington lobbyist.

If you say that I have to choose between a terrible relationship and being single, then that's a choice—I'd agree with that. And I suppose then you could say, "Well, is there something about women who are single for so long? Are they women who always have to be in terrible relationships?" But there are certainly women who get into terrible relationships and still get married.

There's this notion, the Brave New World and the professional career woman blazing that path, and this is just what she wants to do in her life, making those bucks, and this is all her choice. She has decided to forgo the whining children, the inattentive husband, the dishes in the sink, and the obligations of family. . . . That's what she's picked.

I don't really buy it. At least for myself. And I think this is true for other single women I know who have held responsible jobs—we would like both. I would rather have a family and a husband and a nice place to be at night but also have the opportunity to achieve through my work, to express myself through the world at large. Of course, it's hard to do that. Most of the men in powerful positions are married and have children. But the women in the same positions are much more likely to be single. I think it's because the men who do this are often supported by the women who are at home and raising the children and tending to all the needs of their life. There are some exceptions but not many, especially in my generation.

MONICA V., the one who didn't date until college and then partied through the '60s.

And so I started to think of myself, *This is how you've ended up.* You know, like in the song. None of the other times felt like the ending up part. But this time I start telling myself, *You're going to be alone for the rest of your life, and you're never going to have a boyfriend again. You're old . . . you should have married that guy in college.*

So, I'm starting to think of all the "should haves," all the things I should have done. How did I get here? But when I go through the stages of it, I realize I made choices every step of the way. I was engaged in college to a perfectly fine man. I made a choice, and that's why I ended up here. The other choice would have been a bad one. I don't think I got screwed. I think I ended up exactly where I wanted to be.

I'm always better when I'm not with a man. I do better work, I make more money, my place is better, I have my own mind. When I'm with a guy, I lose my mind, I lose my sense of myself. I can't be me and be with a guy at the same time.

BILLIANA'S STORY

An American Life

BILLIANA M., a high school teacher, was born on V-J Day in Camden, Connecticut. We spoke on the same day of the sale of the house she had lived in with her ex-husband and her family was finalized.

I opted to get pregnant when I was a teenager. I came from a very dysfunctional family and felt that if I didn't get out, I would die. So I found a young man. I was fourteen, Bobby was seventeen. I was his first girlfriend. He was very smitten and very manipulatable, to be honest, and I felt very much in control. I was a virgin, I had never done anything with anybody except kissing, but I was very in love with him, and dreamed of starting my own family, and he agreed, so we started trying. I know, it's a new one on everybody. I used to not tell anyone because I thought they wouldn't believe me.

For about five months, we took every possible opportunity to have sex, which of course he wasn't in the least unhappy about. I wasn't orgasmic, so I wasn't in it for the sex, I was in it for the baby. For me it was just: *Get the job done.* Taking my destiny into my own hands had charm for me, but the sex wasn't enjoyable, and didn't become so until much later.

When the obstetrician confirmed I was pregnant, we were elated. Then we had to tell my mother, who was horrified. The look that she shot me I would not want to relive in this lifetime. Until then she had seen me as compliant—a good girl. I was in the ninth grade, and she insisted I finish the year out before she would sign on my marriage. The probate judge was appointed my guardian until I was sixteen. So I was a ward of the court for two years, which is kind of funny. A first, I still lived at home. I remember I had morning sickness, and I had to walk to school. I could only tell one friend. But I guess I'm looking for a Purple Heart for myself. My mother and sister despised me. My sister was twelve, and she thought I was disgusting and felt very betrayed that I was leaving, and she would have to be alone with the two crazies. My mother didn't talk to me at all; she just gave me icy glares. My father was in the hospital at the time for back surgery, theoretically, and certainly with emotional trouble. My father, just so you know, was an alcoholic, and eventually a suicide, when I was twenty.

We were working class but brought up to believe that we were much higher. My mother is Panamanian, and the class she came from didn't really translate in the U.S. They were landowners and had servants, and she was raised with the finer arts, playing the piano, things that were lovely but not practical. My father was a dirt-poor potato farmer in Maine, and they met when he was stationed in the Canal Zone. She always had the attitude that she was high-born, that we are above the common folk, but my father's people looked down on her because she was foreign and her skin was darker. There was a great anger between my parents, and even an undercurrent of physical abuse, though it was never manifested. She said to him, "If you ever raise your hand to me, I will kill you." But my mother was physically abusive to *us*. She was angry most of the time, and she expressed it by slapping us or hitting us with her slipper even though we were pretty well behaved—I was really careful not to mouth off—so it wasn't warranted. My father went away to work, and only came home on weekends. My mother—like *her* mother— ran the house and didn't trust him to do anything. I've tried to neutralize it for my children, but I know I think in a very matriarchal way. I have some inherited sense that men are inferior. Intellectually, I don't think that, but there is something in my bone marrow. . . . It's sad because I always expect that men will come up short, and that's colored my life.

I had my wedding in a little chapel and moved in with my moth- er- and father-in-law. . . . I couldn't drive yet, and my friends were all in school. I took classes on baby care. I had always read, I was not the least bit ignorant about the female body, so I felt confident that I could do a hell of a good job with this. I had always cooked. So I never questioned myself about my ability to be a homemaker and a mother, and I was really looking forward to the baby.

Things were good and uneventful, and the baby was born. At that point the ice melted completely with my mother. She and my moth- er-in-law came every day and helped and adored the baby, and all the grudges were dropped. Then, when my baby was six weeks old, my husband and I were setting up a crib. . . . It was still soon after the birth, and I was not in any shape to be lifting anything, but he wanted me to help him. He had a bad temper, but it had never been turned against me. He just tripped off the line, and he threw this heavy piggy bank full of money at my stomach. Every red light went off, but I didn't know what to do. I hadn't seen it coming because everything had gone the way I had wanted it to, and this wasn't part of the script.

Now these things are all out in the open, and there are people to call and support groups, but there was none of that then. So I just thought I'd better watch myself and not trip him off. I thought, *I made this life, this is my life, and there is no other life.* There was no question of going back to where I had been. I had this six-week-old baby, and I loved my baby and I wanted my life to be this nice ivy-covered life. I just denied and thought of it as a fluke.

After that time with the crib, the violence continued. Classically, with outbursts and remorse. The remorse was almost worse than the violence because he would come to me for forgiveness and grovel for a while. That was excruciating to me. I didn't want him to grovel; I wanted to pretend that it didn't exist. I never was hit with anything except that one time, but he'd pull my hair and slap me and push me. And there were the insults, and the rage—the bulging-eye rage. What kind of insults? After we separated he'd call me a fucking whore or a bitch. I don't remember what he said while we were mar- ried—I have to tell you there's a lot a memory missing in my life.

Throughout this I didn't feel victimized so much as if my infallible plan and will were not working so good. I think it eroded my self-trust and I stopped believing in my ability to make things happen.

The first affair I had, I hadn't been married for very long. I don't remember how we met; I wasn't looking for anybody. But he worked with my husband and knew where we lived. He started phoning and romancing me during the day, and I could not get enough of that. He found some way to come visit me. I would have been happy to continue on the phone. He really pressed me for sex, and I agreed to it because I thought that would keep it going.

Afterward, I was so crushed and devastated, I called and made an appointment to see the priest. I was still too young to drive, so my favorite aunt drove me—it was my husband's aunt, but she was my friend—and on the way there I broke down and confided in her. I felt dirty and sinful. At the time I thought I was the only one who had done such a thing. And she understood. The priest was pretty down to earth. I did my penance and went to church every week.

But I was drawn to this man, and I still saw him every week. What I needed, I don't know. . . . Maybe attention. Being the object of desire. I didn't desire him—I desired being desired. But he was really using me for sex, end of story. He forced himself on me for oral sex, which I wasn't into at all. It was not part of my repertoire: Bobby and I had pretty much missionary sex, mainly to get the job done for him. This man didn't force me physically. It was more his insistence, and my fear of saying no. When this man came in my mouth, I wasn't expecting anything like that; I felt so sickened so violated. In fact, that was the last time I saw him ever. The energy of it was disgusting. It was so intrusive, invasive, there was a selfish violence to it. And in that particular instance I was so aware of smell, and he didn't seem clean to me. It felt like really dirty, filthy stuff.

The second man, he had sweetness, a tenderness, and by then I was open to this. The affair was not his main thrust, no pun intend-ed. He was very kind to me, very sympathetic to my not being happy at home and not treated well. He brought me gifts, and he gave me money for my birthday. I had my sixteenth birthday right around then. He was about eight years older—maybe twenty-five, married, with a couple of children. He started talking about our being together as a couple. That wasn't an option in the other case, nor would I have wanted it. But with him, though, we talked about it, and I considered it. I was pretty much in a life and death situation in my marriage. Bobby would start just smacking me around. This was when our second baby was just an infant. I started feeling I couldn't take it, couldn't do it anymore. One day I started packing up my stuff, but my in-laws came over to stop me. They said, "What makes you think that your mother and father want you back with two little kids at the house? Your father is sick and your mother overwhelmed with responsibility." I'd been too ashamed to tell my mother I was being hit because I feared that she would say, "I told you so." So I said, "OK, but if he ever touches me again, I'm leaving." My one little seventeen-year-old's show of gumption. . . . At the end of six months of relative quiet, one night he lost his temper because of what I was serving him for dinner. He struck me across the head with a rolled up newspaper. And that was it. Two days later when he was at work, I called my mother and asked if I could come home, and, naturally, she yelled at me for letting myself be abused, but she said, "Of course you'll come home." A girlfriend who drove picked me up with the babies, their clothes, and the baby's chair and my clothes. Nothing else.

It took me most of that year to get a divorce. When the lawyer first started to talk to me about the case—he was a kind of fat-cat white lawyer—I told him on my own that I had had an affair. He said, "Forget it, we can't ask for anything but child support." And he treated me . . . I suppose like a whore. Within twenty-four hours of my leaving my husband, the aunt who had sworn secrecy told that whole side of the family about my affair. The wound, the bitterness of betrayal, was probably worse than anything he did to me, and she said she was sorry, but for years I was unable to forgive her. Boy, I was really in deep doodoo. His whole family had turned against me. There was nothing they could say about me that I hadn't said about myself. I felt I had become a creature of instincts, just to get through. I was so remorseful, just ravaged. I wouldn't even go to the mailbox. Once a week my husband came to pick up the kids, and he would abuse me. I thought I had to take the abuse, but finally I just collapsed, and my mother took over the babies' care a while.

Eventually I got myself together to start my life again. My babies were nine months old and two years old. I was single, but I didn't feel it at all because I felt who I needed to be was a mother. My mother instilled in me all my life that if I did that right, I was a worthwhile person, and I took it totally seriously—I felt it to be a noble thing. After several months that other man did leave his wife and contacted me, and said, "I am free and want to be with you." By that time I knew I didn't want to be with him, that it was a bridge relationship. I dated other people, men who were not much older than I was, and were in no way interested in anything permanent. At first, I told people I had two children, but that made them assume I was sexually available because I was a mother and it was no big deal. So generally it was a date or two until they realized that I wasn't into that, and then they weren't into me. One man—a big brother type—was great with my children and very loving and respectful to me, and I found him boring. We did have a sexual relationship, though, and even got engaged, but I kept postponing the wedding. And then I met Wes, it was really love at first sight, so I had the strength to break up with this man. He went over to Vietnam and eventually got killed there. It was so painful because he had called me, pleading a lot about feeling abandoned. When he got killed, I think I relived some of my father's death. I have to say, when somebody dies, it's just such a cleaner ending because you don't have to deal with someone who's still walking, talking, changing—when they're gone you can just deal with whatever is left.

Wes had just come out of the navy. He had sown a lot of wild oats. He wasn't really finished, but he was looking to do some settling, and he was open to a relationship. I was just absolutely mad for him in a different way than I'd been for anybody. He was Prince Charming, the one I'd been saving a part of myself for through all of this. He was somewhat aloof, hard to read, but I knew he felt something for me. I wanted to live happily ever after with him. He was my hero.

It was just before I married Wes that I had my first orgasm. It was at my own hand. As a child, I just don't remember wanting to touch myself. I think I felt I was going to hurt myself. It wasn't really conscious, but my association with being touched was physical irritation, or discomfort, or something painful. It didn't feel like a pleasure site to me. With Wes, something definitely changed. Whether it was because I trusted him or felt something different about him, I don't know. That opened up worlds for me, and then I really did enjoy it, I did seek and love sex. All the time we were married, we had a very charged, very exciting, very sweet, sex life. And it stayed so for years and years because he traveled so much that we were able to experience this honeymoon kind of energy for a long time. With Wes, it was just him; I was monogamous. We did some experimentation and found that we were fairly conservative and that some of the kinkier things just didn't have any kind of appeal for either one of us. I believe he was faithful, and I was to the very end, until we went our separate ways, and he had no interest in me. Wes and I were so much in love, and it was so satisfying that I would really never take anything less than that again. But it had unhealthy aspects. Both of us coming from highly dysfunctional families, we had so many things we couldn't work out. When it came to a head, we just weren't able to ride it out—we didn't have a common goal anymore for what life looked like together. We split up in 1988, when I was forty-three. By then I had three children.

Then I was with someone briefly—just an affair. The sex was fantastic. He was seeking something, I was seeking something, and we just locked in for a moment in time. And after that, I had a short relationship with a man I saw at first as my spiritual counterpart but who turned out to be a major con man. I saved myself, though, because I didn't enter into a physical relationship. He had an air of danger and I didn't want . . . I think we carry other people's energy, and I didn't want anybody else's energy in my body until I was really sure it was an enhancement. I didn't want to have anything imposed on me, in me, with me. Finally, I became celibate. Initially, not by choice, but after a year it was by choice. The celibacy has not excluded masturbation—that's definitely part of my maintenance. You have to keep those vaginal tissues moist, you know. It's like oil maintenance or tire rotation.

The last person I slept with was Wes, my husband, and that feels right to me. Since that time, I've investigated . . . intellectually. I've thought about lesbianism, holding up the model in my head. My emotional intimacy with women has been far superior to anything I've experienced with men. I appreciate women, and I have a sense of who's sexual or sensual, but I haven't been drawn to women. I'm not interested at this moment in partnering. I don't exclude that possibility, but I'm not seeking it. I'm so into self-discovery right now, and I think I want to keep putting that energy into my work. For the first time it's all just me—I don't feel anything diluted—I've learned how much focus I can put into my teaching when my life is not taken up by caretaking. Now, it's been a little bit over six years. For some reason I feel like I need to reach the seventh anniversary to clean the slate.

LIKE GETTING A RADIO FREQUENCY

Understanding fluctuates. But when you feel tuned in, there's an unexpected, profound sense of authenticity and relief. At least for now.

MONICA V. again.

We had that horrible breakup, and I thought my life was over. Not just my life with him but my life with any man. I was in such a state that nobody knew what to say to me. But then I talked about it to a friend who was older and had been living on her own for a while, raising two children. She said, "You don't need a guy; what do you need a man for? First of all, you *will* meet somebody else. But your problem is that you don't want to think of yourself as a single woman. You're not the only single woman ever in the history of the universe, you know. Do some reading. Look at the Victorian women, look at women from the early part of this century. . . ." She got my head open. And she said, "Look at the Suffragettes. There are people in many cultures who choose not to get married. There are women who maybe have a big affair of the heart, physically or not physically, and stay with their parents or take care of their nieces and nephews. This is all *choice*. And there's nothing pathetic about it. It's always happened, and it still happens in other parts of the world. Not every woman has to be a mother and has to be a wife."

I've tried to hang on to that all this time because when I remember it, I know it's the truth. But it's just that every now and then I go in and out of it. It's like getting a radio frequency. Sometimes I get it clearly, and sometimes I just lose it entirely. . . .

BLANCHE W., the endocrinologist.

I went to see my old analyst who I thought had been enormously helpful to me in most regards, and we were sort of reviewing where my life was and where I'd gone. And he said, "But how do you understand that we failed and that you never got married again and that you're alone and not in a relationship?" And I took the question at face value, and I tried to answer it just in terms of historical sequencing, how my marriage broke up, and how my affair broke up, and how everybody in my immediate family died . . . and how trying to get pregnant is not the best way of trying to get involved with men. I was trying to answer his question with these facts. But then I remembered that there had been this woman whom I admired enormously when I was in my late twenties—this woman in my field. And when I met her, I was really in awe of her because she was alone and she had her own apartment in the city and she owned a house at the beach. And she had a career that was going well. And I remember going into my analyst and saying that, and he said, "Oh, but she's paid such a price." By which he was referring to the fact that she was alone. But so then, all these years later, I remembered that session, and I thought back—not to the way he felt but to the way I felt about her—and suddenly I realized that I had become this woman I admired so much.

MARTHA H., the one who loved *Green Mansions*.

I had a dream night before last about a plane landing without a pilot. I was on the plane. And the pilot was a sort of fraternity boy type who was, you know, was too distracted to fly the plane, and talking with some other guys, and people were getting more and more panicked because we were approaching the runway—it was a transatlantic flight—and we could not get him to come back to the pilot seat. He said, "Ah, don't worry, it's on automatic pilot." And I was screaming, "You can't land it on automatic pilot!" And then, in fact, we landed.

ENVY, STIGMA, CONTEMPT, AND THE SINGLE WOMAN

Who Do They Think They're Talking To?

For Most Eloquent Icon of the American Paradigm, in the classical category, I would like to nominate the tumbleweed—the plant that's like a sort of scrawny, spherical tangle of scraggly twigs. In westerns, it's always rolling around the dusty landscape at strategic points in the plot, coupled with a soundtrack of ominous wind. The tumbleweed is the official flower of the unknown and unnamed territory, evoking as it does, at least cinematically, the most attractive of American myths: the melancholy but enviable freedom of the lone individualist somewhere out there near the frontier, riding proud and loose on his handsome and jittery horse, probably dressed in black, with plenty of leather on and about him, afraid of nothing and no one, neither solitude nor death. It's the quintessential moment, the attitude at its most eerily seductive in the ritual alignments. The mute hills in the distance, the solitary figure, the horse, the hoofbeats, the wilderness. And after eloquently wafting about for a while, as soon as the man and the horse start trotting toward the horizon, that old tumbleweed is pushed by the wind machine right past the camera and out of the frame. Dissolve to the lone cowboy, just riding, riding, riding, stopping at most for a night or two among the good settlers of yet another dusty one-saloon town, but only to take a bath and kiss some señorita hello and good-bye and hit the dusty trail again.

Have you seen ever seen a tumbleweed follow a lone woman rider? No, I doubt it, except maybe in a parody or two, perhaps if something really bad is going to happen: oncoming bandits, drought, shriveling. And then it'll probably be in the form of a dust bunny under her bed.

Americans have always had a great romance with solitude, as well as with the notion of tolerating or even embracing loneliness for the sake of freedom. But, traditionally, only the guy got to feel lonely *and* free. The woman, often referred to as "the little woman" to emphasize her dependency, vulnerability, and cloying coziness, got to stay in the log cabin and wait. By way of radical nonconformism, the only alternative was the whorehouse where, according to the conventions of the genre, a girl at least got to wear red and listen to good piano music. But that's still a pretty static setup. And in either case, whether the woman wishes it or not, it's always clear that there's no way the cowboy's going to tie the knot with anybody.

The only women who ever get near a tumbleweed sequence are those waitresses (no less iconic but, since they're alive a hundred years later than the pioneers, much less mythic) who work behind the counter in one of those Edward Hopper diners-slash-gas stations. But that's only after some rough-and-ready trucker finishes his breakfast, hoists himself back into his lonely pickup, and rides on out. She comes out in front to watch the vehicle disappear, and maybe she waves, or maybe she just stands there, her hands on her hips, dressed in a pink diner uniform that shows off her behind, and poignantly sensible shoes. The tumbleweed may swivel into the frame at that point, but it will be immediately flattened by a telephoto shot of the truck vanishing into the dusty haze.

And let's face it, the forsaken diner waitress may be a victim, but she is an attractive victim (which is why she'd get to be in a movie in the first place). Her consolation prize is to be gifted with the masochist's erotic appeal. In real life, unfortunately, there's nothing alluring about the traditional epithets for single women. The most conventional merely desexualize: old maid, spinster, wallflower. These are terms that convey desiccation, evoke the dry flesh of barrenness, emit an effluvium of Darwinian heebie-jeebies. Others oversexualize and patronize: tart, home wrecker, floozy (a floozy would occasionally be married, but essentially she is stalking the sexual jungle on her own behalf). Finally, there are those that frighten the beholder: that old standby, the witch, of course; the eternal, treacherous, gold-digging manhunter (not to be confused with the tart, who is from a different class); and, more recently, the ball breaker who got the corner office. Certainly nothing there competes in desirability with a lonesome cowboy.

But the old slurs are so familiar to their targets that they're less likely to provoke a wounded yelp of pain than a comical eyes-raised-to-the-ceiling groan. It has become clear to most women that these insults are the province of the Obviously Clueless. The never-married woman in her seventies whom we have gotten to know in the preceding pages under the name of Eileen Y. told me that her brother-in-law, with great pity in his voice, still occasionally declares, "And so-and-so, *poor girl,* she's never married." Ms. Y. tells me she chooses not to reply. "It's hopeless with him," she explains. She merely ponders the fact that her sister could have been married for five and a half decades to someone so obtuse, adding, "And I keep thinking, *Wally, look around you. Who are you saying this to?"*

The newest insults, those contemporary with the rise of the single-women-demographic phenomenon, make the old ones seem quaintly retro. They are more primitive, evoking not pathos but disgust. They distort, demonize, cripple a woman's erotic persona—which then provokes even more discrimination. Attacks on sexuality are the deepest signs of fear, the barely noticed poisoned barbs that fly about their targets until there's a soft spot that permits inconspicuous but deadly penetration. They position the single woman not as a "poor girl" but as an aggressive bitch, strong enough to have made herself into a player where she's not invited, a ballsy intruder who insists on making the scene. That's the *real* price of achievement.

One recently engaged young woman in her twenties gave me a candid opinion of her mother's single friends. "It seems like they are all wealthy women," she said. "Like, not from family, but they've made their own money from their careers." I went on the alert here at her tone, which was intended as derisive.

"It's like pariahs who have strength as a group," she explained to me. I remained silent, wondering, *Who does she think she's talking to?* She continued, with confident disapproval, "And they all go out together to theaters and to nice restaurants. It's like this clique of these women who had no choice but to find each other. You know . . . ? These women, I think they sort of suck on each other."

Now, mind you, I am totally aware of the fact that this young person's mother may have an especially revolting group of friends. I know, too, that there must be plenty of single women who are vulgar, grossly bourgeois, pathologically trendy, and so on. But my guess is that this particular group of women is not any more or less au courant and obnoxious than those in their class who are married. Perhaps the speaker feared that if she became receptive to the sensibility of these single women, she would have the same fate: singleness. And, amazingly enough, she expected me to share her distaste. Clearly, she trusted that I would at least understand her message. And, of course, I did. This is precisely how prejudice is communicated—very baldly but for the fact that both speaker and listener disavow the communication. But note the layers of denigration: They *"suck"* on each other (perverse and queasy-making); they are *"wealthy"* women (rapacious, greedy, acquisitive, grasping, tough). What's worse, they are empowered *"pariahs,"* a dangerously desperate *"clique"* (invasive, threatening, and so repellent that they had no choice but to find each other and band together). Clearly, strong women arouse some very archaic fears. Finally, with the weird kind of convolution that makes insult effective, it is as if women who do not have the protection of a husband can be treated as if they are tougher, whether they are or not.

True, countless married women are also sabotaged at work or stereotyped in their personal life choices if they have power, attacked as phallic women, castrating bitches, theatergoers, and God knows what else. But as for single women in particular, even the most glamorous ones, even the toughest ones, have felt hurt by the kind of gratuitous and bristling resentment with which they are sometimes treated.

At the other extreme there's the surprisingly large category of single women who acquire what one can only describe as a kind of aura. A woman in this category is much in demand and becomes sort of a vestal virgin of the social world, almost talismanic. Ironically, it is neither expected nor desired of this type of woman to become attached to a man in any serious way. She must remain an object of desire that lives safely in fantasy. Desirable or not, the single woman is pretty convenient, since there are also many situations in which she can be used to fulfill various social needs, a kind of

cultural stopgap at large. She can be used to help entertain and
seduce clients, she can be any man's escort and any woman's pur-
veyor of a protective presence. She can stand by and stand in for. In
other people's relationships she can serve as a distraction, a scape-
goat, a front person, an instrument of denial, or a buffer, or a status-
enhancing fifth wheel.

Many single women sporadically career back and forth between
being viewed (and perceiving themselves) as distinctly rejected—
"pathetic" is the word that comes up—or as possessing the emi-
nently enviable aura—"glamorous" is the euphemism. My guess is
that many women feel both, depending on whom they're with. After
all, as a rule hardly anyone feels particularly talismanic to themselves, unless they're in the manic phase of their cycle. Conflicting
messages proliferate from the same source: "In my department . . .
most people are married," said one woman, "and they like to have
me as this sort of wandering, sexy, romantic figure, but they would
also like to have me married because they think it would make me
happy and because it would make me less threatening."

Another woman told me of an old married friend of hers who
repeatedly points out how incredibly happy she is not to be single.
"But then she also thinks I go out *every night*, and I have this incredibly exciting, wonderful life that she's just totally envious of.
Whenever I tell her that I'll be home that evening, she says, 'Oh,
you're not going to a party?'"

Why doesn't the aura phenomenon get talked about more? Very
few will admit to it unless they are coaxed. Of course, nobody wants
to seem to be boastful or smug, but it is also confusing to be so
much in demand and at the same time utterly misunderstood. And
then there's the depressing question of whether you want to be
included in the first place.

The rejections are more blatant. It seems significant that so much
of the blackballing goes on over food and drink, in couples' homes
and in restaurants. It's as if one is not allowed to be a participant at
the tribal feast. Older women had few doubts that they were sys-
tematically ostracized. "Oh, yes. I think there's a huge social network of couples. That's the way married people socialize, by and
large: with other couples. Do I wish I were invited? Not as a single
woman, I don't. People deal with single women like people who

have some kind of disease. They're polite and everything but there's some way in which they're afraid."

Afraid of what? As with any prejudice, this is murky territory but, clearly, the roots of fear go deep. There's the neo-Darwinian motif, for instance, which may explain a great deal: an anxiety regarding women who are smart about things other than mating. Of course, not everyone has the biological laws of inseminating mammals on their minds, but perhaps we are more tied to the social patterns associated with those instincts than we imagine.

But there's plenty of bias on the surface, too, and many reasons why the single woman may be seen as being worthless. Financially, she is often worthless. But then women have always been valued less than men. That's why they had to have dowries. By the same token, even the oldest, stupidest, and ugliest would find a husband if the price was right. The others hung out at home, presumably spinning, as desexed spinsters, or else they joined convents. And I may have read of one or two who fled into the forest and became deer.

Meanwhile, what is a single woman to do? "My revenge is to live well," said one. But what about someone who is not constitutionally or logistically or economically outfitted to follow that guidance? What are her choices? Pretend not to notice? Make herself hors de combat? Simply remove herself as a contender from the main social stream? Perhaps just wait it out? There is an uncomfortable friction here that only time may wear away, if combined with awareness and support. Because the worst part of it is, of course, that anything that resembles passivity in this midst of this attack is all but de facto capitulation.

It only occurred to me a couple of days after reviewing Ms. Eileen Y.'s quote that I had overlooked something important in it.

"*She never married, poor girl,*" said Ms. Y.'s brother-in-law.

As you may recall, Ms. Y. chose not to answer. She merely found herself thinking, as presumably she must have many, many, many times in the preceding fifty-three years that this man had been married to her sister, that there was no point—"*It's hopeless with him.*" And thinking to herself, "*Wally, look around you. Who are you saying this to?*"

The phrase rang in my mind. And also its answer: *He was saying it to you!* Just as, I suddenly realized, I had found myself saying to myself, "Who did she think she was talking to?" while recounting having heard the young woman describe single women as "pariahs," and as a "clique of these women who had no choice but to find each other . . ." and as women who "suck on each other . . ." Who did she think she was talking to? Me. She was talking to me. Why didn't I respond? And why didn't Ms. Y. ask her brother-in-law directly and out loud to look around him, rather than just think it silently to herself? True, one doesn't want to squander one's energy on these imbecilic exchanges, but it's not just because some people are Obviously Clueless. More likely, it's because it is less painful to overlook certain remarks. To respond would be to acknowledge the humiliation. We may be thinking, "It doesn't matter. What else is new?" It's just that later that day, or at some point that week or that month, there will be a moment when we are tired, or discouraged about something else, and all of a sudden a great sadness will descend. Or, depending on your background, your spiritual state, and your metabolism, a great fatigue, anger, or, at the very least, an acute frustration, a sense of outrage that someone—it really doesn't matter who—could have talked to *you* that way. It's the direct, raw experience, not just of prejudice but also of contempt.

And now and then, perhaps, we should be not just *thinking* but also *saying*, "Wait a minute. I'm a single woman, and I don't agree with you." Or just, "Are you kidding or what?" Or how about: "I'm sorry to tell you this, but you are utterly hopeless, Wally. And I am really glad to take the opportunity, after fifty-three damn years of listening to this drivel, to inform you that you are not only a lout, but you are also Utterly Clueless about the moment of history you are living in."

Maybe we don't have to say it every time, to every Conclusively Clueless person we encounter—there are too many of them—but we should certainly say it more than we do. We fear being perceived as victims—which would confirm the stigma. But the truth is that the humiliation will be neither greater nor lesser for expressing our sad surprise at the bias, and if we are reluctant to do so, it may be because we have so internalized the attacks that we take their legitimacy for granted.

Of course, not all women would agree. No doubt some would read this account and scoff. "I don't even think of this stuff," such a woman might say. "It never occurs to me. I'm too busy. And who cares about those people, anyway? Or about any of this? Life is too short for this garbage. I have other problems."

Some take a very different stance and they don't even have to work at it. I hope they're right. They may be dissatisfied, but it certainly doesn't necessarily lead to self-hate. Certainly the stigma has been considerably weakened. And the less prejudice there is about all women, the less discrimination there will be toward single women. After all, the only explanation for the attack on sexuality is that on the most profound level, the real target of bias is not singleness but womanhood. Singleness is merely the excuse.

And bit by bit, a different sort of tradition *is* being constructed. "I'm always, like, maybe there is something wrong with me. . . . ?" admits one more woman in her late twenties, "But then I see how other single women live, the ones I admire," she says, to explain why she chooses this way of life. The older single woman may still be a "poor girl" to Wally, but to those who are even now sketching the future, she is viewed as a role model, a most desirable friend. "Yes, I still have some friends who are single women who feel pathetic or desperate," says one woman. "But then, I remember when my whole circle of friends was like that. Now it's exceptions."

How much social restructuring will eventually result from so many women remaining single is still unknown. But already one has a sense of a great and growing number of single women "out there," and if they are lacking the power and organization of a self-identified constituency, they are nonetheless what women have never been: an amazingly free-floating social unit—freer than women have imagined themselves being, albeit at least sometimes lonely, too. Or should I say "lonesome"? Ah, it's too bad we don't get the use of those eloquent old metaphors men always got to keep—that desert which can look so empty and forlorn yet turn out to be replete with eerie surprises; that horse trotting away, the rising winds, the hoofbeats, and that old tumbleweed rolling and wafting about and tumbling right out of the frame, leaving the scary, vast unknown wilderness on the screen, waiting only to be transversed by the cool and brave cowboy. Surely we will soon stumble onto new metaphors of our own, allowing the cowboys and cowgirls to stay on their old horses, while we zoom into the twenty-first century in our new spaceships.

THE CLASSIC LINES

It was never the good old days for single women.

EILEEN Y. from Gloucester, has gray-blond hair and moves with graceful deliberateness.

These days, it depends on who you're with. My brother-in-law still says, with great pity in his voice, "And so-and-so, poor girl, she's never married." And I keep thinking, "Wally, look around you. Who are you saying this to?" But it's hopeless with him. And my sister has been married to him for fifty-three years.

So, yes, you still do encounter that attitude. But back then it was ubiquitous. My family would have been happier if I had been married. They were not comfortable, and I was certainly aware of it. I probably would have been better off if I'd shown defiance, but I was much more apt to get sad and feel longing. Since then I've come to understand that they don't even hear themselves. I have occasionally said, "Listen to what you say."

GEORGIA L., 70 years old, has obviously always been stunning looking. In the '50s, when her marriage broke up, she and her two kids remained in a suburb where all her neighbors were couples.

You were considered used. You were used merchandise. The husbands of my friends would call me and say, "Why don't I come up to your house and bring a bottle?"

MARGUERITE M., for all of her dignity and social standing, doesn't get much better treatment from the local Don Juans.

I had two couples over to dinner. After dinner I served liqueur, and it got to be sort of late and everyone started to leave. And this man's wife even said, "We have to go. It's getting late." Well, he wouldn't budge.

They had come in separate cars, so she went home. I really was angry at her for going. And I don't want to put into words what he wanted, but when he sidled up to me, I said to him, "You leave this second or I'm going to call the police!"

Finally he left. He'd had too much to drink, anyway. I have not had him back in my house since.

Sis N., 61, poet and translator.

Oh, you always went to cocktail parties where drunk men would look down at your chest and say, "Why is a pretty girl like you not married?"

I remember, I had a friend once who was approached by the predictable drunk, and he asked, "Why is a pretty girl like you not married?" And she said, "Why is a big slob like you married?"

Susannah W., who has affairs but lives alone.

Many married women are perceived as needing help, and they get it. They break down and then recover. It's an option for them. Some of them, anyway. But what I have to do is keep putting one foot in front of the other and keep going. What choice do I have? I'm a single woman. So in a way I get resentful when people keep telling me how strong I am because I exist as a single woman and I don't collapse. Adaptation to a difficult situation, yes, that's good. But what's bad is going ahead but with bitterness and resentment, and that's sometimes how I feel. Though, obviously, not often enough to make me want to be on the other side of the chasm.

EVERYDAY PUT-DOWNS

*What's most poignant is the wide range of emotional responses,
as if women were at their most creative in trying
to process attacks on the self.*

Christine L. is still incredulous.

It's not something I ever wanted to change, but being smart was a handicap in terms of dealing with who I was perceived to be. And yet it never dissuaded me from wanting to do well. It just meant that I always had to deal with a potential reaction to that on the part of those boys I wanted to perceive me as interesting and attractive and desirable, however scary that was. And the thing that was amazing is that it wasn't only true in high school. I was shocked when I went to college. I went to Yale—for me it was such an exciting accomplishment—and I was shocked because I thought there will be all these guys who are smart and intellectual, and I will be perfectly accepted, but that wasn't so.

Another thing is, there's this restaurant everyone in town tries to get reservations for, a French restaurant, and I went to dinner there one night with a friend who is a single woman. And we were seated in the back section, which is nice but less nice than the front. And when we left, my friend said to the maître d', she said, "You know, I noticed that everyone sitting in the front is a couple, a young couple, and the people in the back are either women together or men together or two and one or something." She raised it and he denied it. I couldn't tell whether she was right about it being deliberate, but it certainly was true: That was a little showcase for the couples up front.

PAULINE M. shakes her head, bemused.

One friend who was married, she would just drop by—on her way to work, on her way home, on her way wherever. Without calling ahead. I would never have presumed to do the same to her, but the presumption was, I was there all by myself, what could I possibly be doing?

BLANCHE W., like many women, finds herself helplessly regressing in the presence of patronizing relatives.

My aunt, an enormously successful, respected professional woman, who is fortunate enough to be married to a very wealthy man, will say whenever I complain about being tired and working hard: "Well, you know, Bibi, you really don't need to work that hard except that you want to have a house at the beach. You wouldn't have to work so hard if you would just accept something more modest." This said from the vantage point of eight rooms on Park Avenue.

"Maybe you want to go to law school?" she says. Yes, she actually says that. I remind her that she's the one who wanted to go to law school and that I am quite successful in my field, and it would be major-league bizarre. Needless to say, she and my mother were quite competitive.

AMELIA J. was able to talk about something that almost all single women feel but few are willing to confront.

I hadn't thought of it as status. I hadn't phrased it that way. But when I was married, there was this presence, there was this man in my life. Even if I was unhappy about it or worried about it, still, I was identified in relation to that. I really felt like I had a position, like a woman in society. So what I believe is that one of the things that people get married for is a position in society. I don't know if it's something they're aware of or not. I know that they may not admit it.

I don't know what to think about women who are married and feel trapped. I mean, they could do what many of us did: They could give it up. I gave up everything. But it would have been harder *not* to do it than to do it. That's true.

WHO ENVIES/PITIES WHOM?

This was the sort of question my subjects enjoyed pondering.

GINNY O., 29, would be cast as a heartthrob any time except when she's talking about herself.

I don't know. I feel self-pity sometimes, and I don't know if people who are in couples pity people who are single. I've never asked.

Even my sister has said things to me that make me think that at times she thinks I'm a fool! It's a kind of relief, because when I was a kid and I did so well in school, I thought at times, *Maybe she feels bad because she's not getting good marks.* But she must have felt that socially I'm an idiot. So that's OK. I really don't care. But I see how her marriage is going. . . . I couldn't take that kind of tension. I would have to be in a fairly easygoing relationship or I couldn't survive it. I couldn't be putting pressure on another person all the time or taking it. So I feel sorry about that tension, or sorry that my sister doesn't get around to doing things she might like. But she's very happy with her two sons, and each of them is a handful. She loves her life, and she prefers it by far to mine, I'm sure.

SOPHIE K., 61, admissions director in a private college, has been rebuilding her life in the year and a half since her husband died after a long illness.

One of the first things I learned as a single woman is that it's very difficult to be with people who are even very dear friends, as married friends, and the other thing you learn is that you never tell them anything about your private life because the women who are in their long-term marriages are very jealous.

JENNIFER B., the one who discovered that not being afraid of men is often problematic.

I think probably my married friends feel both sorry for me and they also envy me. I don't think any of them wants to be out there dating. And yet they envy the fact that I have "freedom."

ABIGAIL Z., 37, an architect, widowed after three years, is an emotional seesaw adept.

I often vacation with women who are married, without their husbands, and they are very jealous of me and their vision of how glamorous my life is. I may not have regular sex, but I have boyfriends. And freedom. Of course, their vision is exaggerated, but they can't think of it another way. I know that's true because I talk to them about my life, but they don't hear.

I've only had small tastes of being part of a couple and didn't even realize until years later . . . like when married people have pet names. . . . It's absurd, but I remember how that was with my husband. A lot of it is ridiculous, but also you know every Saturday afternoon when you come home from the supermarket you're going to get in bed, have sex, and then take a nap. And that didn't vary. At the time that seemed to be incredibly boring and not exciting, but I look back on the predictability of our sex— which was by far not my best sexual relationship, not the most satisfying to me at all—but I look back and think, "Oh, God, I don't know *when* I'm going to have sex again." And I'd just love to get on a plane, go home and find John, and go to bed and have sex and take a nap!

MONICA V., the divorced entrepreneur.

I have a married friend, who's a good friend, and an old friend, and I can see that she thinks my life is so pathetic, she's so happy that she's not in my situation. And then she also thinks I go out *every night*, and I have this incredibly exciting, wonderful life that she's just totally envious of. Whenever I tell her that I'll be home that evening, she says, "Oh, you're not going to a party?"

As if there were parties every night. But in fact, we're not living in a fun time. Look at the newspapers: We're encouraged to think that cooking at home is an exciting thing to do. I mean, where are the articles about all the great restaurants where everybody goes and hangs out? Or the great bars where people go out to meet and talk?

SUSANNAH W., who told us she fights against resentment.

Well, I have one friend from junior high school I see about once or twice a year. She met a young man just out of high school. They dated the appropriate period of time, they were engaged for two years, they got married, they had twins, the twins have graduated from college now, and I meet them every few years. In the '70s I was embarrassed to tell my friend Marilyn, "Well I'm separating from this guy" or "I'm moving again" or "I'm giving up this career and I'm doing this or that." She always knew what she wanted. And I always thought that Marilyn wanted to be a big fish in a little pond. And when I've seen her in the past few years, I am so grateful that I have my life. She has this man who is a very sweet man, but there's no interest there, it's clear. There's control, but no interest.

So I find that I'm enjoying my privilege of singleness with this friend, and the privilege is that she says, "Well, what's going on?" and I say, "Well, I'm going out with three men." And it's very cruel of me, I know, but for all those years, she didn't intend for me to suffer, which is the cruel part because I intend for her to wriggle a little bit. She was totally unaware of being judgmental about my life. I know I'm punishing her but I've always felt disappointed in her because she made a choice; she made a deliberate choice to take that comfortable path and, unconsciously, make me pay for it. She probably couldn't allow herself to question herself directly. I think that's why she's pursued me all these years. I don't keep up with her. She's the one who calls me.

ANDREA H., 48, a social worker.

There's a perception that single women go through life with a chip on their shoulder to be like men. And that it's a mark of infamy.

I would be just as willing to believe that as anybody. Like, *What's wrong with me? How come I'm single?* And I've gone through many years of therapy trying to figure out that central concern. I look around at married women and I think, *Well, how come that one or that one? They're really crazy or not that smart or interesting. How come they're not single?*

You always hear about somebody who was abused and psychologically damaged and so forth, and then you hear that they're married with three kids and you think, *How did they do that, and why can't I?* And you start to feel like you're the problem.

BLANCHE W., 50, the endocrinologist whose aunt suggested she go to law school.

Right before this place, I had a two-bedroom apartment, and it was quite nice. And my mother, when she saw it the first time, said something like, "It's going to be something for you to get involved with any man because they're going to be completely intimidated by this place." So now that I live in this duplex, it's even worse. . . . Not that there have been that many people I've brought over. One of the things I hate when people come over here is when they say, "Oh, you're brave!" That makes me feel stupid. Like they know something I don't know.

But also, I know that when I have business meetings here, it leads to all sorts of speculation about me and where this money comes from. And it provokes a lot of envy, and that's sometimes hard. The men don't articulate it. The women do—especially older women or women who are married. I think there is something about having this home by myself that really profoundly disturbs them.

JANIE A., wearing a suit and stenciled cowboy boots, is a lawyer. I spoke to her on her first day off in two weeks.

I threw a party with my sisters and my brother a while ago. It was one of those crowds of high achievers, and there happened to be a lot of single women there, older single women. And a friend of mine—he's in a very traditional relationship; he was married when he was twenty, and they go to the Hamptons every weekend and have two kids—was also there. And I asked him if his wife, Laurie, had a nice time, and he said, "Yes, but she thought it was so strange that there were so many older single women there." You know, women in their twenties, thirties, forties. She's thinking the exact opposite of what I'm thinking. She's thinking, *They're losers. Can't find a guy. It's pathetic.* And I'm thinking, *Now, we've got a real interesting group of women here.* I'm thinking, *These women haven't settled. These are really strong strong women.* And Laurie thinks that the men are thinking what she thinks, and I'm thinking the men are thinking, *Well, we have some interesting stuff here. These are women with careers and goals.* Laurie's the kind of woman who would have shot herself in the head if she wasn't married by thirty, you see? But at a party with all of her friends who got married in their early twenties, I'd probably be wondering, *What's wrong with them? They really missed out.*

CALLIE S., the real estate agent who has raised her youngest daughter as a single mother.

Envy them? Never until I had Reiny. And then I became reacquainted with the fact that the whole world is in twos. I never saw a marriage that made me say: "That's what I want for me." But being with somebody and being a part of somebody, that's what I envied.

CHRISTINE L., the woman who discovered that her intelligence was not necessarily an advantage at Yale.

I feel that even by having this discussion, I'm sounding whiny. But maybe that's the problem. Why is it whiny to talk about your life? Or to acknowledge your longing? I think there's an issue of shame, sort of, that's very deep.

You think that women who are married have shame too? I hadn't thought of that. Well, good, they should feel that. Because I always assume that women who are married, whatever else they may think, they're really glad they're married and they have children.

JOCELYN H., the African-American nurse in her 40s, has real assurance about her situation.

Yes, I do believe I have much closer friendships with other single women than I do with married women. I believe so only because I think they have more time. They don't have to say, "Oh, I have to go home and make dinner for my husband." They can take more time and do things with other people.

Do I feel that there are things I'm not invited to? I never thought about it, but, yes, I think that would be the case. I had a girlfriend I went on a cruise with a long time ago, and she got married—and now we talk on the phone, we don't go out anymore. It's true, it became a different relationship.

I don't know if there's a stigma or if married women consider themselves, or are considered, higher. I've never thought about that. I personally would not. I think single mothers have the status of being in a higher position because I think they can get themselves to do more. You're out there, you're supporting yourself and your children. If you're married, you depend on a two-income setup, and you don't have to be saying, "I have to do this." If you're at home, sick, you don't have to say, "I still have to go out and do it." You think, *My husband is going to bring home a paycheck.*

LISA C., 33, by contrast is timid, soft-spoken.

Am I envious? My married friends . . . I don't think marriage changes them; I think having children changes your life—a lot. But, no, most of the people who are married I look at and say, "Thank God I'm not in that."

REGINA M., 40, clearly has done a lot of work on herself.

The ones who have good marriages I deeply envy. I wouldn't want one of those marriages, but I would love to have a true companionship. People see marriage as a right—that's the problem—and it's actually a grace. I do know a few really good ones. These two men I know have been together thirty years, and they still make love every day. Remarkable? Yes, with gusto. I'll call up and I'll say, "How are you?" And one of them—the one who talks about it—will say, "Well, we just had a lovely nap." And then there will be a pause. And then I'll say, "I'm so jealous," and then he'll say, "You should be."

SISTERS

*Some of the most penetrating barbs come from
other women, starting with sisters.*

JANIE A., the lawyer, worked in a bank before going back to school for law in her 30s.

At one point when money got sort of rough, Marianne, my sister, who is married with children and lives in a wonderful, huge house, suggested I rent a room in a terrible neighborhood. I mean, move out of my apartment! She assumed I should just have this pathetic life. As far as she was concerned, going back to school was a total insanity.

You know, it's like that game—where little plastic heads pop up? It's a game for, like, one- or two-year-olds. And the kid has a hammer, and every time they pop up, the kid has to keep them down. They pop up, and the kid has to go *whack, whack, whack, whack* and keep them down. And I guess every time I pop up, Marianne goes *whack*, and I go back down.

CINDY M., 34, feels that not having taken her elder sisters' paths really simplifies sibling rivalry.

It's funny that I have two sisters who went in such very different directions. There's the martyr, the helpful one, the one with the terrible marriage who gets so excited when her husband goes on business trips. He is an alcoholic. He doesn't know it yet, but he is. And there's the selfish one, who has the great marriage. So that's kind of a hard lesson.

It's my sister Rosemary who has the wonderful marriage. She's amazing because she has always been able to get what she wants. I think I'm a little resentful there that she's such a hard person. She could look at my mother and say, "Fuck you"—and here was a woman on the verge of a breakdown. And Rosemary likes her job. It bores me to death, but she really likes her job, and she's got a great husband who does fifty percent of the work, and he's a wonderful father. But the way she relates to my situation, you know . . . sometimes she's a little insensitive. I tell her about dates, and she tries to act supportive, but she's never done anything to help me.

But still, she was the first one in the family to recognize my positive attributes, and so I'm always grateful for her, because everyone else would really sort of ignore me. She was the first one to say, "You do a great job," and that's hard for her.

I think my [other] sister sometimes forgets how it is to be single and alone and . . . I don't make my desires known to my family because I think they'll get some satisfaction knowing that I'm feeling unfulfilled. They wouldn't feel at all badly for me. Not that I want anyone feeling sorry for me, you know. But so it's especially annoying that I can't get this relationship thing off the ground. Yeah, I think my sister unfortunately would have a lot of pleasure out of my misery, and it would make her feel good. There just wasn't enough love to go around when we were growing up, even before my mother's suicide. I mean, it's not all animosity, we have a lot of fun. It's only that I'm in analysis three times a week, and I really have to think about these things.

LAURALYNNE A., the schoolteacher, is the second oldest of four daughters.

With sisters, there's just this built-in competition, and like it or not, it's always there. On the one hand you sort of feel this intense rivalry, and on the other hand, you can feel pitied as well—that they feel sorry for you if for the third or fifth Christmas in a row you show up without a guy. And then when you do show up with one, you feel that there's envy, as well. So there's sort of a strange mix.

In my family? Are you kidding? No, nothing ever gets said. It's a feeling—a feeling that they're sizing you up, like people are passing judgment, like, "How come there's no one to share her life with?" That kind of thing.

Even if you're not participating in the competition, everyone is out there like, "Oh, she's got more money" or "She's the pretty one" or "She married the nicest guy." Especially when there are several of you. The best way to deal with it is accept that people are going to do it. And you kind of get labeled as "She never got married" or "She never got children." It's sort of melancholy.

JENNIFER B. has no sisters.

You know what else you should ask single people? What they think their responsibility is to their parents, versus a married woman's. I think I, as a single woman, I will bear the brunt, whether it's financially or emotionally, of the later years of my parents' lives. The question is going to become whether they are going to live with me, or whether I can afford to have them live on their own in a style I feel comfortable having them live in. And I'm not looking forward to it.

My brother? He's got a wife.

JOCELYN H., like many youngest daughters, gets little help from her older sisters.

Two of my sisters were out of state, and the third was here in the city, but if I'd say to her, "Can you look in on Mommy?" because one weekend I wanted to go away, she would say, "I can't do it." She didn't go to see my mother for the two years she was really sick.

No, I don't really understand why. One of the things I thought about over the years that might have done it, I guess, was the fact that my mother was really supportive of me when I had my son. She did more for him than for their children, who had fathers. . . . I don't know if they understood.

HAPPY COUPLES

And then there's the guilty detail of comparison.

EVELYN B. Despite the fact that she is a respected mathematician, Evelyn once had all the attributes needed to be a Class-A wife.

I could be wrong, but I can't imagine that most of the couples I know have anything close to pleasurable sex. One of the things you learn when you get a divorce is how many of your friends' husbands hit on you immediately. It's amazing. The couples we had spent eve-nings with, our kids went to school together. . . . He was the model husband, uh-huh. And of course you can't say a word because she thinks she's happily married. And these are the "happy marriages." . . .

PAULINE M., who doesn't care for schleppy men.

And when you think about it, there are plenty of men around; you just don't necessarily want them. Most of my friends who are married or are living with men, I think they're so much smarter or so much more interesting than their husbands are. And who knows what the terms are, but it seems a compromise that in many ways is too bad.

MONICA V.'s husband took a powder when she had breast cancer.

Thank God I have my friends, because they keep me oriented to the viewpoint that this isn't it. . . . Linda and Michael, and Annie and Brian, and Valerie and—you know, all these little couples. When I was first divorced, I called them "the happy couples.". . . You know how when people are just coupled, and it becomes their principal identity, you want to throw them both in the river. "Well, *we* think . . . and *we* do this, and we're going to fix you up with him because you can't be single, because we're married and you're a threat, and we don't like it, or it's pathetic, it's just too pathetic; you have to be married just like us. . . ." Well, I don't say to people, you have to be single just like me. . . . Give me a break. People who are married constantly have to have that kind of affirmation.

It's not taken seriously when we object, but men complain about this, too. Bachelors complain about this with their married male friends. It's a cliché already; you know, "He's trying to get me married. . . ." But it's just as true with women too. And if you don't have a child, there's something wrong with you for not having a child . . . and I find myself having to explain that I tried to have a child. "Oh, OK, well, that's OK, as long as you tried. . . ." Or I *was* married; I'm divorced. "OK, OK, as long as you're divorced . . . as long as you're not one of those *weird* women who has something really wrong with her, who doesn't want to get married, who doesn't want children." Give me a break! I mean, who's defining the norm? But the problem is that we—single women—are defining it that way, too. In my worst moments, you know, I feel pathetic and alone, and, *Oh, my God, I've got to meet a guy. And please fix me up with whomever . . . somebody coming into town. . . .* You know, that kind of thing?

NINA L., the 28-year-old aerobics instructor. Like many of us, she says very few of the marriages among her acquaintances beckon to her as models.

I only know three couples I would consider have good marriages. And two of the couples are people in their sixties, so they don't count.

FELICIA C., 49, says that postdivorce she suddenly found herself retreating into an all-female universe.

The community of single women can feel like a wonderful, comfortable place to be, or it can feel like a ghetto, and it only depends on my own feelings of self-worth, I guess, which for me is a problem.

My relationships with my married friends? I can't remember who my married women friends were because I don't have them anymore.

ODD WOMAN OUT

When one of us is suddenly one of them.

ABIGAIL Z., the architect, is still wistful.

I'll never forget the first time I went to a wedding alone. It was after John. I just didn't have anybody, and for two years after he died I didn't have a date, and I went to things alone, and I felt like everyone at the whole room was looking at me.

Even now, all these years later, I have a hard time knowing if I want to be alone. I have a great life alone now, and yet I wasn't brought up thinking it was OK. I still feel terribly uncomfortable. I go to everything *alone.*

MARGUERITE M., when she was widowed, noticed that she was immediately dropped from certain functions.

Like dances and things like that, you know. Balls. And some dinners. Actually I think a lot of people don't know how to handle a single woman. And I think men are intimidated by these women, especially the ones who have been single very long.

CALLIE S., a decade younger than Marguerite M., responded with the same kind of good humor to a question about social discrimination.

Oh, probably, sure. Parties at peoples' homes? Oh, sure, definitely. I know dozens of married couples who never invite me for dinner. They might come to my house for a Christmas Eve or something. And any kind of a family function—a wedding, a funeral, a bar mitzvah—those I'm always invited to. But you know there are dozens of dinner parties on Friday and Saturday night. I never see those invitations.

ANDREA H., 48, the social worker.

Are you kidding?! There's plenty of public discrimination. If you're alone in a restaurant, for instance. And I think there is when you're shopping if you're not wearing a wedding ring. A wedding ring is a sign, and people look at it. *I* look to see if they're wearing wedding rings, *I* look to see if they're married, to see if they're on the other side. My friend Pamela, who had to take off her wedding ring when she was pregnant because her fingers swelled up too much, told me that people treated her completely differently, even on the subway, because they assumed she was a knocked-up single woman. She told me that she wanted to scream at them, "I'm married! I'm married!"

Oh, yes. I think there's a huge social network of couples socializing. That's the way married people socialize, by and large: with other couples. Do I wish I were invited? Not as a single woman, I don't. People deal with single women like people who have some kind of disease. They're polite and everything, but there's some way in which they're afraid of single women.

I do feel defensive. It's so easy for married people or people who are with someone to feel pity for single women, and I sometimes feel what I have to do is take great pains to make it clear to everyone that I am not in the category of single women to be pitied, so that I have at least the illusion of equality with them. So that they'll think that my being single is a choice.

MONICA V., as the months passed after the breakup of her marriage, felt her life had less and less in common with that of her married friends.

I decided that for the time being, I shouldn't focus so much on my married friends because they have different kinds of lives, and that I should get single friends. And I did. I went out and I got a whole new group of friends who are single women, and then they all got married, and then they all had babies. So here I am, all over again.

FELICIA C., who was divorced two years ago, says that though she is relieved the relationship with her husband is over, she feels deprived in ways.

It surprised me how complete the rejection was, after the divorce, and how sudden it was. Not that I ever wanted to be in the mixed company that I was in when I was married. . . .

Yes. Dropped by people who were his friends, and the problem with it was that I really had very few friends of my own because they led such different lives from me, the ones I had known before I was married. They were much younger than my husband and his friends, and of course I knew many more men than I do now.

Why do I think his friends dropped me? First of all because it's awkward to have an extra woman at the table, and dinner parties are still rather formal that way; they like to have more or less equal numbers of men and women, and there are just too many single women to be thought of, and in my case it was—Once I actually was invited out with, or rather just had friendly conversations and talks with one of my ex-husband's friends who was a neighbor, and my ex-husband found out about this—it wasn't a big secret—and he told our neighbor, who then told me that he had said that if his friend ever went near me again, he wouldn't talk to him. So that was that. It's not even that I would want to talk with any of the people I knew when I was with him, but it's plain that he was more useful to them than I was, which was why we were invited out so much in the first place. Because of his work there was always the feeling he could do something for them.

Oh, yes, my family behaved very differently after the breakup. You get treated more like a child because the only reason you weren't treated like a child was out of respect for the husband. And the illusion that your family was interested in your opinions is really shattered for good when you realize that nobody wants your opinion anymore. You thought they wanted your opinion, but they really only wanted your husband's, which they assumed would be yours. And they were right.

BILLIANA M., 52, teacher, says she didn't even have to wait to get divorced before the social exclusion began.

Oh, I do definitely have a sense of stigma. I just have handpicked more conscious people. Am I defensive? I think it's tied up in a complex way. There's a part of me that feels that people will see me as unlovable because I'm not anybody's significant other. I question myself, as well, to be honest, so it's painful for me because I sometimes wonder.

JUNE W., the state senator, is someone who did remain in her own milieu, and she experienced less and less discomfort as time went by.

This year was the first year when I was invited to the benefit galas where I didn't have to have an escort and they did not supply some gay fellow.

MARY ANN B.'s slice of society is much more casual, but she has noticed a similar progression.

There may be social events that I'm not invited to because I don't fit. But I'm not aware of them because I'm not invited to them. I can't think of any group I want to get into but can't because I'm single.

I still get invited as a single woman to couples events. But I've found it changed in the last few years. People feel today much less compulsion to have a partner for you there. I don't think any of my friends feel that at all. Even in the Midwest. Although in the Midwest, when I went back home last year, there were a few occasions in which I noticed a single man was also invited to the dinner. We were not necessarily seated next to one another, but the boy-girl neatness of the arrangement was somehow met. And I only noticed it because that's rare now. At least that's rare for me now. People don't try to fix me up. Or maybe my friends think I've become unfixable, and they're resigned now. But I think it comes much more out of respect than pity.

PHILLIPA C., the well-known artist.

I don't have many friends in couples. Also, many people see me as famous and successful, so they get confused. They might look down on me for not being married, but they know I'm a celebrity, so they don't know what to think. I've noticed that my married friends are very eager to have me paired off. And it may be because they love me and would be happy to see me paired off, but it may also be something else. But it's strange that often when I go somewhere with a man, they will just assume that he's the new man in my life and proceed accordingly. It's almost as if they have a need to see me paired off.

What's amazing to me is that I go to a party with some guy, and the next thing I know is people say to me, "Where are you two going to send the kids this summer?" Suddenly we're a couple, and he's going to be taking care of my kids. It's as if their brain can't take in the possibility that I'm alone.

HILLARY P. was in her mid-20s when I first interviewed her, at which time she emphatically declared that promiscuity made much more sense than monogamy. Now in her late 20s, she's about to move in with someone.

One thing I've realized, especially at work, is how people seem invested in my relationship. You know, even people who don't really have the emotional right, in a way, they seem awfully invested in my couplehood. There's definitely a "one of us" feeling to the way people ask questions about Eric and how they relate sympathetically to me. And it always feels like, "Oh, you kids . . . " You know, like, "You're not married yet but . . . " What I'm trying to get at is that there is an "Us" and a "Them," and I went from "Them" to "Us." It doesn't really affect me one way or another but it feels a little strange. Like I'm being admitted to a club, and I don't really know what that club is. Or it's like being admitted without applying.

THE GLASS WORKPLACE

For all of its advances, the American workplace is
astonishingly static from a social point of view,
each small change hard won and not all that secure.

JEAN I., 48, the divorced director of research at a large company, is one of those women whom many people think other people fear. She's smart, politically sophisticated, outspoken, and not given to girly-girl displays, even though she knows which Armani suit to purchase. The double whammy is that she is therefore not only forbidden to rise above a certain level in her conservative company but also not allowed her due as a woman.

For example, one of my intermediate bosses, whom I've now removed myself from, has never, never acknowledged that I've had a baby-sitting problem. He'll always assume that I'm available, and then I'll always have to say, "I can't be here 'till midnight, I don't have a baby-sitter." And then the next time he doesn't take it into consideration, he never says, "Can you make arrangements?" He always asks so that I have to say it again. The other women have standing arrangements with husbands who'll cover when they have to work very late, and everyone knows that very well, including him. It's a hostile power maneuver that goes on time and time again. But that's so pervasive.

JENNIFER B., 32, who says she intimidates men, works as a portfolio manager at an investment company.

Yeah . . . I definitely do feel I was discriminated against in my company. But I think a married woman would have been even more discriminated against. You know, the Boys Club. But I think one of the reasons why I'm able to do well in the business world is because a lot of people say that I think like a man and move on and don't get too emotional about certain things. Which I think stems from the fact that I was the only girl on the block when I grew up, and I was the tomboy. And I think not being married enhances that image.

Also, married people just have many more commitments. Married women have to leave and go home whereas I was able to work ten, twelve hours a day. But that's why I left, too. The line had to be drawn. But a man would probably have left much sooner than I did.

MARTHA H. got fired, had to pack all her stuff that very day and put it in cardboard boxes, and leave her corner office without a backward glance. She's got the suits, and the Joan and David shoes, and the Donna Karan pocketbook, and the Isaac Mizrahi blouses, but she's got nothing in her bank account.

Oh, my God, it drives me crazy. For instance, my married friends who were let go by the firm at the same time I was keep saying things as if they're in the same position as I am. They're constantly saying, "I know how you feel." They have absolutely no idea what I feel like because it's a completely different proposition to be a single woman who's lost her job. It's like that poem—Who wrote that poem?—"She's not drowning, she's just waving." She's clearly drowning, and people on the shore say, "Oh she's not drowning, she's waving." It's astounding to me that there are women who were fired at the same time as me who talk about how are they going to survive or get work and whatever it is they say, and they're married to men who are partners of law firms and making $150,000.

I do understand their fear, but the fear of monetary collapse and actual monetary collapse are not the same. And it's basically a way not to listen to me. "I know how you feel" means "Shut up."

JEAN I., the director of research, who has to "ask" each time to have some notice taken of her childcare problems.

Is there a couples culture in this company? I don't feel that so much. There are many things you're expected to go to on your own. Like a lot of these big benefits—you're expected to attend without a spouse, even if you have one. So it evens out.

There are two types of events—a lot of corporate evenings for which they're paying $10,000 a table and where you're not supposed to bring spouses, and then there are Christmas parties where you are supposed to bring spouses. . . . I don't know, maybe I've just done it for so long it doesn't feel like pressure, but I never even think about this. You always have a choice of whether to bring a date or not, and these days I always choose not to bring a date because I don't want to be trapped with some guy.

ELEANOR D., 38, a buyer in a department store in Akron, Ohio.

In my department, I think my stock goes down when I'm involved with someone. It's sort of disappointing to people. Like with Bob now—people like it because they want me to be happy, but it' s a little bit boring, and my entertainment value has gone down. Part of my character was that I was always in these quixotic, romantic, long-distance things. It goes both ways in my department. Most people are married, and they like to have me as this sort of wandering, sexy, romantic figure, but they would also like to have me married because they think it would make me happy and because it would make me less threatening. But then when I am with someone, it's like part of my value is gone because I'm no longer the arty, romantic person.

EILEEN Y., the well-known New England watercolorist, came of age in the 1940s.

Luckily, there were enclaves. And of course the arts. And there were certain colleges. But even during my graduate work I had problems. The women were sort of jealous of me because I was in the class with their husbands, and the husbands didn't totally accept me because I was a woman. I think I felt threatening to some of the wives. I mean, I felt that to be inevitable. I'm not the most threatening person in the world, but I've definitely had that sense—and it sounds very funny to say this, but I'll say it anyway—that sense of not wanting to be too powerful. But that was one thing that I certainly was brought up with, that as a woman I should not be too powerful. Especially if you're around a man, with my talents, such as they were. I was really brought up to always let the man win, in some sense. That was another layer of difficulty.

SUSANNAH W., you may recall, had her desk taken away at age 10, right around the time she thought Perry Mason's Della Street should be elevated.

I became a film critic for one of the news weeklies when I was about thirty-two. In my early thirties I was perceived perhaps as more of a sexual threat than I was in my early forties. But now, the last thing I would have dreamed of, what I never thought would happen in my forties, was that I would be perceived as someone who achieved something totally on my own. Not through a man, not through a marriage or mentorship or some affiliation. As a single woman I'm perceived in a way as somehow more mysterious or powerful because no one knows how I got to where I got. The only assumption made is that I did so through my own energies. And that gives me a certain aura, more personal power. It's almost like a Horatio Alger story. I don't know if this would be true at a corporate level, but in academia, it seems to have changed. Every decade that I've been in there's been a change. I'll be entering my fifties in three years. Let's see how it is in my fifties.

MEGAN'S OPTIMISM

Am I Depressed? Not Really.

Born in 1970 in Korea, MEGAN L. was brought at age 2 to America by her parents. They soon settled in a wealthy suburb. She now lives in a rented walk-up apartment, which she shares with several other women.

I'm twenty-six years old, and I haven't dated very much since I've been out of college. I think it's interesting that I really haven't been giving it as much weight as I did in college. In the age of assumed feminism there are other weights to carry, especially what you want to do, a career. I am of an age where nobody expected to get married. I went to Barnard, and absolutely nobody expected to do anything except work.

My parents are from an age where everyone would set up marriages. In Korea, if you have a daughter, it is very common to find a family with a son and match them up. Even through college, some of my friends whose parents were more conservative and traditionally Korean were constantly hounded by them to marry a certain kind of Korean guy. That certainly wasn't the case in my family. My parents knew my sister and I were living with people. We were very progressive. My parents were more expatriates than immigrants, even though they did come at the Golden Age of America, when there was an American dream.

And they're very liberal regarding the way I've gone about dating. But it's gotten to the point that if you have freedom of choice and you have a whole spectrum of options, you're standing there in the middle wondering what to do. I almost feel like saying to my parents, "Why don't you send me out to meet somebody because I don't know what to do, and I don't have the time to do it."

I think as an adult you become very tired, and adulthood becomes about being tired all the time and having to use your basic instincts to survive so that the choices that you make aren't really ideal. You often behave in a way that you wouldn't admire, you know? And sometimes I am aware of a certain feeling of not wanting to grow old alone. I think of that as the most primitive cultural instinct—going back to something that must have existed at some point, when women had to struggle to exist. Some days, I'm too tired to care what happens to me on that level.

The last time I was in love? I'm not sure I'm being honest, but I could almost say I've never been in love. But I'm not sure I'm being dishonest because I don't have any internal or theoretical sense of love I can refer to. Classical Asian love? I don't know if it ever existed. People married for status. I don't know why my parents got married. I never even saw them kiss, you know? And most of my childhood, I hoped they'd get divorced. I think at certain points it was probably a really close call, and it was obvious that they had bad spots. Ultimately, it seems to me that they were comfortable and enjoyed each other's company and laughed, and they had us, but I feel that if love was part of that equation it would have been apparent to me. So I can't really say it exists. But I'm twenty-six, and for some reason I feel that emptiness. . . . Is it going to hit me one day and am I going to say, *I'm in love?* I can't fathom what that's going to feel like. . . .

How other people think of me definitely works into the syndrome and plays into the worry of how people will treat an old woman in New York. *The spinster!* That threatening, horrible idea of being an old maid gives me an equally horrible Scarlet O'Hara idea of *I'll think about it tomorrow.* I say to myself that if I'm going to prevent that, I have to put some serious thought into relationships.

Yes, I was in therapy through college, because that was a very confusing time. Being single right now is much more than a situational thing; it's the combination of situation and the choices you've made to be in that situation. And the choices are highly psychological—fear of intimacy and fear of control and self-esteem. Like, this is the kind of thing I would talk about in therapy when I was doing it. I think it's the combination of all of those things that I would rather not think about right now, mostly because my physical situation isn't all that secure. That's part of why I have all these theories. Theory is therapy, there's no doubt about that. . . .

When I do fantasize, it's about a situation rather than a person. It's because I don't know what that person would look like. I have never gone out with anyone Asian, and I wouldn't know how even if I wanted to—and I am starting to want to. Because that's one of the things that's driving me crazy, which is the whole white-guy/Asian-woman thing. It drives women crazy, especially the college educated.

A lot of the reason I am presently single is I could never put a face on the man I could be with, and for years I was not a face in my own fantasies. Even if I was fantasizing, masturbating, I couldn't put my own face on that. I think it's a whole amalgamation of not having an identity as a person of color in America, a classic problem of alienation and lack of identity as an Asian in America. And as clichéd as that may sound, it was years of pain. So for years I didn't look in a mirror. And if I didn't have a face in myself, I don't think there was any way I was going to have a face with a partner. All of my old boyfriends have been white, and that annoys me, and it annoys me when I see Asian women with white guys, even though I'm in the same position. I try really hard not to say that he's doing something wrong or that she is—it's just the situation that annoys me. It would be amazing one day to remember all the things I've blocked out because they were so painful. I'd have to be a really secure person. Most of the time I feel upset by my formative experiences in those areas. You see, I wouldn't call myself a cynical or bitter person, I would call myself an optimist—but I just know that everything sucks.

Am I depressed? Not really. I've just always had a sense of acknowledgment that things sucked. I faced it. From a very early age I faced the fact that people were going to be against me because I wasn't white. Academically, socially. Everything that existed was wrong for me, and everything that was right didn't exist. It would have to be modified first before I'd be with someone—and it would have to be somebody who wants to take me home as a girlfriend, somebody who doesn't want to think of me as a victim so that I would feel that I have nothing to be victimized about anymore, that it's all past, all that taunting, spooking me.

I see this whole—if I can summarize it—this whole grand age of repression at the end of the century as a symbol for my own Asian repression. I just have to find a nice repressed Irish American. I've decided Catholic Irish Americans are the cross between repressed WASPs and neurotic Jews.

SOCIAL CHANGE & PRIVATE COMPLICATIONS

Betrayal becomes too simplistic an accusation
when trying to figure out what's happened.

MONICA V., the entrepreneur.

Betrayal of what? For a while I felt this whole situation . . . you know, I was betrayed by the women's movement. Did you ever have those feelings? Like in the mid '80s or late '80s, I just felt, *Wait a minute! They said it was going to be better!* I had imagined that it would be better, you know, to be alone and to be working and this and that. Where are they now when I need them? But betrayal of *what?* That's the thing with our generation. We all think that somebody says something and it has to work out, or else we're going to sue them. Life isn't like that. You have to think things through, and nobody knows these answers.

AMELIA J., the researcher, is a veteran of the woman's movement heyday, twenty to thirty years ago.

I started to feel that it was getting sort of hard to be with this group of friends. In fact, it became awful. It was a group of professionals. I was the only unmarried person. For three or four years, we met once a month. At my house. Why my house? Because there was no one else to disturb. There were no arrangements that had to be made. And we would read nineteenth century novels. You know, it's great; You bring in your food from Dean and Deluca, you have your meeting, your intellectual exchange, it's personal, and then they would leave—and they would always forget to pay me, and I would be left with the dishes. Though, of course, the privilege there is that I'm at my own house, so I don't have to go anyplace. Anyway, so there was this group, and they were all married, of different marital generations. One with grown kids. Two in their forties, with little kids. . . . And one of my friends said to me, that, well, yes, she does look down on women who are not married. And she says it with great irony, but, in any event, she says it. That she's the success, and that the other ones are the failures. But somewhere I know she knows that long ago she compromised her relationship to the world of women who are achievers, feminists. . . . It wasn't her marriage. It was her need for comfort.

GINGER G., a 34-year-old landscaper, has been involved with a married man for years. Without the official status of marriage, her family feels there is no need to respect their relationship.

Of course, I've also had to deal with the kind of disapproving thing with Eric. Because they've known it was going on for years and years and years. They figured it out after a couple of years, so there's a certain amount of resentment that I sort of deal with.

Like not getting invited to a Christmas dinner party. I remember once my aunt who's ultraconservative—my father's sister—she knew Eric's name perfectly, but when she was making introductions, she said, "What's your name again?" She's to the right, the Pat Buchanan right, and she thinks it's like Living in Sin and all that.

ELLEN P., our curator.

Well, I think that the relationship between Eros and curiosity— which I think need to exist in relation to one another—has been in this moment, in this culture, virtually eradicated. I don't think late-American-capitalist puritanical culture has any real interest in Eros as a place of subversion or understands the value of being truly curious about the self and the world. All of this exploration is seen as too dangerous. I think people are frightened. And if you're seen to have it, that subversive curiosity, it's very scary to them.

What this culture wants to do is tell us what we desire. We need to reimagine what passion and loyalty and commitment are really about. I don't know who'll take a chance on doing what you have to do—as I think my generation did. You have to have a generation that once again says, "We want to find out whether these terms, which are not in themselves deadening and cauterizing, whether we can't define them so there is a genuine human exploration going on." And not just the passive reassurance involved in a commitment like marriage. I think a lot of younger people are more interested in marriage now because everything is so insecure. But I don't think that's a good reason to marry somebody.

ADELE U., 40, wishes choices were made unconsciously because she just can't stop debating with herself.

I'm always, like, *Maybe there is something wrong with me. . . .* But then I see how other single women live, the ones I admire.

ANNETTE F., 34, recently divorced, has felt mystified as to what kind of self-image she is even *supposed* to have.

I realized how much had changed because of Princess Di and the way she was deified. I mean, she was a single mother. There she was, a divorced woman who was out on a date. . . .

HATEVILLE

It's only in dreams that oppression is clearly defined.

BILLIANA M., who got pregnant and left her family's home at age 14.

I dreamed I was in a compound surrounded with barriers. There were other people there, contained in this compound, and these people were both male and female. The buildings were comfortably utilitarian, more like dormitories or congregate living. And we were definitely being kept in there by some force, implied or expressed. . . . The compound had a rectangular shape. Just outside it, at one end, there were warheads, missiles, and they were all dead aimed at the compound.

The place was nicknamed Hateville, at least by me and those of us in there. That was because we were hated by whoever was around us, by whomever the oppressors or the authorities were; we were despised somehow. Because all basic needs and comforts were being met, there was a lot of passivity on the part of the people there. I knew that if any of us tried to escape, the missiles were right there, and we would be obliterated, but I knew I couldn't stay there. And so I went back to my kind of cubicle, my own little space, and I put on some black Reebok aerobic sneakers, and I put on a black leather jacket with the sleeves cut off and some of those black gloves that have no fingers—you know, street-fighting gear. And I had on black pants and a shirt—you know, very functional, very sturdy. And I started to walk in a very . . . not a marching fashion but very resolute, walking with arms swinging, and I had my hands kind of in fists, swinging but ready. Then, as I was walking through, right where the warheads were, and I was going to walk out, little by little people started to gather with me. We were sort of like a parade marching out of there. And that was the end of it, we were going to go. It was "Give me liberty or give me death" at that point.

THE ENDGAME

Breaking Down and Breaking Up

That divorce may be good for marriage is an idea that's been gaining ground. More and more people have come to feel that real choice may be healthier for both the married and the unmarried. Like "The personal is political," a phrase often heard among women in the '70s and '80s, it articulates a paradox that brings a historical dimension to daily life, but mainly it's a way of pointing at something that can't be expressed. How else do we maneuver around the problem that nobody wants to break up a marriage, but most people can't stay in one? And, at the very least, it's a real idea—the only salient new thing that anyone has heard about relationships in ages.

It's like the proverbial ugly linoleum that we eventually manage to stop noticing. We are so bombarded with exhortations to save our relationships, to welcome intimacy, to be in touch with this or that within our repertoire of difficult feelings, and to connect with our partners' desires, sense of loss, willingness to grieve, capacity to feel joy, hopes, fears, limits, needs—and their various attempts to be in touch with ours—that the subject of relationships begins to seem monotonous, if not exhausting, and eventually, therefore, quasi-invisible and inaudible. It's not that there hasn't been any good theorizing and writing on the subject of couples and their problems, or their future; it is that whatever good ideas may be floating around are either obscured or simplified to the point of distortion by the endlessly voluble sermons of the self-help pedagogues.

So many people seem to have given up—and in this case I don't mean the ones who aren't in relationships; I'm talking of those who are. I would like to propose that the barrage of calls to be in touch with our feelings may actually accomplish what it is designed to prevent. Numbing out, fragmentation, myopia become the escapes of choice. Clarity is forsaken. Let the obnoxious repeated pattern blur underfoot.

And it's spreading, as if to cover every inch of the emotional space. You can't turn on a TV or open a magazine without pressure by mental health professionals of every stripe to face the Problem of Intimacy, to express, to allow, to free, to open, to reach out, to *connect*. The most desperate emblem, I think, of everything wrong with being hectored to connect is the jingle that informs us that if we only pick up the telephone, we will finally be able to reach out and touch someone—since, of course, that touch is predicated on the other person being out of town.

But then, too, dependency ("co-" and every other type) has come to be regarded with dismay. The "relationship industry" sabotages the very reality it supports by relentlessly inspiring us to engage in reaching out and touching on the one hand and to "be your own self" on the other—and seldom helping us work out how the twain should meet. What is the woman to do who has been in an abusive relationship with someone she should not have reached out and touched in the first place? For all that as a society our official position is still to deplore the divorce rate, she is likely to encounter the moral imperative *not* to stay in such a marriage, for her children's sake and her own. An ability to break up with someone (the ultimate assertiveness training) has become no less a sign of self-esteem than the capacity to attract a mate. Divorce as self-help, it's here. So then, why badger a woman to "reach out and touch someone?" After all she's been through, when she hears the culture's call to connect, all her circuits have to blow.

For all of this, the divorce rate remains steady at 50 percent. While the real rate of unhappiness must be even worse. We are so browbeaten that we often lose our sense of humor, but surely one of the more amusing inverse ratios of century's end is that of the ever-increasing call for More Intimacy vs. the ever-decreasing percentage of successful conjugal and/or romantic relationships. The more the institution of marriage falters, the more families dissolve, the more community becomes atomic, the more frenetic the injunction to connect. The more relationships break up, the more agitated the self-help press and the talk show media become about the necessity of Expressing our Feelings or Hearing our Partner's. Yet nothing is better designed to make us lose our awareness of one another. Personality, ambience, interaction—all forfeit their singularity when they are neatly packaged into dense clusters of shoulds and should-nots. If we diverge even slightly from the contemporary model of mental health, we are accused of causing and/or operating from a position of "misunderstanding." Scan the cover lines of your average self-help paperback bookshelf, and you will notice how often you're invited to learn how to **PREVENT** the *misunderstandings* that sabotage relationships, or how to **EXPRESS** your needs and/or fears so as to **AVOID** *misunderstandings*, how to show the kind of **CONCERN** and **CARE** that **CUTS THROUGH** *misunderstanding*. The implication is: All that's required to save your faltering emotional connections is to obliterate *misunderstanding*. So just keep **PREVENTING, EXPRESSING, AVOIDING, CARING, AND CUTTING THROUGH.** These days, you don't even need a professional. Everyone's an expert on relationships, and you can hardly say two words to a friend about your personal life without finding yourself the target of passionate reproaches regarding your deplorable passivity, being goaded to be "up front" and to "just say what you want/need" and not to forget to "just be really clear." All that is clear is good.

One begins to suspect that this may be bad advice. What if, on the contrary, it is *understanding* that is causing all the damage? What if many unions end precisely because people do indeed express their feelings much more than they used to, triggering the exposure and exacerbation of an amazing amount of resentment that hardly anyone knows how to deal with? Perhaps the call for ever more understanding merely serves to distract us from our helplessness in facing problems of competition within a couple, grudges due to unequal emotional contributions, painful regrets at paths not taken; terminal weltschmerz; classic modernist alienation; greed and egotism; disparate views on the need for fidelity, loyalty, money, style of living, social status; miscellaneous aesthetic considerations and the raising of children; indifference or habitual bad will; or plain old hate—which is to say, all the conflicts whose resolution used to be preordained by marriage. That the misunderstanding about which we are so often admonished to neutralize may lie buried, impacted in, inextricable from, the incomprehensibly deep human structure is not examined. What is precluded, therefore, is addressing the real problems—dealing with our very inexact fit to what we call civilization, now that we question many of the rules that once bound us to it and one another. The merger of the timeless ideal of marriage and the contemporary vision of good mental health is problematic in that, in the course of all the changes of the last several decades, men and women have not kept step with one another.

Perhaps the intimacy ruckus actually prevents us from even beginning a cool and effective evaluation of the problems, as do the other clichés of our era. The "angry woman," the "uncommitted man," the "incommunicative spouses"—it could be argued that these are results, not causes. The moralists' familiar condemnation of Americans' lack of reverence for marriage (these days often prudently euphemized as The Family) only winds up serving as yet another distraction from the bald fact that many men and women in couples are hopelessly out of sync with one another, and their best hope of staying together would not be to come closer to the old models but, on the contrary, to find new formulations.

What women seem to complain about the most is that, in effect, men really haven't changed enough. The philanderer, the work addict, the unfair competitor, the bore, the freeloader whom you will hear invoked in the pages that follow, these are familiar types. It is the same old dynamics that are disrupting the couple's chances of happy union, the difference being that this defeat is then made public and the spouses liberated from one another. We have the same old power struggles, the same old disloyalties, the same old claustrophobic infighting as always. It's just that the lead-up used to be codified, and now there are myriad ways to arrive at the same point of despair, exasperation, or severe emotional entropy. The resulting relationships are reminiscent of one of P. T. Barnum's many ingenious schemes. Ambling through his circus sideshow, visitors would notice signs that read: THIS WAY TO THE EGRESS. Predictably, almost no one could resist the urge to follow the signs

and find out what the mysterious "egress" looked like. The tantaliz-
ing lure of the egress only turned out to lead the way to the exit door,
but it wasn't possible to realize that until it was too late. Meanwhile,
the dazed visitors were quickly hustled out so that fresh patrons, still
waiting on line for admission, could be invited to come right up and
purchase their ticket. Most of us hope for so much more, but for all
the complexity and mystery of what can happen between two people, it often turns out that what we are headed for is only the banal
end—yet another divorce, or the even more unceremonious breakup
of a long-term live-in relationship.

And so the answer to the question "What's wrong?" only gets
acted out, not really comprehended. Of course, people are voting
with their feet, but someone leaving a marriage hardly intends to be
announcing to the world that he or she is sick of the intimacy rack-
et, feeling oppressed and powerless and surfeited. People don't leave
relationships because of general considerations about the state of
marriage, because the economic system has changed, or because
the demographics indicate that the stigma won't be too harsh.
People break up when they can't take it anymore or when they're
pushed out by someone who can't take it anymore.

There is little possibility of summing up our "problem" with the
kind of easy catch phrase that we've been depending on all century
long, such as Roaring Twenties, cold war, generation gap, sexual revolution, me decade, hippies, yuppies, buppies, guppies, and, my personal favorite, quality time. The only new catch phrase we've come up
with lately is the ubiquitous and tedious "politically correct," which is
so reductive as to have contributed to the ongoing destruction of the
possibility of anything politically interesting. But perhaps that's the
point. We move so fast and often seem to skip over the transition that
would let us take stock of what just happened, never mind preparing
for the next phase. One reality morphs into the next without warning.

Instead, in our minds float all of the debris of potential catch
phrases: the book titles and minislogans and quick characterizations
that stand for all the valiant and contradictory and futile attempts to
wrestle the problem to the ground: women who love too much,
women on top, codependent no more, men from Mars and women
from Venus, the dancers of the dance of intimacy and those of the
dance of anger, Peter Pan, Cinderella, Iron John, et al.

And yet love is still invoked as the ultimate panacea. I suggest that we are in fact in the midst of a love backlash. Between men and women it's relationships that are idealized, not love. I so seldom heard the word from my single women interviewees that I took note whenever I did hear it. People do *love* things, houses, clothes, movies, babies, and pets, but when talking about an adult of the opposite sex, the word is usually invoked in the context of falling in love—a locution that is invariably designed to indicate either the foolishness of youth or the humiliation of immature behavior in adulthood.

Between men and women, love is a source of interest principally as a form of growth—yet another illustration of our ever augmenting emotional utilitarianism. Like the neglected old linoleum, whatever it is that we used to call love—a state of consciousness, let's say—lies under many layers of fin de siècle malaise, only glimmering through now and then in the bald patches.

One thing's for sure about us citizens of the turn of the millennium: No one ever says anything nice about us. I find it telling, in view of the ardor with which we are goaded and beseeched to stay nice and close to the significant other, that there should be precisely at this time a phrase as unspeakably ugly as "couch potatoes" to describe staying at home for the evening. Notwithstanding the fact that if anything deserves to be spared from epithet in this era, it's the need to rest, terms like "couch potatoes" rob men and women of the possibility of seeing themselves as capable of behaving with valor, honor, courage, dignity, or sexiness. We forget to notice that we live at a time when there is an extraordinary dearth of pleasure and spontaneity, in which we are entitled less and less escape. We're actually stricter than the Puritans: Even those who channel their vitality into their work are accused of being "workaholics" and of forgetting "what is important."

If no one's going to say anything nice about us anyway, some of us start to think, "Well, why *should* I be nice?" Just as with children who are deprived of routine gratification, it all begins to come out in tantrums. Or else some very bad behavior occurs when no one's looking—or simply when it's possible to get away with it. There is one place where the moral/spiritual free-for-all is let loose, down and dirty, and that is the phase when there is nothing to lose in the course of a relationship that's perceived to be already lost: the end. The charm and romance of the past feels all used up. In the present, the relationship is riddled with unarticulated signals of estrangement. In the bright light of "understanding" there is the feeling that this person may have become one's worst enemy, and the "misunderstandings" are suddenly seen to have been very effective screens for unbridled aggression. Ahead, there is the deep dread of impending old age with unhappy partners facing each other in an intolerable no-exit stance.

There is no protocol established for severing these relationships. True, one occasionally hears of that very modern thing, the truly amicable breakup, but that is a great, great rarity. Many people behave horrendously. The discourse is conducted with sloppy nastiness, on the brutal terms of the least scrupulous of the partners. I believe this is one of the least noticed but most influential phenomena of our relationships. Many women describe breakups so traumatizing as to make it impossible to innocently meander into another commitment.

Before it is truly over, the endgame, moving in the kind of slow motion associated with car crashes, provides plenty of time and opportunity for the parties to sink down as low as they can go, through the crazy-making uneasiness of pulling back from someone to whom you've been connected, into the terrors of the unknown and the darkness in which unfold all the primal stuff: monsters from the id, bared teeth, vicious hand-to-hand combat, name calling, comparisons to frightening animals, dominance and submission games, ritual exploitation—all to the tune of the clanging shut of the gates of sex as the relationship wafts into total abstinence, or else on the contrary the grotesque hypertrophy of the couples' sexual complicity. In some breakups this is explicit; in others, it is not. It's hard to say which is worse.

And then there's the hate. "It was just like being poisoned," says a woman of the conversation she had the night she was in bed with her lover for the last time. "I felt ill for days." Indeed, poison seems like a good metaphor, as if something inside her is still paralyzed with hate. Some women look back with horror at the state they were in, remembering how they behaved, the feeling of utter emptiness they had, the numbness that led them to walk out of a relationship, the guilt and dread they felt, the loss of the self they had turned out not to be.

Do women behave as badly as men? I don't know, I didn't listen to both sides. Certainly most of the women I spoke to think they gave much more and took much less. This isn't about male bashing, but the subject of breakups is bound to produce a less than flattering group portrait. For every woman who was able to look back at the end of an affair or a marriage with a feeling of affectionate resignation, several described struggling with despair, rage, or crisis of meaning. And, mind you, the accounts that follow don't even include any horror stories of the nightly news variety—beatings, thefts, kidnaping of children, lawsuits, to say nothing of homicide. (We all know those, and my feeling is that, in many ways, these extreme manifestations also serve to obscure more "normal" illustrations of maladaptation.)

If you listen to the way women tell their stories, very often what they seem to be narrating is less the history of a marriage than the story of a breakdown. And in the manner peculiar to hindsight, the end provides a vantage point to see that throughout the relationship everything that caused it to end was already in place. Mr. and/or Ms. Hyde were murmuring in the background all along.

Still, for the ex-wife there is a period of intense discomfort and spiritual desolation that comes with a change of identity. There is no automatic replacement persona. But at least now when the "worst" happens, a woman may stay comfortably single rather than feel obliged to either hustle back into neomarriage with a neoex-husband or be ostracized from "polite" society. The newly free male has always fallen on his feet. He is not unmanned by the end of a marriage—quite the contrary. The newly free woman, however, may still be womanly, but that doesn't work to her advantage. From biblical times on, a woman who loses her virginity also loses her original value. Indeed, historically, the newly alone female was often simply in trouble, even in America, no matter her background, from Hawthorne's scarlet letter bearer to Edith Wharton's passionate eccentrics. Today's newly free woman, however, will find friends and supporters among her peers; there's hardly a place in America that doesn't have at least a cluster of single women.

Then, too, she is more and more likely to feel that she doesn't have that much incentive to remarry. What accounts for the precipitous drop in remarriage? Consider the possibility that a woman who has more financial and emotional independence than any in history may feel entitled to be a different sort of wife. She is more than pulling her weight financially now, and yet her "rewards" have remained static. The organization Nine to Five reports that in 1994, some 54 percent of mothers of infants were employed. In families where both spouses work, 23 percent of the wives earned more than their husbands. More than half of employed women provide 50 percent or more of their household's income, and 18 percent of working women provide all of their families' income.

Though no one can bear to hear about the dishes anymore, it is impossible to discuss divorce and not mention the figures shown by research. According to a 1993 report by the Family and Work Institute, working women do 87 percent of the shopping, 81 percent of cooking, 78 percent of cleaning, and 63 percent of bill paying in American households. Yet women are still punished in the workplace for the lost "face time" that results from their second shift at home. And once home, women still do much of the emotional housework. "There used to be a deal," more than one ex-wife said to me. The deal was supposed to be that men provided money and security, and women provided the rest. But that deal (dubious to begin with) has little relevance now that most women work outside the home. According to a 1991 *Working Woman* magazine study, "Career women participating in the study tended to boost their output, win higher performance ratings and feel more motivated and satisfied with their jobs after a marital split."

But, in any event, in *Cutting Loose: Why Women Who End Their Marriages Do So Well,* author Ashton Applewhite tells us that, despite the well-known decline in women's income (around 30 percent) when they become single, "Even women whose standards of living declined significantly prefer their present situation to the economics of an unhappy marriage."

For all the talk of alimony and child support problems, and the problems of single mothers, there is little acknowledgment of the metamorphosis that many women experience with sudden independence. When their primary relationships break up, women feel that it's not only one man they're leaving or being left by, it is a way of living; the task is not only to deidealize and mourn one man, it's to relinquish a way of thinking.

"It's the first time in a long time I have felt I am myself" is a remark I heard many, many times from my subjects. One woman told me that she'd been eating oysters for years—and after separating from her husband realized with a shock that she didn't like oysters. It was he who had liked them! In fact, one hears rather often of a favorite food—or favorite author, or close friend—that was abandoned during marriage, resumed afterward. No wonder both men and women so often sound much less confused after a breakup.

Women have traditionally been more likely to seek divorce than men, but what is new is that remarriage appears to be a significantly less attractive option than it was twenty-five years ago. While the 50 percent divorce rate—the highest in history—remains static, rates for remarriage have plummeted. From 1970 to 1988 the remarriage rate for all age groups dropped by 40 percent. It is one of the most flagrant instances of sexism that there is still such a widespread belief that this drop is because women cannot "find" husbands. It is actually ludicrous to explain away the fact that better off, better educated women marry less and fail more often to remarry by saying that men don't like strong women or men are afraid of powerful women. Sure, strong and powerful women are frightening, but isn't what is really frightening the fact that they're just tired of getting a raw deal?

It has been demonstrated again and again that divorced women—those with an adequate income—fare better than divorced men in well-being, attitude about the future, and even health. Some studies have found that divorced men suffer as much as three times the mortality rate of their married peers, while mortality rates for divorced and married women stay roughly equivalent. Clearly, something happens to those divorced women that makes them want to stay alive.

Perhaps we could think of it as P. T. Barnum meets Lewis Carroll: The egress, as it turns out, leads a late-twentieth-century woman directly through the looking glass. She's on the other side; she couldn't duplicate her former reality even if she wanted to. And she doesn't want to. Many women I asked expressed wishes for new, improved versions of conjugal life. Not a single one wished to have her ex-husband and her ex-life back. "I went into every room in the house and saw every room with a kind of relief" is a dream one woman recounted to me.

Are there no solutions?

"It's ridiculous," opines one of my friends—a young person, as it happens, now in the kind of the relationship that is referred to by an older generation as "happily married," "to expect marriage to fulfill all emotional needs . . . to expect that a single relationship will provide everything."

Would it not be good sense to put less pressure on relationships rather than more? Won't we be better off if we emphasize tolerance, permission for individual will, and above all to value friendship when the going gets rough rather than continuing to struggle toward an ideal that does not allow for even partial failure? But that is so ambitious a thought, and we are so tired. The last time we had such an ambitious thought, we got hit with the '70s. It's easier to make fun of the '60s than to reconcile ourselves to the disappearance of a real interest in examining the rules for relevance and fairness, which would stand us in good stead now. It's easier to bring up tie-dyeing and the muddy fields of Woodstock than to recall what felt fresh and vital then: a tremendous, widely shared curiosity about how our institutions might be adapted to the future.

Let's at least admit the possibility that there is some interesting thinking to be done about the role of intimacy in our lives. If we were to be more honest about our conflicting need for both freedom and love, we might be better equipped to honestly ask ourselves some important questions. Is it necessary to have intimacy in order to live what we call a fulfilled life? To stay spiritually alive, is it necessary for a woman to feel desired? Yes, say many women, all this is necessary—but that's not what they got in their relationships.

Not a few people blame the divorce rate and, generally speaking, the bad state of heterosexual affairs on women who have wanted too much (and, the presumption is, gotten too much). People often point out that women "paid" for feminist gains with damaged marriages. But of course what many women felt was preciscly the opposite: that the marriages were already damaged and this is what propelled them to action. But even then, way back then, there were already some really radical women. Not the ones you're thinking of perhaps. One of the important, least document- ed developments in sexual politics was that many women simply began to take the imperative of marriage less seriously. It's mostly forgotten now how radical women's humor became as a result, but some of us still remember laughing out loud the first time we heard of journalist Blair Sabol's notorious phrase, "I have met Mr. Right and he is me."

The phrase "The personal is political" was coined in an essay of the same name in around 1970 by Carol Hanisch, a member of the radical feminist group Redstockings, around the time when many women felt that there was no way their struggle wouldn't triumph. But since then, in "Feminist Revolution," Hanisch wrote wryly, "We thought it would only be a matter of a few years before we would have male supremacy conquered." In retrospect, she decided, they may have been "a little naive—silly almost."

What has been gained *and* lost by women is clear when you look at the income distribution: As we've seen, more than half of employed women provide 50 percent or more of their household's income. *More than half.*

But the problem is undoubtedly less having to bring home the money than it is having to bring home so much else, as well. "Of course, he was devastated," said one woman of her husband of his miserable reaction when she became pregnant with their first child. "It was the end of the gravy train."

Indeed, one may safely imagine that many marriages don't break up despite the children but *because* of the children, whether unborn or born. It receives little currency in general conversation, but again and again among the statistics relating to divorce, one finds women saying that the men are not pulling their share of the emotional work. Women have honed a certain kind of survival skill in the American workplace, and it doesn't make sense to ask them to always leave it outside at the kitchen door—or the bedroom door. Men are struggling more, some graciously and some not.

It's foolish to mock the complaining about housework and the eternal and avowedly tedious questions about who does the dishes.

But I don't believe this to be spite or pettiness on most women's parts. Many of them are simply exhausted. If you listen to what they have to say, you will see that they are full of not hate but sadness.

Even when a breakup is clearly necessary, it's not easy. "He used to drink in front of the children," says Evelyn B., who split up a seventeen-year marriage. She says she doesn't miss him, but it's true that it's difficult not having anyone to talk to about the children, about how things are going, someone to sit down and have a glass of wine with and talk over the day's events. "Sometimes," she says, "I miss someone to talk to after dinner." When she left him, she didn't bargain for the solitude that ensued, the years alone. But if she had been forced to bargain, that's still the deal she would have gone for. Nonetheless, she is someone who loves men.

What then? Trying again is one option, and this is where divorce may indeed be good for marriage—when we can hope for a chance to fall in love with our eyes open, knowing that we're playing for real because we want to. And then perhaps we can better accept that others will be freed not to. Perhaps we should put the problem differently and set ourselves to wondering whether it isn't our search for that ineffably lovely bird, the egress, that makes us believe our lives are worthwhile.

WHY AM I HERE?

Otherwise known as: This is really stupid. Good-bye.

EVELYN B.'s husband had trouble understanding why she wanted to divorce him.

The kids saw him drunk. And he used to scream at Timothy. He would pick Timothy up in the crib and scream at him, "I hate you! I hate you! I hate you! She used to love me before you!" And I said to myself, *Now divorce is in order.* You know? *Now. Really. I married him, but they didn't marry him.* So that was it. A typical story, don't you think? And we were married seventeen years.

The kids don't quite know the degree to which the divorce was so very unpleasant. I mean, my husband cornered the housekeeper and grabbed the key and pushed her around and came in and tore the house up, looking for love letters. He had a private detective following me. And the clincher is, the divorce cost me—and this was way back in the golden years of the '80s—$127,000. It cost every penny I made from writing these math books, which of course would have been for the kids because, under New York's Equitable Divorce law, he was entitled to half of what I had, which was fine, except he wanted half of my income for the rest of my life, on the grounds—are you ready? This is in the divorce suit—"I taught her how to think." I mean, that's got to be a feminist's nightmare. . . . I want that on my gravestone: "He taught me how to think." He was claiming that I was a silly young thing, and he taught me how to think, and so everything I made for the rest of my life he was entitled to have. So, I got a very good lawyer. And the sad part is, in New York, there are many judges with whom he could have won. I mean, men win these things all the time. This judge gave him nothing, but that *cost*. And years later, Kevin said to me, "It's such a shame we had such an acrimonious divorce. We wasted so much money." That was when I considered actually running him over with a Mack truck for the first time.

SUSANNAH W., just before her excruciating breakup. They'd been together ten years.

I guess it alternated. In the very beginning he wanted to get married, and I wanted to wait. Then I wanted to get married, and he wanted to wait. And he always presented his objections to marriage as being on political grounds—"Oh, it's bourgeois. . . ." Blah, blah. And then I realized at some point that because of his family's history in politics . . . and he would be seeing himself as kind of capitulating to middle-class bourgeois life. So when we went on a Caribbean vacation, he said, "Well, I'll marry you in the Caribbean." And I thought to myself, *Sure, you can hide, not tell anyone, not be public*. So I craftily, accidentally on purpose, forgot to bring my divorce certificate. So we couldn't get married in the Caribbean. And he never forgave me for that. He always held that up to me: "I wanted to marry you, and you deliberately didn't bring your divorce certificate." And I said, "Yes, and the reason was, I could not tell you at the time, but I really felt that you were ashamed to marry me, and

I could not marry anyone who was ashamed to marry me, nor could I confront you about it. It was too shaming."

Do you think I'm really crazy?

BLANCHE W.'s situation is an egregious instance of how crazy breakups combine with crazy passages in a woman's life, setting her on an irreversibly different course.

I was broken up with on the day my father died. A lot of people get broken up with on the day their father dies. And my sister was broken up with on the day after.

Why? The man I was going out with was getting very upset for the two weeks my father was in intensive care because I felt compelled to go out and see him. My father died in February. There had been a snowstorm the day of my father's car accident, and it continued to snow on and off those weeks. And since he was about an hour from the city, when I started going back to work, I wasn't finished . . . until after seven, and I felt nervous about driving an hour alone in the snow after a twelve-hour day. So I asked my boyfriend of five years to come with me.

"But I've never met your father," he said.

"That's okay," I said. "He's unconscious. You don't have to say a thing. All you have to do is sit in the waiting room."

So it took some cajoling, but he did drive me out one night. Partially in exchange for the ride and partially because my father seemed to be better, we had a date for the following Sunday. I was really looking forward to it. I had planned to go out to the hospital at twelve o'clock and be back in time for a dinner date with Sam. But the first call came at ten o'clock from my sister. My father was in cardiac arrest, and they were working on him. I gathered my things to run out to the hospital. Before I could leave the second call came: "I think I have to tell you that your father's dead," the resident said. After getting to the hospital and taking care of my father and the funeral parlor and seeing my stepmother, who was also in intensive care, I called and told Sam I wouldn't be able to make it for dinner—my father had died—and I couldn't talk just then, there was too much to do.

The days went by in that kind of stupor that follows death. In error, there were two funeral announcements in the newspaper with two different funeral parlors, and my ex-husband showed up at the wrong funeral.

Did Sam come to the funeral? No. I didn't hear a word from Sam. Granted, I wasn't home much since I had to sit shivah in two places, with brief breaks to speak to my mother to see how the cancer that had spread to her liver was doing.

At the end of the week of shivah, still no phone message from Sam. But the doorman did give me a bunch of dying flowers that Sam had sent some time during the week. That was it.

During that period right after all those deaths, I . . . wound up talking to people who had [suffered a] death. . . . I was just shocked at the numbers of women who described how the men broke up with them when they were in the peak of mourning—or the depths, or whatever you would call it.

Oh, yes, and they often want you to fuck that night. I mean, sometimes you want to fuck that night, but often you don't. But clearly what's intolerable to them is that you are consumed with the loss of someone else.

ADELE U. says there was no way to avoid the oppressive dishonesty between a boyfriend and herself. It was intolerable to go to bed together.

We just . . . we weren't connecting. There wasn't . . . I always looked at sex as a form of communication, you know. Sleeping with someone . . . being with someone . . . there is so much communication in that connection. And we just weren't. . . . So, that last time—I remember that last time—basically we just did it. We knew what was going on. We had had a very intense relationship. We spoke a lot, we were together a lot. It was close, very intimate. So we knew what was going on, that something was wrong. And there were excuses: He had just come back, we hadn't seen each other. But it was very telling. I didn't say there was something wrong. Not at the time. I thought I should go a little slowly. I mean, it was a marriage. We hadn't seen each other in days. He said he was sick. And the plane ride. And so on. . . . So I just left it. It was the only time we had sex like that. I mean, we did it, and then we turned over and went to sleep.

Afterward, when we were having those discussions, I told him. I said, "There was something wrong with the last time we slept together."

He said, "Yes, I know."

And I said, "Well, it's telling about what's happening right now; I mean, you are not there."

And he said, "No, I'm not."

And that was it. It was over.

MARIA A., 40, Norfolk.

I once walked in on my husband with his pants down, having sex with someone on his desk at the office. . . . The woman he was with, one of the other attorneys at the firm, had taken her underpants off, but her skirt was just pulled up around her waist, and her panty hose were around one ankle. And her shirt was open. She hopped down to the floor and pulled up her panty hose and pulled down her skirt and buttoned her shirt as she walked out.

So, needless to say, our lives are changed. But ever since that event, I don't think of myself as married. I don't wear a wedding band. We're staying together, but that's mostly for financial reasons and for the children. . . . We may seem really married but we are totally demarried.

What do I tell people? Oh, anything. People don't really pay attention.

No, I don't see other men. And now he doesn't see other women, either, which is interesting. He wants to make it work, but it's a very angry relationship, which to tell you the truth works for both of us, anyway.

Yes, I was five months pregnant. And I had two children who were waiting in the outer office, chatting with the receptionist. They'd wanted to come in, and something made me say, "No, you guys wait here for me."

There are different rules now, and what matters is what's in people's heads. You're married on paper, but you don't act like you're married. Or you're not married on paper, and you act like you're married. I just think there's a much broader range.

I think people ask now, "Are they together?" rather than "Are they married?" or "Are they seeing each other exclusively?" That's the '90s. As opposed to fifteen years ago, "Does she have the ring?"

ANITA S.'s lover expressed incredulity when she told him that she thought they should split. After four years together, she wanted to have children. He informed her conclusively that he didn't—he already had two from a former marriage. She was turning 40.

I felt trapped, I was bored, I was angry. I told him I really would feel better if I could go back to my place to concentrate on finishing my project. And he said, "You're too compulsive, you're too obsessed with your work." He, of course, wasn't working well at that time. He was bogged down in his own project.

Oh, and then around that time we went down to Washington and met two couples that I called the Mirror Couples. The men were friends of Marty's who were both his age, and they were both going out with women who were somewhat older than I was, in their midforties. And I felt that Marty wanted very strongly that we be like these couples, because these men had children and ex-wives, while these women may have been married before but had no children.

Marty at that point, I guess, was fifty-eight. And so we went to some sort of conference in Washington, and I basically went around and looked at paintings, which was great. And then we went to dinner with this one couple and it was awful. . . . I had read this guy's book, and I was curious about his subject, and so I tried to talk to him about his book, but he just wasn't very interesting. And I realized the book wasn't that interesting. And then he immediately just started to talk at great length about his ex-wife. And her therapy and selling their house. He kept on talking about his ex-wife and kids, and on and on. Marty hardly said anything; he nodded and said yes, but he didn't see that was a problem.

At this point I turn to the woman sitting next to me, trying to start some conversation. She looks really bad. So I say, "Are you all right?" And she says, "I'm having a migraine." And I start to feel like I'm having a migraine, too. So here is that guy rattling on about his ex-wife, and this woman is sitting there saying she's having a migraine, which she seems to be prone to. She says that chocolate sets it off, but I'm thinking, *I know what sets it off; it's setting it off in me.* So I can't start a conversation with her, but I don't want to listen about the ex-wife, so it's really boring. I just started thinking about what might be interesting to remember in order to save my mind.

And the worst thing is, we go back to the hotel, and the guy says, "It was really nice to meet you," and then sotto voce to me, "You should really take care of Marty. He's a really good man." That just sent me into the stratosphere. I was so mad. I just kept thinking, *Everything's about them, about taking care of these guys. And they have everything. They don't care about other people, they don't even try to make things interesting for everybody. It's just about them. And I'm supposed to take care of him?!*

So I was thinking about all of this on Christmas night, after this really, really awful dinner with his kids. We went to bed, and he just turned off the light and got into bed; and he lay there and wouldn't say anything. And I remember thinking, *This is really stupid. Why am I here?* I was really still pretty mad and hurt about the way that his kids had ignored me at dinner. I mean, what a dismal Christmas it had been. . . . So I started to get dressed. It's like one or two in the morning at this point. I thought, *I'm just going to go home. I don't have to stay here for this. I might as well be alone.* And then he said, "You can't go," and we had another huge fight. And suddenly I realized that he was afraid I would leave; it would be embarrassing for him because two of his kids were still in the house. And I said, "Well, why should I stay when you're acting like this?" And so we fought again, and finally we went to bed again.

But it was just like being poisoned. I felt ill for days afterwards. I hadn't been that angry in years. It was just . . . I felt really poisoned.

And then right after New Year's, I went to visit with a friend and had a terrific time. And I remember that before I even came back, I called him from the street before I got on the train because he wanted to know what time my train came in. And I really felt great, and I was talking about the trip, and he said, "Oh, you sound so good. How come you never sound this good when you're here?" I said to myself, *Hmm, this is something to think about.*

SAY WHAT?

Then there are the same convoluted, obsessive stories one has been hearing from one's friends for years about their relationships. You feel like yelling, "Say what?" because they

don't make any sense at all. In the old days women would
spend years—lifetimes—in those. Now they seem to come
and go more quickly, as though women just don't get
stuck as much, for as long.

JENNIFER B. had to consult a therapist to figure out what her boyfriend was talking to her about.

And finally I understood that what he was trying to say was that he was going to marry her but he wanted to continue having an affair with me.

What? No, of course not. I'm not that far gone.

TAMMY F., 27, divorced, and feeling "spaced."

He just uses me in between his real relationships.

JEAN I.'s sense of fragmentation has become so global she can no longer make sense of the categories.

I don't even know which one of my relationships would qualify as the last one. You know, they quit qualifying as relationships somewhere in there. Does that mean the last person I slept with more than once? Of the last serious affairs I had, one ended very badly, and one ended very amicably.

I would say that the worst one was over the pregnancy, but it was already over before that.

The old classic was the guy caught in bed with the secretary; I mean, there's no worse behavior than that. And the modern one is a lot of torture and passive aggression and withholding and weirdness. If you believe that cheating is the worse behavior, as opposed to just being a low-level jerk day after day after day, then nothing has changed.

ALICIA D., early 20s. Her account is of one of those gruesome endgames where lovers drift into hopelessness but become too helpless to move away from one another.

The worst was, I remember, the blizzard of '96—his wife was a schoolteacher or she worked in schools or something, so we could only talk during the day on certain days—and school was canceled, and I was livid because I couldn't call him. It was snowing. You could barely go outside. And the moment I got the guts to take the dog for a walk, he had gone to the A&P and called from a pay phone and I had missed it. . . . I remember playing the message again and again with the fucking snow falling. And you know how tedious it is when there's like a weather condition and there's nothing else on the news? So there was nothing to do but stay home and watch TV, watch Connie Chung or whoever talking about school being canceled, and I was in a rage for those four days. That is when things sort of took a downhill turn.

The day of his birthday. . . . Of course you couldn't get him a present because he'd have the present to deal with, and where would he put it? His birthday was in January, and I was going to take him out for a fabulous lunch, and I found out from my friends where's the best place . . . because we were never outside together. And he called me and said he wanted to meet me at the apartment. So I changed the sheets. And he came over and said, "You know, it's not fair to her."

Yes. On his birthday This was all of four months or five months ago or whatever.

My birthday was a month later, and he said, "But please, please let me call you on your birthday." So I lived like I was always waiting for this phone call. Actually, what he first said was, "I want to stay in touch with you, and I want to be your friend." And I said— and it was true—I said, "I take extreme pride in my friendships, and I'm an extremely good friend to people. And I put a lot of work into those friendships, and I don't know whether I want to do that with you." Which was my one moment of strength in the whole thing.

BILLIANA M. dreamed of her ex-husband.

I went into every room in the house and saw every room with a kind of relief; it was not sorrow. Then when I came to the last room in the dream, at the center, or let's say the heart, of the house, in a classical upholstered upright chair with his back to me, was my ex-husband, sitting with his eyes open but almost dreaming, slightly unconscious, if you will—which was probably no accident. And I went up to him, and I put my arms around him in a loving way, still crying, and put my head down on his shoulder. And somehow he came around, and I saw his face, and he—I suppose telepathically because there were no words—he said, "I know." That added to my feeling of rightness, appropriateness—healing, I guess would be a good way to put it. And from there I stepped away from him and stepped into a very large . . . it was like a Japanese public bath. . . . I was naked—I don't know how I got undressed, but you know how dreams are—I was naked, and I stepped into a rectangular space to bathe, to wash, and the water was still coming in from the spigot, so it wasn't full yet, and just after I'd gotten settled, seated in there, Bobby came in, and he sat close in close front of me, with his back to me. All different members of my family—my sisters, my mother, one of my daughters and one of her daughters, family members— came into the room and were surprised. Not surprised that we were naked in the tub, surprised that we were together. And I would say pleasantly. Bobby was still silent and not really awake. We talked for a while about very mundane things while still in the bath. And I started getting cold, and everyone else either disappeared or left. And then I realized the water was cold and then realized Bobby was cold. I had my arms around his chest from behind, and then when I picked him up and held him around and saw him, he looked dead, he looked desiccated, his eyes were sunken, dried out. His mouth was contorted. And he had no arms and legs. And I held him the way one would a baby and was alarmed about this and felt responsible because I hadn't noticed that the water was getting cold, so I hadn't noticed that he had died in front of me, and I didn't see it happening. I put out a yell to see if there was anyone near to get help. And there was no response. In the meantime I blew onto his chest, at his heart area. And I blew into his mouth, and I was trying to breathe life back into him; really, though, I was giving him my life to be alive once again. And I called out to anyone who was there, "Call 911!" And I could hear some sounds of rustling, that someone was moving or coming toward us. And at that point thinking, *It's too late; he's been dead too long.* And I was still trying to breathe into him.

RENNIE N., the composer, talked to me about two years after her disastrous breakup, and by that time she could be analytical and could attempt to tidy up the perspective.

We had been together for several years, and by that point I wanted to get married and have a child. But then I noticed the pattern.

The first step would be that we would get a place together, and he would change his mind about it every three days. We'd look at a loft and he'd say, "No, I can't do it." We went on and on like this. We broke up a few times. Reconciled. We had a fantastic sex life. It wasn't even an equation of the more we disagreed, the better sex was. I think it was that sex was a separate part of life, and we communicated very differently there than we did in our verbal exchange. And so the sex kept getting better.

For me it was very hard to part from that. Very difficult. But I finally did it. I was still in love with him, but I knew it wouldn't work. I'd been tormented for so long. By the time we broke up, I remember, I was able to call him up if I was lonely, and I'd say, "Why don't you come and visit for the weekend? It doesn't mean anything except that I just would like to sleep with you."

We broke up for good that spring, and I was basically shut down until this summer. I couldn't go out of my house, I couldn't work, I couldn't do anything. I became a recluse.

Oh, I was pretty catatonic in those days. I guess what happens is that you find that another person also can be a mask to your own self, that you've been sort of avoiding your own problems that you've had since when you were a kid. And then it's really, *Oh, fuck! Now I have to really accept myself, I have to really like myself, I have to do all this garbage that I read about and didn't think I'd ever have to do. . . .* And so what happened, finally, is that I was able to distract myself this summer with a twenty-two-year-old.

MONICA'S BRILLIANT HUSBAND

*His idea of a relationship is one that
maxes out at two and a half minutes*

MONICA V. is an entrepreneur who thinks of herself as a '60s person. Growing up, she loved to read and felt out of sync in the rural Midwest. She didn't date until college, but then there were many boyfriends. Afterward, following several fairly long-term relationships, she married. Divorced two years ago, she is once again without a relationship.

Why did I get married? Because it was the '80s man, you know. . . . Because it was the '80s, and you had to be married in the '80s, and you had to have a child in the '80s, and you had to be a mother, and you had to be a parent, and you had to have real estate, and you had to start to learn the computer, and I got swept up in this thing that I *never* thought I'd fall for, ever in a million years. You know, ever, ever . . . and I really did fall for it. I don't know if it was Reagan's fault or whoever's fault it was, but, man, I really went for it. Plus I was, what . . . thirty-six, thirty-seven, something like that, and it was my "last chance," and there was all this hysteria about biological clocks, you know? I had had two abortions. I never wanted children, But now, all of a sudden I really wanted kids, and I really wanted to be married, and I really wanted a husband. And then this guy popped along. I think if it had been another time, we would have had this, like, fantastic affair because he's really very charismatic and charming and silly and wonderful and nobody would *think* of getting married to him. He's not a guy you get married to.

And I knew right away I'd made a mistake. From the start, we began to have some bad luck. Right after we got married, I got pregnant, and then we lost that first baby, and he . . . instead of bringing us closer, it drove us apart. And then losing the next baby drove us farther apart and. . . . Well, I mean, there were many reasons why it didn't work. I was trying to start a business in the city, and he insisted we had to live in Nowheresville, New York, in the middle of this incredibly rural part, and I had to commute, which was really hard on my health, and, you know, he just was a . . . He's actually a horrible person; he's really mean-spirited and horrible, and none of my friends and none of my family can stand him . . . and none of them can believe I put up with him as long as I did.

And why did I? I like men who are extreme. I don't like guys who are boring. I mean, I am bored by guys who are sort of normal. And, well, those are the husbands, right? Those are the guys who stick with you through the whole thing and who are by your bed when you have cancer, and they're great when you lose the baby, and if you're starting your business they listen to you, and this guy . . . He's completely egocentric and self-involved, totally, and everything was about him, but *so* interesting, you know? He's brilliant, he's a fabulous actor, he's crazy, he's silly, he's funny—I mean, he's a wild man. He's known for

that. It's not my opinion only. And, of course, he cannot sustain a relationship for longer than two and a half minutes. At one point during
our marriage, he said to me, "Well, you can't ever say that this was boring, or that I was boring." And he made me laugh because it was really true, you know. Whatever I can say about it, I can't say that.

When I got breast cancer, that's when he let me know he wanted
to split up. But we worked it out so that he agreed to stay until I was
finished with the chemo. Then that was it. When we broke up, I
couldn't bear to sleep alone in my bed. I concocted this thing where
I have lots of pillows—which I still do, six years later. I have four pillows on my bed: two here and one over there; you know, like a body!
When I wake up, often I'm grabbing a pillow . . . these big thick pillows that take up half the bed. . . . Well, so already then I couldn't
bear to sleep alone, and I remember going out to these business
lunches and coming back to the apartment and just crying and crying, crying, crying, crying, and stopping and then doing another
thing and then stopping and then crying, crying, crying, crying, crying. . . . I just couldn't bear it. And I remember, I had a masseuse. . . .
I found this fabulous masseuse, who's really wonderful, and I had a
doctor, and then one day I had the thought, *I have to pay people to*
touch me. This is my life now. I have to pay people to listen to me, to
touch me, to care about me, to do my laundry or make me food. All
these things that I have around me . . . there's nobody who does it just
because they love me or just because I'm here, just because I exist. And
that thought just completely destroyed me. It all seemed, you know,
just horrible, horrible, horrible. . . .

No, no, I didn't grow to hate him then. Not until recently. I stayed
in love with him. Yeah, I did. Through all of this, through all of the
horrible stuff that he did to me, despite the fact that he left me. Of
course I knew that it was horrible that he walked out on me when I
was sick and vulnerable, but I just wasn't angry at him. I mean, I
was, but I wasn't. Not really, inside. It wasn't until . . . we recon-
nected a couple of years ago, and we stayed connected for about a
year, and I could just see the same thing was going to happen all
over again. He's that kind of passive-aggressive, you know, push me-
pull me; he likes to draw you in so he can push you away. And I
mean even now I don't hate him. I just realized who this guy is. . . .
I could see the whole thing happening again, and I thought, *I've got*

to get out of here. . . . This guy really is fucked up and sick, and I'm just . . . I'm out of here, I'm gone.

Oddly, in some ways, it didn't leave a void. Socially, for instance, it didn't make a dent. Even when I was married, I did things on my own because he would never go anywhere with me, so I feel like I've been alone, whether or not with a man, for so long, anyway. I've always gone to parties alone. I remember living with someone in Seattle, and it was the beginning of the women's movement, and I would make a point of going out with my female friends at night. So I've always done that. . . . I often felt lonelier when I was with someone.

I don't think there's anything else I could have done. No . . . it wasn't a matter of, like, two people coming together and not being able to work it out, it was more like a normal person meets a nut case, and the nut case drives the normal person away.

Well, there just aren't any men. Yes, I do think that other women have lower standards, absolutely. I think women will put up with stuff. . . . I can't imagine how they do it . . . or why they would want to. I couldn't put up with that stuff in my relationships. No, I don't wish I could lower my standards for the sake of companionship. The guy would drive me nuts. And the older I get, the worse it is because I'm so much more set in my ways, so much more aware of who I am, so much more demanding.

But also something has happened. I don't know if it was the times, or if it's our age. I'm really stressed out. You know, it's one thing to work hard and everything's fine about it, but when work is really tough, and you have to really try extra hard, and it's not always great, you really want a home life, you want another life to balance it all. . . . I remember being with my creepy husband and being able to come home at night and say, "And this happened to me and that happened to me. . . ." And there'd be somebody to talk about it with, and we'd have dinner and then talk about something else, so I was able to drown out my life. I don't have that now. And I've had a whole fucking year of bad news, and toughness, and I just am sick of it. I don't think I'm depressed. . . . I think I'm angry. I've put the word out that I'm ready to meet some men, you know? But, depressed? No. I don't get . . . I don't know . . . that down.

WAIT A MINUTE!

Relationships break up, and one imagines that one will go on as "before"—which is to say, one will have something of a hiatus and then one way or another be back in a relationship. But it turns out that you break up and . . . that's it. Suddenly it's one year, or three years, later. There's a point at which every woman in that situation suddenly realizes that she's slipped through the looking glass into a different cultural reality.

CALLIE S. remembers the point in the relationship when there's nothing more important—hardly anything matters at all any more, by comparison—than ending it.

The end of the marriage was a hard-fought battle. Was it devastating? I don't know. I wanted out more than life itself, once I figured out it was something I could do without the world coming undone. And even if it did . . .

And I don't think I really thought too seriously about what would happen, and it didn't occur to me that I wouldn't soon again be a married person, in relatively short order. But that sort of never happened.

AMELIA J., the one who felt that she was somehow more grown up after her marriage dissolved sixteen years ago nevertheless hadn't bargained for being quite so grown up that she would remain unmarried in perpetuity, that the relationships she'd find would turn out to feel like unsatisfying limbos at best.

Yes, when the marriage broke up, I did assume that I would be with someone else. And I thought it would be pretty soon. I thought I would have a kid. I thought I would get that.

I don't know, maybe I couldn't do it in a marriage, maybe that's why I'm not married. But there's nobody in my bed. I don't have that. I don't have a body. I only have sex twice a year.

I think my desires were always mixed. Right after the breakup I wanted to go and sleep around a lot. Which I hadn't done before. But then I met someone and quickly fell in with him. He was the first person who would be in the right category—you know, the right type?—but like a year later that was still true. I mean, I sort of still thought he was the right type. I wanted to marry him. . . . The underlying truth is that I didn't really want to. But my fantasies were that we'd do this for a while, and then we'd get married.

And then the urgency to get married never defined itself in an inevitable fashion, and nobody else really came along. But in my own self-defense, I have to say that it's not every person who was in the right category. When you've broken up with someone, Mr. Wrong is ubiquitous. I didn't feel that strongly about that many people. I'm not the sort of person who just falls in love. But there were three or four, you know, major relationships that weren't in the right category. And then, somehow, it's now.

EILEEN Y., the watercolorist who, in her youth, cancelled her engagement three weeks before the wedding.

So I went back home to take care of my father until he died, and by then, of course, this young man had married someone else. So when I was twenty-five, I felt that part of my life was over, and I felt I had really messed things up in my emotional and sexual life. I was really very unhappy about it. And I went to New York and absolutely loved my work, but was terribly lonely in every other way. So . . . I had an affair with the first man who presented himself after that, which really was quite risqué.

You know, I really had the sense at that moment of my life as a kind of a mess.

That was my first affair, yes. Which was late, you know.

He was perfectly well behaved. He was a very interesting man. A lot older than me, European. But it was a disaster because I was not . . . I mean, I did not enter into that affair for any of the right reasons. It was about equally both our faults, I think. No, it didn't last very long. He got interested in someone else, and I knew that I had just really made a drastic mistake, but . . . It left a lot a scars.

EVELYN B. was understandably clear about the need to divorce a man who gets drunk and screams at the kids. She sees the breakup of the family not as a tragedy but as a deliverance.

Oh, you want me to talk about the joys of being single? Yes, I guess there are some. Like being rid of your ex-husband.

But now what, when it comes to men?

I never thought that would happen. It just was inconceivable to me. From the time I hit Smith College at age sixteen, perhaps primarily because I had a southern accent, there were just always men. And in graduate school, you always met men. In graduate school, when you ran out of guys, you went to the library and picked two more . . . it was like going to the grocery store. I mean, we had systems. You walked in, you spotted the guy you wanted, you didn't look up, you sat down studiously, and you read for an hour without looking up, and then suddenly you would look up and say, "Excuse me, do you know what time it is?" He always asked you out.

I just assumed there would always be men, always. This is the problem with therapy. To reach healthy sanity is very depressing because you can't kid yourself. I told my therapist the worst thing in the world for me was to get sane because now there are no eligible men. I used to be able to pick up these lost, lonely souls who really needed you and borrowed money from you. . . . Now I don't go out with them anymore, and it's like there's hardly anybody around!

So it's been two years—a really long time for me. And everything is clearer, and then it gets harder and harder to talk yourself into it. Sometimes you meet a guy, and there's an attraction. But then you tell yourself he's probably married, or he drinks, or he's going to turn out exactly like your ex-husband. By now we're all smart enough. We know the end of the story.

ALL THE MR. WRONGS

There seems to be an endless variety.

PHILLIPA C. on Mr. Last Month:

Yes, well, so after the few months of being in a state of totally intense love and lust . . . it's already not what it was.

When the magic wore off, I found out he's a miserable human being just like everybody else. So what do I want to do? Be one miserable human being or be part of a couple of miserable human beings? I mean, where is the relationship going to go? I certainly don't want to get married.

LAUREN R. on Mr. Right Now:
But he's twenty-five years younger than I am!

ABIGAIL Z. on the Mirage:
I'm getting real worried about myself, because I like really hand-some men, pretty men. . . . I've always had this great conflict between the guys I really like to talk to and the guys I really like to fuck, and there are a lot of people I thought I should have sex with, and I felt I was just *dying* to have sex with them and I did. But I'm starting to wonder. . . .

I've had several affairs in the last couple of years with men who were . . . I'm not sure I thought any of them were possibilities.

There was someone in one of my engineering classes who was so great looking—this was one of the two affairs I had when I was married. After my husband died, I waited, and he got a divorce. What a surprise! In the middle of the year, this guy got a divorce, and he was so gorgeous but . . . And since he was also an architect you'd think he'd be interesting, but he wasn't. I had to end it because it wasn't enough. I was also looking for someone I'd be able to talk to.

NINA L. on the Sexless Wonder:
I don't know if he's gay. I didn't think he was gay. Maybe he's scared. I don't know what he is.

CALLIE S. on Availability:
I work in a heavily "womened" industry. I probably know more women and homosexuals than anything else. Heterosexuals are few and far between—and grossly boring for the most part, especially the available ones. Well, it's probably why they're available! I guess just 'cause they're the leftovers, wouldn't you think?

HILLARY P. on Sssssss—the guy with whom the air goes right out of the balloon:
But I was really not in love with this guy. It felt like love, but it was only gooey anticipation. And he had a big red warning sign stamped on his forehead. . . . On our first date, he actually told me that he was in therapy or had been in therapy and that he was work-

ing out the problem that he had with commitment. And I remember thinking at the time, *Boy, you don't really know enough to not tell me this! . . . And couldn't you have a more interesting problem? If you told me you were in love with your dog, it would be so much more interesting than this. . . . Oh, so you can't commit? At least have a new problem, Jesus.*

RENNIE N. on the (increasingly common) Competitor:

What happened was, I decided I could live a monogamous life because this mission I was on, this music mission, was so great. And I finally found this profound spiritual companion, in a way—I romanticized it—who was on the same mission, and I thought we were mutually inspiring each other with our art, that we could both be great musicians and I never thought. . . . I never thought he'd have such a retro attitude. And I never thought there would turn out to be this incredible competition. . . .

MARY ANN B. on the Postmodern Freeloader:

I didn't have a relationship with a man for years—for the entire period I think of as the last trimester of my kids' childhood. For one thing, I always had to make money. When Murray and I separated, it had a lot to do with him not having gotten involved with us as a unit. We broke up right as the kids were entering high school, and the main reason we broke up is that we were living in a two-tiered family. I was still a single mom even though I was living with a man. I was also working—we had never combined our finances in such a way that we'd ever become a nuclear family. I was still totally responsible for the kids. So I was a couple with him, and I was a single mom to those kids. It just wasn't feasible anymore.

ROSA M. on the Batterer:

My last serious involvement lasted for about two or three years. That one was a disaster because even though there was the romance and the passion, there was also violence. I never thought I would ever experience that, and now I can relate to stories of other people who have that happen.

I wasn't in love with him, no. I was addicted to the passion. A part of it was that romance I had always been looking for.

He'd hit me if I made him angry for any reason. Sometimes it was . . . because I had made him jealous or out of possessiveness. Oh, yeah, I tried to stop him, but it was impossible.

Yeah, I left. I was in bad shape when that relationship ended, but not in the same way as I had been with my husband, when I was so unhappy. Because this man had been successful to a certain degree in manipulating me into a position where I quit communicating with my friends and my family. It was a control thing. So during the relationship I lost a sense of myself, and I wasn't able to do the things that I'd been used to all my life, social things, the things I'd always enjoyed. All my releases had been cut out, and I felt like I had gotten into a shell. It was weird. So afterward there was a great relief to be on my own again and getting into my own thing.

RENEE G. (90) on the Excessively Libidinous Suitor:

It wasn't long after my husband died. Around six years ago. I had gone back to study. Not to an adult education center or to audit courses or anything like that, but really back to study and to get a degree. American History. I've slowed up since my fall, when I broke a hip. But I only have thirty credits to go. I think I'm going to make it.

Well, so you meet many people of all kinds in those classes. I love being with young people. I feel young myself, and I feel they revitalize me. A few older people, too. Though no one is taking these classes for credit, and doing the homework and taking the tests, you know? I'm the only one, I can tell you. *Oy*, it's so hard, I can't tell you. But in my Civil War class, there was a man who kept talking to me. A professor. He came from Belgium during the war. Nice enough. Smart. A widower.

So it turned out that my friends who used to go to Temple Emanuel knew him, this Belgian professor, because apparently he lives in that neighborhood. And they said his wife, who died eight or nine years ago, was a wonderful woman. A younger woman—so you see, you never know what's going to happen.

So now that I knew he was all right, I became a little friendlier with him. And then, all of a sudden, he wouldn't leave me alone. He was always waiting for me after class, or asking me to go for coffee or out to dinner or something like that. So I went for coffee once or twice after the class—Sanka, of course. And I enjoyed conversing with him. He was intelligent. Except that he was flirting a little too much. And so I said to him, "It's too soon. Let's be friends."

So one day, it was raining after class, and the coffee shop was full, so he came back home with me, and we had a nice cup of tea at the table here, and then afterward I said, "Why don't we go into the living room." And so he sat down on that blue armchair over there, and I was just going to bring the tea dishes back to the kitchen—because I don't like to leave a mess. We'd brought our cups and saucers to the living room. I was just going to clear the rest. I brought the empty teapot back to the kitchen and then came back for more.

And he was standing up in the living room, and he came over to me, and he said, "We could be so happy together."

And I said, "What are you doing? We're having tea. Let me bring the dishes back to the kitchen." So then he came closer to me and tried to kiss me. I pulled back and I said, "Please don't do this. It's too soon. You are brutalizing me."

"Just kiss me," he said.

"No!" I said, "Stop! Can't you control yourself?"

And he said, "I can't help it. It's the way I feel."

I said, "My husband just died."

And he said, "But we're here and we're still alive. We should make the most of life." Actually, I didn't mention that he's a little bit younger than I am. Seventy-two or seventy-three. So he said, "You're a beautiful woman."

And he came closer again and was trying to touch me. He was brutalizing me. It was too soon. He was too brutal. "Maybe you should go," I said.

So he said, "I can't help it, when I see you I get excited."

So I said, "Well, if you're excited, take a Valium."

ADELE U. on the Pulchritudinous Creep:

The trouble is that the sort of men that I'm attracted to are not necessarily lovely people to share my life with. And the people I'm friends with who share my head, my heart, are often seminerdy, lovely, kind men. So to me love and dating are two completely different things. Good sex and lovers are one thing. Good, interesting, kind men . . . that's something else. So you know how people are always saying, "Well, how can you sleep with someone you don't find loving and kind?" And the answer is: Very easily.

CLAIRE O. on the Phantom:

You can sort of see the big picture when you're older. What's strange about all of it is that we're all sort of struggling with the same fantasies. We're sort of looking for ways to find this perfect person. We're all kind of groping around out there, and in my experience, whatever I have seems to be the very thing I no longer want. As if it were just the act of *getting* it. It's the concept of a relationship as opposed to what the relationship really is. I've *never* been able to commit, so I've had a series of broken engagements, and that was really humiliating. And yet I can't stand being alone. That's the other side of it. I see that there are these choices, and I think that I probably could have had an OK life. . . . But this horrible fear of ending up in something that I can't believe or don't trust—that fear prevented me from taking these choices, and I just don't feel it was a mistake to listen to that in myself.

MARY ANN B. on the Widower:

He was actually hoping for a wife; he was a widower, and he wanted a replacement. And so I found myself in a situation where I was with someone I could tell was thinking, *Are you the right one for me? Well, you seem right. It wouldn't be embarrassing to introduce you to my friends, but you're not perfect.* And then he started sharing his reservations about me, and I found he was expecting me to change myself to be perfect for him. I thought, *This is astonishing that he thinks I would be motivated to change,* and it was a big jolt to realize how much I'd evolved because twenty-five years ago I would have expected it, and now I thought it was his job to learn who I was, and he thought it was my job to be who he wanted. That relationship didn't last. I don't know if any of them will last with this new framework, but we'll see.

BEATRICE H. on the problem of true love. She is a friend of my mother's (who wouldn't give her age because, she said, it can be

used against a woman). When I asked if she had ever considered remarrying, she gave me the classical, ageless answer, and I felt it should appear in these pages at least once.

I'll say it to you, but can you dress it up? When you've really given your heart and your mind and your entire being to someone, there can be no one else.

PHEW

What I kept hearing is that, eventually (though often sooner than one could have imagined) there was an abrupt feeling of relief so succinct, it was almost eerie.

ANITA S., the one who had to endure the dinners with the Mirror Couples, wound up to such a rhetorical pitch that I thought the end of her monologue would be quite poignant. Instead, as would happen many times in these conversations, the mountain shrank to a molehill with no further ado.

So we broke up and it was painful, but I immediately started to feel better.

LISA C. had braced herself for the worst, experienced prospective retroactive nostalgia, rehearsed the parting conversation with friends, even warned her parents.

I was devastated for twenty-four hours, and then I was fine. It was really a funny thing, because my therapist, who's obviously a very influential person in my life, used to tell me this—that you cry and then you get over it. And I did. And I was sort of relieved not to have to worry all the time about whether this relationship was strong enough.

JANIE A. had thought she was headed for hell.

When we broke up, he said he wasn't seeing anyone, but then I heard that he had taken up with a fashion model. And her face was pasted everywhere, every magazine cover, every billboard you could imagine. . . .

Well, it should have been a nightmare. It sort of was, at first. But then afterward, not long after, actually, I found I was really enjoying being single. I was having a really good time, even though I was having one terrible date after another. Basically, it wasn't such a bad place to be at all. My life went from that incredibly confining situation to this new phase where there was nobody to think about. There was no one person kind of cluttering up your head; it sort of cleared some space there. I remember thinking, *Oh, God, it's going to be awful*. You know, I definitely had a dating binge for a couple of months, and that was . . . I think I sort of needed to do that. But then I just realized . . . *This is nice!*

REBECCA S. In her late 70s, she recently redid the living room. The number of photos of her late husband had dwindled radically since my last visit.

He was my husband, and I was traditional. Oh, he had a very authoritarian personality. Ohhhhh, his personality. . . . If I'm moving—I've got to sit down. If I'm going shopping—I've got to hear something else he has to say. If I'm talking—I've got to be quiet. The friends I have now didn't ever know me then because I never said a word. I was a submissive mouse. And when he passed, that's when I broke out. . . . And I became very talkative. I never stop now. It's been going on since he died, I don't stop talking.

JANE H., 39, had a marriage that ended in a sort of *Gaslight* meets *Gone With the Wind* extravaganza.

My husband and I had a very difficult separation because he became violent, and after we separated he began following me. Yes, he stalked me. I threatened to call the police, and that sort of ended it. He fortunately decided to move out to LA. He was a very nice guy. He wasn't a batterer, but he was on the edge of becoming that, and he realized he was in trouble, and he left New York. It was a very smart thing to have done. And we wrote to each other and spoke to each other and—Oh, you know; he said, she said. It just went on. After six months I told him that I'd found that I was attached to him but that he was a very unappealing person. I felt terribly relieved. I mean, I even went through the smelly little pillow syndrome. You know, when they leave, and you're supposed to sniff their pillow and say you miss them. That kind of . . . romantic-novel stuff: *Oh, the*

bed is empty. I remember the first morning after he left, I was totally miserable; I could barely see out of my eyes, they were so swollen
from tears. And I flipped over the pillow, and then I thought, *I don't
give a shit about this pillow. I'm glad he is not here.*

AMELIA J. is honest enough to remind us of issues around prestige, which, as is well known but seldom discussed, can sometimes take a vertiginous dive for a suddenly single woman. At the
very least, the sense of emotional place and social role are permanently disrupted.

And there's a comfort in having a relationship. As much as you
might want to be outside institutions . . . I mean, you know, I was
very aware of my husband being a professor and that by virtue of my
marriage, I then became something that had to do with his being a
professor. I left because I felt like I needed to be outside of it; this
institution was driving me crazy. But, also, I think for the possibility
for creativity. Yet I was pulled back toward an institution, for a position and security, so I was so scared. But finally after a long period
of staying home just limping along, I started to emerge, and then I
was moving forward while he was moving backward. As difficult as
it was, it made me feel like a grown-up in a way that I hadn't when
I was married. . . ..

SUSANNAH W., like many of us, had one relationship that went
on and on, long after she should have ended it.

It's just that I didn't have the strength at that point to just leave
and act on my instincts. No, it isn't that I was scared to be alone. I
thought no one would want me. A lot had to do with bearing children. I had so much invested at that point, and I wanted desperately to have a child. He was sort of holding out the carrot; like, if we
solve our problems, then, yes, we can.

I was in my forties.

What I feel for him is a powerful hate. I saw him not long ago in
a restaurant. I had thought that my hate was so powerful, I'd be
afraid of my physical reaction if I saw him, that I'd want to damage
him. But it's funny. I saw him, and I wasn't even taken aback, not
even aghast, nothing. And I thought, *Well, I just don't want to see
him.* But I didn't have that physical outpouring, so I think that's

good. But I blame myself a lot, and I hope that I learn from this experience, enough to say, yeah, he misled me, he's compulsive, pathological, but I learned something about myself. I hate him profoundly, but I don't hate myself profoundly. I just realized what makes me tick more.

So I lost something that's irretrievable. But I played a role in it. I really did.

I'm extremely relieved. I can't imagine how I could have continued. I feel like myself. I feel like I've gotten myself back.

ROSA M. in Tucson expresses irreconcilable certitudes with a total lack of self-consciousness.

I don't know if I ever got over it. I thought I did. The first year was so painful that I thought I was mentally ill. If I looked at a beautiful scene of nature, it looked sad because it didn't have the love of us in it. And if I went to the lake and saw a couple sitting on a park bench, I didn't feel I could bear that, either. A cloudy day with rain felt like death. In fact, the first part of that year was scary. Almost like the fear of death. I hated that feeling; I never wanted to feel that again. And then the second year, it started to fade. And by the end of the second year, I was completely healthy again. . . . I really think I was and am healthy. I guess I've changed, though.

Damaged? I don't feel damaged, I really don't. I just feel wiser.

No, it's not really like shedding my old self and having a new one emerge. I like to think it's my real self that emerged. Because it feels really comfortable where I am now. More comfortable than when I was married and wondering where my husband was and yearning for him. Fifteen years ago, and I can bring it back just like that.

THE SO-CALLED
NEW FAMILY

*Why, Decades Later, Do We Still
Think of It as New?*

We know that the "New Family" exists because . . . well, because everyone knows. Even sticking strictly to the *A* section of the newspaper it is increasingly hard to avoid, as people fight one another, companies, co-op boards, courts, over sharing apartments and health insurance benefits for unmarried cohabitants, maternity leave for an adoptive mother, or maternity-leave equivalent for a childless worker to care for an elderly parent. All this is the bustle of the new family. Droves of little Chinese girls are adopted by graying urban professionals. There are waiting lists at in vitro clinics, and sperm banks are doing sell-out business. Surrogate mothers advertise. Lesbian couples improvise with old boyfriends and turkey basters. People argue on television shows about the merits of biracial families. People are interviewed in magazines about the experience of growing up with a transvestite dad. Older women marry younger men, younger men marry other men (in Hawaii, anyway), younger women use their mothers' wombs to bring a baby to term. Divorced spouses take vacations together with their children (first set and second set) and new spouses and, occasionally, their new spouses' ex-spouses.

Like "single woman," "New Family" refers to a negative space. It has come to serve as an umbrella category for anything "irregular," that is, anything unlike the "regular" mom-dad-kid unit. Beyond this evocation of the norm, the term rather fuzzily brings to mind clusters of nonconforming adults and children thrown together as a result of divorce, remarriage, single parenting, infertility, homosexuality, adoption, various housing-without-wedlock situations, and all manners of combinations of the above. And, of course, bizarre custody suits are now among the most favored national media spectacles, although they are probably less iconic of the troubles of the New Family than of our reluctance to abandon the old.

The "old" continues to be seen as *the* family, the traditional family that alone can provide good values, good kids, good marriages, the good life. Some still call it the "natural" family, and this is a matter of contention. But then so is everything else. Conservatives, neoconservatives, liberals, progressives, and civil libertarians, the Christian right and the old Christian left, and the Orthodox Jews and the New Agers—all factions have a certain view of what is natural and good, and most refuse to support the others or even acknowledge the contradictions of the rest. Somehow, in the midst of this cacophony, politicians still campaign on a family-values platform, insisting on keeping up appearances, as if we were just one big family whose members should present a united front. Anyone who says anything else is a spoiler, according to this view. Yet everyone knows the truth: We are many things in America at the end of the century, but we are not one big family. In this climate of inflamed controversy, however, no distinction is made between questioning a traditional view and attacking the family.

What we call the old, however, is relatively new. "Before the eighteenth century no European language had a term for the mother-father-children grouping," write Frances and Joseph Gies in *Marriage and the Family in the Middle Ages*. From Roman times through the middle ages and the early modern period, "The meaning of the Latin cognate, *familia*, from a common Indo European word signifying 'house,' . . . referred to all the people who live in the house, including servants and slaves."

Similarly, the American family started out as a "little commonwealth," with the father as sole governor. In the colonial family, only the father sat on a chair (others sat on benches, chests, or stools). Child-rearing manuals were addressed to him. His wife called him "sir" or "mister," and he was likely to address her as his "dear child." This authentically old family was quite diversified, and, then as now, the extreme natural and economic conditions of American life shaped the groupings. In Virginia, for example, half of all marriages were ended by death before the seventh wedding anniversary, two-thirds of all children lost one parent by their eighteenth birthday, and one-third lost both parents. This country has always had more than its share of single-parent households. "For over three centuries, Americans have bemoaned the decline of the family," claims *The Reader's Guide to American History.* "Even in Puritan New England, community elders decried the fragility of marriage, the selfishness of parents, and the rebelliousness of children."

Of course, noncolonial America was even more diverse. Each of the 240 Native American tribes had its own kinship system—some matrilocal, in which husbands joined their wives' households in "longhouses" shared by some ten families, others in wigwams that held two or three families, and yet others in what we would today call extended families of three generations. As for African Americans, they were prohibited from establishing legal families. Many slaves did not live long enough to even marry "unofficially," or else they had very brief unions.

The "little commonwealth" system began to weaken toward the end of the eighteenth century, when marriage was seen less as a property arrangement and more as an emotional one, and for the first time the conjugal bond became the household's central organizing principle. Parental control weakened, sexual mores loosened, and illegitimacy rates rose, and people became more affectionate to their children. The family's social and economic significance declined, and schools, almshouses, and businesses took on many of its functions. It is only in the nineteenth century that middle-class families began to take what we now imagine to be traditional form, with husband as breadwinner and wife as full-time homemaker. Not until then did motherhood come to be glorified in the American way and parents begin to keep children home into their teens instead of sending them out at age seven or eight to work as servants or apprentices. It is only then that the many customs we think of as ancient and universal family traditions first appear: The family vacation did not arrive until the mid-nineteenth century, nor did Thanksgiving, birthday parties, or decorating a Christmas tree. By the end of the nineteenth century, there was much worried talk about the disintegrating American family: The birthrate was declining, the divorce rate rising, and young women balked at remaining within the "sphere of domesticity." Despite legal efforts to restrict divorce, the rate rose fifteenfold between 1870 and 1920—the period in which women first went to college and held jobs outside the home in significant numbers. And this is the point at which the ideal of the "companionate family" originated, calling for the spouses to be friends and lovers and for parents and children to be pals. In the 1920s there emerged a call for liberalized divorce laws, sex education, birth-control information, and permissive child-rearing styles.

Even in the Great Depression, often invoked as an era in which material problems were acute but the family was close and strong, although divorce rates fell—people couldn't afford to divorce—the rate of desertion was astoundingly high. By 1940 more than 1.5 million married couples were living apart. During World War II, the divorce rate surged up again, as did juvenile delinquency, venereal disease, and the prevalence of latchkey children.

And so here, then, is the tangle of central dilemmas. The smaller the family gets, the more it depends upon the parental couple's bond. And the greater the expectation of emotional fulfillment in family life, the less rigidly a single "governor" can control the family. The less control there is, the more freedom everyone has, the more sexual activity among young people increases, the greater the number of children are born out of wedlock, and—since freedom and sexuality combined create their own synergy—the more either partner might want to, at the very least, look around some . . . and, therefore, the more the parental couple's bond is threatened. Something's got to give somewhere, and it has.

On only one general point are we all agreed: All factions invoke "the good of the child," and all factions then invoke the single-mother rate as the enemy of the child. In 1994, some 28 percent of all American births, more than one million, were to single-mothers. This is a statistic that is invariably greeted with expressions of horror, undergirded by images taken from the painful lives of our least-privileged citizens: poor, unwed teenagers. True, most unwed mothers are poor and uneducated, and the unwanted pregnancies of adolescent girls are hardships and sometimes tragedies for them and their children and the rest of us. But it is seldom noted that in the 1990s the birthrates of unwed teenagers actually decreased. The steepest increase was seen among white, educated, professional women. By the beginning of the '90s the demographics had changed so much that almost a third of single mothers had some college education. You can see by the figures exactly when it happened: Between 1980 and 1989 the birth rate for single white women between the ages of 30 and 39 rose more than 90 percent. In 1970 less than 9 percent of white children lived with one parent. In 1995 some 21 percent of white children lived with one parent.

And to make a full assessment of single motherhood, you must add the uncounted thousands of single women who adopt children. (State records are often not available because court records are sometimes sealed, and, incredible as it may seem, there is no national clearinghouse for local adoption statistics.) But it is estimated that families maintained by women with no husband present nearly tripled between 1970 and 1996, rising from three and a half million to nearly ten million. It may still be news to us, but the so-called New Family is decades old—at the very least. One could certainly make a case that the demise of the "little commonwealth" style of family power heirarchy was the true beginning of the New Family, which would make it around two hundred years old.

Personally, I only saw how large my own lag time was when one of my friends, a working single mother, mentioned in passing that her child seemed in some ways better adjusted than many of her friends. "Molly doesn't have to live with all the tension of a couple, or get used as a lightning rod for the conflicts between two parents," said my friend. She spoke very casually, as if repeating a certitude no longer questioned.

My friend had found her daughter, then aged eight months, in an Eastern European orphanage, the kind where photographers surreptitiously get shots of children lying in rows of uniform cribs, many increasingly lethargic and depressed for lack of human touch. Most of us who have seen the photos in the paper can never forget them. What we hardly ever get news of, however, is the happy humdrum everyday life of these children after they are adopted. They were begged or bartered for and snatched away from their terrifying fate, yes, but soon their main concern shifts from survival to getting their own phone, learning to Rollerblade, loving their grandparents, pleading for computer classes, and resenting the very idea of having to take naps. Even I, who should have known better, had been too focused on the initial drama to note that the quotidian had eventually imposed itself, and life had gone on to take up all the available space. Molly is now almost five, a bright child, boisterous, mischievous, open and tender, endlessly curious. "She's something, that one," people say about this little girl. And what seems extraordinary is not her history but her energy and intelligence.

As a working single mother, my friend has millions of peers, some of whom have raised children now already raising their own children. So why has the aura of newness stuck so tenaciously to it? To evoke a kind of faddish impermanence? To set aside the difficult issues so as to address more pressing practical questions? The term "New Family" is a sloppy generality that gets everyone on all sides out of having to look closely at the specifics of the new single mother, the new single mother's lover, the new ex-housewife and the new type of stay-at-home mom, the new birth mother, the new ex-husband, the new ex-husband's husband, the new stepfather, the new modes of conception, and the world of offspring resulting therefrom, to say nothing of the mixing and matching of these. And of course there is the new childless person—or "child free" as some prefer to call it—and all of the diversity she brings to the new parameters of family. And then there are the many shadings: the married couples who live in separate cities, the lovers who don't live together but have been monogamous for the last twenty-five years, the "cohabitants" who live in symbiosis more intense than in many a marriage. Some may prefer to call themselves companions or live-in partners or even, most discreetly, roommates. We don't even have names for all the new categories.

The decline of the mom-dad-kids family as a real-life mainstream is already a fait accompli: This is family only for a minority of Americans. The changes "traditionalists" are trying to prevent have already happened. For example, by the time Vice President Dan Quayle made his outraged pronouncements on Murphy Brown's single motherhood, the statement was outdated enough to provoke laughter. Mr. Quayle must have thought he could get away with it because the words "single" and "mother" used together faithfully raise the specter of moral decadence and degenerate deviance, to say nothing of relentless housing problems, to say nothing of sexual freedom, to say nothing of the unstated fear of violence from the poor and/or people of color, mixed together with what appears to be a primeval horror of women in suits.

While the statistics of single mothers have (like their married counterpart) somewhat slowed from the vertiginous rates of increase of the 1980s and early '90s, they are already much too big to be contained by other people's moral code, and they are staying on a steady upward course. Right now 11 percent of households are headed by women; in 2010 that figure is estimated to rise to 12 per-cent—a significant increment. In 1995 six and a half million fami-lies were headed by unmarried women; in 2010 that figure will total seven million. It is estimated that half of all children will reside in a single-parent family at some time before they reach age sixteen, for an average period of six years.

But why is that necessarily all bad? Change is not an attack on the family, it is part of its evolution and survival. Is it possible that what we call disintegration is, in fact, adaptation? Throughout his-tory, many of the most moving attempts to constitute or reconsti-tute a family have been in highly unusual arrangements. The above mentioned African-American slaves are a good case in point. From the eighteenth century on, many more Africans were imported into the colonies, plantations grew, and life expectancy went up so that more families formed. When the Civil War ended, there were freedmen who roamed the country for years, trying to reunite their families.

Similarly, ninety years later, many Holocaust survivors, bereft of spouse, parents, or children, ended up living in highly unusual arrangements right after the Second World War—in collective homes or in couples out of wedlock—but they never stopped look-ing for kin, and kin of kin, no matter how distantly related: This was hardly a matter of conservativism or of tradition, or even consan-guinity.

There is such a thing as the family of the heart, and this is as like-ly to be *new* family as old. The current new vs. old battle is a false one. There are not two sides, there is a continuum. But we stay focused on the split between that part of the population still in "reg-ular" families and that which isn't; we still think in terms of "mainstream" (a.k.a. traditional) and "alternative" (a.k.a. independent) as if these referred to irrevocable distinctions.

But why are these figures cited only with horror? Why can't single motherhood or the New Family, the irregular family, be trusted to uphold any ideal, except in second-best, morally tainted fashion?

And no wonder, then, that we see only evil in the divorce rate, that we see only dissolution and harm to the children: If the ur-family is idealized as somehow magical ("good") in one form only, then the central couple's severance has to be demonized in equal proportion. Therefore, to speak of all the so-called new variations as not only common but potentially honorable and even desirable is to threaten the taboos that serve to keep the family romance intact. But as more happy kids growing up in these "new" families prove how possible it is to thrive in them, one does begin to wonder what the taboo is really trying to prevent.

If remaining unmarried destroys a collective sense of comfort, if independence tears a crucial bond, if a woman's choice or acceptance of solitude disrupts everything, what then are we to fear if women have *babies* without men? Or, even worse, most catastrophic and unthinkable, if they choose to have no babies at all? You could see why their mothers and fathers would be upset. When you then provide women with modern fertility possibilities, artificial insemination in every variety, sperm banks, in vitro pregnancy, surrogate mothers, the possibilities of having babies with friends—with homosexual friends even!—and rearing them on their own or with other women or in temporary, serial relationships with men, you are really, really threatening the supremacy of the old-time phallus. For what is supremacy if not ultimate necessity? Their predecessors, at least, were soundly punished. Modern single women get off scott free, by those standards; they have jobs, they have homes, they have lovers, and they have babies, with or without the lovers.

"Single mothers are terrifying to everyone," a therapist specializing in fertility issues told me, "because they trigger the ultimate fear of castration: Men won't be needed at all!"

Traditionally, the Oedipal verities' magic spell has been perpetuated not only by tradition but also by law and rite, and those rituals that incarnate the most powerful kind of belief, whether they are major ceremonies such as formal weddings or minor ones such as boy-girl-boy-girl seating at dinner. But now even the hallowed old rites are succumbing. What family, loose or rigid, can live through such a pregnancy without changing? What so-called values can resist the power of a baby, no matter where he came from and how? To insist on maintaining those values condemns us to separating ourselves from our emotions, sentimentalizing an invented ideal from which we are exiled.

This is how historian and sociologist Stephanie Coontz defines the family crisis in *The Way We Never Were*. In a chapter entitled "The Way We Wish We Were," she writes:

> Like most "visions of a golden age," the "traditional family" . . . evaporates on closer examination. It is an ahistorical amalgam of structures, values, and behaviors that never co-existed in the same time and place. The notion that traditional families fostered intense intimacy between husbands and wives while creating mothers who were totally available to their children, for example, is an idea that combines some characteristics of the white, middle-class family in the mid-nineteenth century and some of a rival family idea first articulated in the 1920s. . . . The hybrid idea that a woman can be fully absorbed by her youngsters while simultaneously maintaining passionate sexual excitement with her husband was a 1950s invention that drove thousands of women to therapists, tranquilizers, or alcohol when they actually tried to live up to it.

And so, just as an example, even while sexual abuse in the family is nowadays a hot topic in every American medium, we have elevated the 1950s to the pedestal of kinship systems, the innocent Eden of family affections. What a defilement it would be to even *think* of incest when living in the same iconic universe as that undying American dream—the girls in crinolines (no hips, no groin), the boys in crew cuts and loose pants (no sexual threat), all the kids in saddle shoes (no fetish, no perversity), doing the Lindy (no pelvic contact). We illustrate our memories of the 1950s with stills of family groups: Ozzie and Harriet and their kids, Robert Young and his, Donna Reed and hers, Beaver's family, Dobie Gillis's, Desi and Lucy's, mothers in pageboy hairdos, bringing snacks in on round trays, ponytail/crew-cut-sporting kids lounging on the floor of the den, the inevitable dads flashing the inevitable boyish grins with sparkles bouncing off their teeth.

And if we insist on seeing this setup as the "real" family, what are we to make of the reality of the present? "The most common reaction to a discordance between myth and reality is guilt, . . ." writes Coontz. "Perhaps the second most common reaction is anger—a sense of betrayal and rage." Indeed, many in this culture are furious, but I propose that they are furious at the wrong people—and addressing the wrong issues. "Women and children bore the brunt of poverty within 'traditional' two-parent families just as surely, if less visibly, as they do in modern female-headed households, . . ." says Coontz. "Twenty percent of American children live in poverty today: At the turn of the century the same proportion lived in orphanages, not because they actually lacked both parents, but because one or both parents simply could not afford their keep." As for the violence that is perpetually cited as a direct result of the current decline of family values, it might be useful to recall that the United States has had the highest homicide rate in the industrial world for the last 150 years.

The guilt that results from experiencing the discordance between myth and reality and the ensuing blame has fallen most heavily on those who abandon the model of Mom-and-Dad as an inseparable unit. A "broken marriage"—a telling poetic expression emphasizing the pathos of a breakup rather than its more obvious rage, hate and pettiness—is always deemed to be sad, no matter how much physical or emotional brutality led up to it. Similarly, no matter what the circumstances, the children of broken marriages are always evoked as the most prominent victims of the breakup, never as possibly the beneficiaries. And yet what of all the wonderful little Mollies walking around? They are living evidence of another reality.

But if single women will now point out to one another, in private, that they think that their children are, at least in some ways, doing as well as a child can do, this is still a perception that is not often expressed in public.

As far back as a couple of decades ago, I heard a black woman on a talk show tell the host that children raised in single-parent families didn't necessarily have a bad home. At the time, though, I remember being surprised by her statement. The very fact that I remember it still is testimony to how seldom I have heard it echoed since then.

Just a couple of weeks ago, I watched a talk show on the theme of single parent adoption and heard a rabbi insist that children would be better off living in institutions or foster care than with single parents, and a seemingly liberal psychotherapist inveigh against single-parent adoption. The styles were different—the former expressed himself in a paroxysm of aggression, the latter in a miasma of regret—but the message was the same. Most painfully, even the lone adoptive mother on the panel insisted at every opportunity that she agreed with these men that it would have been better for her son to have had a father, but he still had a lot by having her for a family. The reality is that this child of color, adopted long past infancy, would have had little chance of ever getting into a nuclear family and would have joined the more than 500,000 children in foster care in this country, instead of living with someone who wanted to be his mom. The idea that this generous, caring woman might be offering the child a wonderful home, a wonderful future, not second-best in any way, was never once considered by any of the participants, including, sadly, the mother herself. This is the problem that plagues the New Family: Even its supporters often condemn it with faint praise.

But for better or for worse, the progenitors of the future will include the 75 percent of all children who have had some experience growing up of living in a single-parent household, and perhaps they will correct these distortions. Newt Gingrich (himself adopted and divorced) notwithstanding, not all of them are going to be crack-addicted criminals. My guess is they will be at least as decent as we are, in a ratio that was perhaps genetically embedded in our species to begin with (though we can try to improve it tiny bit by tiny bit.) Maybe the leaders of the future will choose to direct more energy toward preventing hunger and war rather than waste it stigmatizing every conceivable kind of unwed mothers.

Why can't we give praise to the mothers who do it all rather than consider them as selfish freaks? Why can't we honor the families of relations who are eager to provide housing, education, amusement, and protection to the children who otherwise are labeled unwanted? Why is the ideal of the "Old Family" constantly elevated, while we only see the New Family in its ugliest, most frightening forms? Just as we might say of one child that he is lucky to have such a wonderful dad, why can't we say that another is lucky to have such an amazing grandmother? Just as we praise the stability of one child's home, with her two siblings, her mom, her dad, her dog, why can't we praise the incredible luxury provided to another of having a nanny of her own who takes care of her when her mom is at the office? In the era where in many circles there is no greater reassurance to utter to a child than "You're special," why do we fear and demean nonconformity with such vigor?

None of the myriad ways in which people can damage one another in private is new, and—unless the species actually mutates—violence and dysfunction in one form or other are probably with us for the duration. But it doesn't seem like our capacity to love other human beings is going anywhere fast, either. I haven't noticed a decrease in our need to be loved by others or in our propensity to form lasting bonds with our families both of election and blood. Adopted children are often even more desired and more cherished than biological children. Is the new view of the adoptive parent-child bond based on a new imagined ideal? Absolutely. And, as a group, single women undoubtedly idealize friends-as-family, a notion that was invoked by nearly every woman I interviewed. But what we think of as "Old Family" has given a hefty chunk of humanity safety, succor, and meaning precisely because we have been able to idealize it.

The New Family can succeed the old—or rather, complement it—in our hopes and dreams as well as in our reality. Ideal visions enable us to stretch a little further, to seek solutions from within our situation. Americans are now extraordinarily educated about their own psychology. Even the talk shows, for all that aspects of them are so gross, voyeuristic, and exploitative, also represent a powerful collective urge to see and understand, and many basic problems are now out in the open. There seems to be a great impetus to uncover what was once unspoken and criminal. It does force us to betray the fantasy of the past of the beautiful, all-giving family. If we can cope with that, we can move on to less grim observations and conduct our explorations of the possibilities of relationships with a lighter heart. Dropping sentiment in favor of real emotion may prepare us for deeper connections, whether we call them old, new, or nothing at all.

And the future of the family can be anything, for just as we remember our own aunts and grandmothers, children now are memorizing the people who compose their family. Think of the mysterious and interesting role of childless single women in the life of the culture. While there are remarkable women who are mothers in a new way—married or unmarried—there are equally remarkable women—married and unmarried—who are not mothers, and they, too, have a great deal to contribute. They are not only improvising their own present, and their own future, they are also the role models for millions of little nieces and nephews who can see now that there are real alternatives to the Mom and Dad roles. And they are available for whatever kind of emotional engagement they choose.

"You know, I met with the guy in the official admission committee for the law program," a woman told me, apropos of family. She's in her late thirties, and she recently moved in with her lover. They had an affair for over a decade, but he had decided to stay in his 15-year-old marriage until his kids were grown. Meanwhile, though, since my friend wanted to have a child, they had tried for several years. Although they had gone through quite a lot of complicated procedures, she never did get pregnant. Eventually she went back to school full time and has since decided not to try anymore. But without her saying so quite so explicitly, I have the feeling that what he went through with her in those difficult years made her feel that they were as connected as if she had succeeded in getting pregnant. "It was the same thing," she said of her feelings about him even before he moved in. "Even while he wasn't there, he was always with me."

This had come to mind while she was being questioned for the law school. "When I finished the interview and the tour and so on and said good-bye to the man at the admissions office," she recalled afterward, "the last thing he asked me was, 'Do you have a family?' And I felt, *I do have a family!* But I guess I knew what his definition of family was, so I said, 'No.' But I was really thinking, *Well, his understanding of the word "family" is very different from mine. I have a family."*

YOU MUST GO HOME AGAIN

And again, and again, and again. For the single daughter it's harder to separate.

JEAN I., the director of research at a large company, is the one whose boss always "forgets"—when he asks her to work late—that she'll have to scramble for a baby-sitter for her four-year-old.

For one thing, if you don't have a husband or a child, you never get out of the child role on holidays. Usually the way that's manifested is you're the one who has to travel to someone else's house. But once you have a child they all have to come to you, and that sets up a superstructure for the shift. Everything is now focused on the child, and that's a different arrangement, which winds up deflecting a lot of the old family conflicts. You don't get into the same arguments you've been having for twenty years because now you're involved in a whole different set of activities—depending on what the child wants and needs.

CATHY D., a 44-year-old entrepreneur, says her relationship to her family has improved several thousand percent since she adopted a child. Her parents have stopped hinting that she should find a second husband.

Before I had a child, holidays were an obligation, and I had to brace myself for conversations that would hit on the sore point—about men and dating. I always felt unconnected, like there was something I hadn't done right. Whereas going down with the baby is just fabulous. Nobody bothers me about anything. All the focus has gone onto him. And I suppose there's a feeling that I gave them something, and I can just relax and kind of feel . . . a much more integral part of the family. In the same way that having a child makes me feel an integral part of the human race.

MARTHA H., 45, no kids, confirms the points made by the single mothers.

I *always* have to go there. It's always at my sister's, year in, year out. Not just Christmas, but every holiday. I have to get on a bus and go to Connecticut. And I'm always the one who has to pick up my mother and take her there. Since my father died, we never even have it at my mother's anymore. And it's been almost thirty years since my father died. . . .

NINA L., 28, divorced, prefers blatant avoidance.

Every Thanksgiving I go with some friends to a Chinese restaurant and then to a movie. It's one of the best days of the year.

RAFAELA Z. has no children but plenty of siblings. She's the oldest of nine.

How do they view my life? They probably have their opinions, but essentially they're pretty impressed. The one thing in the family that's really a problem for me is that they think that I should spend a lot more time with their kids. I don't have my own family, so I'm supposed to make myself available. "You're missing the girls growing up," they say, completely lacking in understanding that I actually made a choice not to have a family.

JANE H., 39, divorced. Surprise, surprise: Money and power make a difference.

Really, the whole attitude to my being single changed dramatically once my company became very successful and I moved into a great house. All of a sudden nobody bothered me about anything. There were trade-offs, I guess. Whatever I did must be right because I was living well, and taking care of them to some extent. In a way I became the matriarch of the family. At this point my singleness would be described as an idiosyncrasy more than anything else.

CAMILLE O.'s parents are both artists. They view these matters differently, and none of the children is ever deemed to grow up, anyway.

In my family, there are almost rewards for being single, like you get taken on holiday more and that kind of thing. And as a matter of fact, with my married brothers and sisters, there was a certain amount of resentment on my stepmother and father's part of not being able to see their children without their spouses.

SCRAMBLED CODES

Issues of competition resonate more clearly when the daughter abstains from following in her mother's footsteps.

SUSANNAH W. felt that she saved herself by rejecting her parents' assumptions and expectations.

My mother did have ambitions on my behalf. The earliest was that I'd be a movie star. So she was a stage mother during the early part of my life and schlepped me around to various studios. I was a princess for a day. In New York there was a show, I think on Dumont Television, I guess it was channel five then. And it was sort of modeled on *Queen for a Day*, but for children. But you didn't have to tell a sob story or anything, you just became a princess. I remember my mother hounded the producer; she dragged me to the studio constantly, until I finally became princess for a day. My prize was a Little Lulu doll. It was a little mannequin, a dress dummy—so you could make clothes for Little Lulu, you know? I'm getting off the point, but in a way not. Her ambition was that I be glamorous and beautiful and charming and that I marry well.

And then, of course, there was my father who wanted me to quit school and go to work. So I had two wonderful choices, didn't I?

LISA C., 33 years old, seemed unaware of the contradictions in her own account.

My mother was very supportive, very interested in my life. She loved to hear about everything. No, I don't think she lived through me vicariously. No. There was a little problem there, as a matter of fact. In some way she was thrilled by some of the things I did, but I also got the message, *Don't go too fast, too far, or have too much fun.* I think there was a jealousy, too.

My mother talks a lot about the fact that she never went back and did her master's work. She was a historian, and she really does know a lot of history of Europe. It is incredible to play Trivial Pursuit with her. She was very well educated. None of us went into that area; we all went into the sciences, and I think it's because everyone felt, *This is Mom's territory; if we even slightly infringe on it, she'll crumble into the ground.*

CHRISTINE L., the Washington lobbyist, is very aware of the fact that her way of life may be fulfilling her mother's unstated fantasy.

My mother has never been the kind who would say, "When are you getting married?" I never felt that kind of pressure from her. I did feel this pressure to succeed, either in a profession or some creative realm, to "be somebody." I've always been struck by that lack of pressure about marriage from either one of my parents and felt irritated by it. Instead of thinking, *Thank God*, I thought, *What? They don't think I can get married?* Or, *They don't care?!*

And the other thing is, my parents had a very unhappy marriage—which they have to this day. So I'm sure I looked at that and took it all in.

CAMILLE O.'s adult life has been centered around not imitating her mother.

The fantasy of having a life when I was younger was, *I'm going to make my dad happy.* I just remember wanting to please him, not in a sort of horrible, unhealthy way, but just wanting him to be OK.

When my father was alive . . . I wasn't crazy about my father, but I was very close to him. I think that, in many ways, saved me, the way very close friends save me.

My parents did not have a good relationship. My mother . . . she wasn't my idea of a mother, and she wasn't my father's idea of a wife. My father was the one who got us off to school, he did all of that. And there was my mother the whole time saying, "I'm your mother, don't just ask your father questions." And I remember thinking, *I never want to be a woman who begs for my children's attention, for my husband's attention.*

MARINA T. is a widow and mother of a grown daughter.

I'm fascinated when I hear women say that you don't have to

have a baby because I think: *Yes, right*. But I always felt I needed to—whether I would be a good mother, or a bad mother. But it's true that very well may have been part of the era. And maybe my own family because my mother had four children, and it seemed to me that there was something very unnatural about not using my body to have a child. I remember having had the discussion over a martini with a friend I worked with. We had both turned thirty, and we used to go out for dinner from work and have martinis and talk about life and so on, and we got into a terrible argument one night because I said I couldn't imagine I would be happy if I didn't have a baby, and she said, "You are ridiculous. Women don't have to have a baby." I said, "I'm sorry but that's how I feel," and she was furious. She was much more politically aware than I was.

If this was all happening now, and I wanted to have a baby, I know I could do it without being married. But for myself, I still think that would be very difficult. Whether or not the person I could have a baby with could change diapers and be a politically correct husband who did half the work . . . It seems to me that having another person there, when you're meeting the exhausting demands that children make—exhilarating but also draining—that to have another adult who knows this child the way you do and knows you is an enormously useful and practical arrangement.

But I also have the sense that something new is happening, that people are finding their own families in different ways. Because families, birth families or natural families, have become so broken up with divorces or geographical distances that we as single people are now in the position to find and to make our own families in a new way. And I think you have to be as careful about that as you would be in the old days about picking a husband. But there are so many people living alone now. And everybody needs . . . I mean, people need each other. It's a lot easier.

But these new families . . . there's something about them. Marriage was set up as a rather clever way to take care of children, and we haven't quite found a substitute yet, though we're working on it. So many contradictions. We're all trying to find our way in the world. We're born, we grow up, we have to figure all these things out. Then we do it again with a baby or a child, and we figure it out—or maybe we do all sorts of bad things because we *haven't* figured it out. And then we grow old and we die. And we're trying to figure out all of this, and it seems to me it's much easier to figure it out with someone else rather than to do it by yourself. It's better if you don't have to do it in isolation. And that's the thing I feel now, this sense of isolation that feels wrong. Yes, I'm independent and separate, but none of it seems to me to mean much, unless I feel very connected. If I didn't have a daughter, I think I would be spinning out into space in the aftermath of my husband's death. And by "daughter" I mean someone very close to me that I care about enormously, who's just part of my skin in some way.

JEAN I. feels tremendously distanced from her more conventional sister, and exasperated.

My sister's been married three times, one guy twice. She's sort of a case study in the fact that there are no fairy-tale endings. She keeps trying to get married, and the pathetic thing is that as she approaches fifty, the whole focus of her life is still who she's dating and whether she's going to find a man.

Well, that's true. That wouldn't even have been questioned a decade ago. But, I *mean* . . . !

MY PARENTS' MARRIAGE

Early lessons are well learned. The codes were often scrambled generations back.

PAULINE A. received quite overt messages from her parents, though they were later disavowed.

None of my brothers or sisters is married, and my mother has said, "What did we do to you all to make you not want to get married?"

And in fact what they did is they said: "Don't get married! Don't get married! Don't get married!" Like a joke, but not a joke.

RAFAELA Z. had a similar problem.

I really didn't want a marriage like my parents'. And also I had the sense that my mother would really have liked to try being alone. When they started to split up, I was twenty-three or twenty-four. They sort of temporarily split, and then my mother died. It's sort of a Gothic tale to me because I had the sense that the marriage had killed her.

SARAH O., 25, is of a generation of children who took their parents' marital problems for granted.

I probably have a funny way of looking at marriages, or sort of a skeptical way of looking at them, because my parents aren't divorced, but they have one of these relationships where they probably should have gotten divorced a long time ago. I can't even remember a time when they really had a close relationship. Basically, they both adore me and my brother. And so our family life . . . there is no sort of bond at the top; it's sort of all attention directed at me and my brother.

They're in their early fifties now. They were really a part of the '50s generation, and so they thought that they had to get married when they were twenty-five. They didn't understand . . . about the revolution that was coming. Or their sensibility just wasn't attuned to it, even if they were right in the middle of it. I mean, they have the same friends, but essentially they're just two very different people than the ones who got married thirty years ago.

LISA C. I asked her what her family was like.

We always blamed my mother for everything because she was so easy to blame—she was drunk half the time. I'll never forget the scene where my two sisters, who were in college, had driven across the country, and they had come back home for Thanksgiving. This was before my mother died, around the time my parents were supposed to get divorced. One of my sisters, Tracy, had taken on a lot of the maternal role. And so she had cooked the dinner. And my mother insisted on sitting in this chair—this sort of chaise longue thing she always sat on when she was drunk instead of at the dinner table because she wanted to watch us as we would be without her. But by then she was really drunk.

So she started eating and she started to choke on her turkey, and the chain reaction that went around the table . . . you know, one person turned to the other and said, "Is she choking? Is she choking?" And Dad said, "Oh, she always does this." And then Holly finally panicked and said, "She's choking!" And then we all ran up. You know, as much hell as she was, we didn't want to see her expire right there. I took her plate, and Holly instructed Lawrence on the Heimlich maneuver, and Lawrence did the Heimlich maneuver, and Dad just sat at the table. And then we all went back to the table and continued. And then afterward we were cleaning up, and she got up and looked at her plate of food, which we had taken away from her, and she said, "Oh, who didn't finish their meal?" She was just so out of it.

You experience a kind of humiliation. . . . It's funny, but that is how I feel. I feel very humiliated by my parents, and yet they are listed in the social register—though I think Dad had his name taken out—but that was important to Mom, and they were on these committees, and Mom was in the junior league. And there was my father most of the time with his fly down, just kind of vulgar. There's an ugliness that goes on. I want to get back to your questions, but I think to answer, it is that my parents were not able to solve their problems as a unit. And it's funny that we all blamed my mother; and then after she left, we saw that Dad had real problems.

BLANCHE W.'s mother was a talented architect whose career was stunted by her marriage.

My parents did set a really bad example of a marriage. Both sets of parents. But beyond that, I felt like I betrayed myself when I got married. In fact when I look back, the women I admired were always women alone. Those women were my heroes.

CATHY D. had no special problems with her mother, but it was her father who was her role model.

She couldn't imagine living *out there*. Within the limits of her life, she took advantage of opportunities, but really she preferred where she was. But I thought my mother was much more capable than she thought she was.

I didn't particularly feel pressure to get married from her. She was probably more concerned and involved in the issue than she let on, but she was intimidated by me because every time she would say something about it I'd snap at her. And managed to control her. But she'd always be giving my name to people. I'd say, "What did you do, write my name on the bathroom door?" And she'd say, "You meet the peaches through the pits."

I think I've wound up living out my father's fantasies much more. He always wanted to travel, and he used to imply he had given it up for his wife and family. And I always hung around my father and his friends, almost all of whom were small-business owners.

JOCELYN H., the one who has closer friendships with single women than with married women.

Would my father have been disappointed to see I've ended up a single woman? I don't think he would have, but my mother would be. My mother wanted me to get married before she died. This gentleman that I'm in a relationship with, she even said to him, "Take care of her." Even though I kept telling her I didn't need someone to take care of me. Yeah, I guess she did expect me to follow the same pattern she had, I think so. My father—he just let you go on your own. It was funny because even though he had all girls, he was very easygoing with us. He was always very easy to talk to, and my mother wasn't. I could talk to my father about anything and everything. He wouldn't give you advice, but he made you feel that whatever you decided you would do, that you were on your own. Whereas my mother always said, "Well, this is what you should do."

To be honest, I think I did prefer my father. I really cared for my father a lot more than my mother. But I think I grew to see my mother in a different light when she got sick. I saw her in a different way, and that's when I saw that I loved my mother in a different sense.

PERSONAL ANTECEDENTS

These are characters from childhood who were much admired and romanticized. Often it is a fondly recalled grandmother or aunt who lived alone.

ANITA S. knew her grandmother as a proudly independent widow.

Her husband drank a lot. Eventually, he was hurt in a mine cave-in. And in the end, after all that, when your husband died you were free. My sisters and I would talk about my grandmother a lot when we were girls. She was haunting in a good way. She had a garden, she lived well, she didn't seem lonely. We never saw her as needy. There were always millions of people around, and she would cook for them, but then they always went away. She was very proud in some ways.

She kept a rifle, a shotgun. And when we slept over, she would say, "Be sure to tell me if you get up in the night." One night my sister Elizabeth got up to go to the bathroom and didn't tell her, and all of a sudden she heard a noise—and there was my grandmother in her nightgown with a rifle pointed right at her.

It's funny, but as a role model, no one ever really replaced her for me. After my sophomore year in college, I had only male teachers. It was just the beginning of the feminist movement, so I was always looking for a female role model, but I couldn't find one.

I had a fantastic dream about my grandmother. She was standing behind the table; there were all of these candles lit in the front room. And then I went into the dining room, which had a big table in it, and everyone was there as they usually were for Sunday dinner. It was almost like a Last Supper vision, but instead of Christ, it was my grandmother. When I knew her, she was in her sixties, and her eyes were blue and rather faded, but my mother had told me that when she first met her, she had these brilliant, brilliant blue eyes. And in my dream she was looking at me with these incredible blue eyes. The dream was wonderful, somehow filled with blue and candlelight and green. I felt wonderful, like that solved everything in a certain kind of way. When I woke up I didn't need to ask myself quite as many questions: That was my female mentor. I remember thinking, *Wait a minute, that's supposed to be the solution to my problems?* It was a lot about her living by herself with so much autonomy, amidst all these colors. There was something so vivid about her, so beautiful, and I felt she was looking right at me.

ANTONIA C. was influenced by her mother's heroines.

My mother grew up in a family of eight, with alcoholic parents. She was the oldest and had to take care of all of the others all of the time. Her father died early on. The story was that her mother moved them all into a place over a stable, and they had to help take care of the stable, and also she got a job cleaning toilets at night in a big department store, and that's how she paid for the apartment. She had no American education, so she could never do anything here, though she was a bright person and loved to read.

Periodically one of several aunts, all single, would come up to her house to help. They looked after her very well, and taught her how to shop for food, and taught her about money, all kinds of things. The kids would sometimes go over to her long-widowed Irish grand-mother's house, whom I never met, and the grandmother would help her out. They were very strong minded—very bright, indepen-dent types—and that was a very lucky influence, I think. So my mother respected unmarried women, and I never heard anything derogatory. And she became someone really not inclined to be abused by anyone in any way. She expected to be treated fairly, and she certainly believed she was the equal of my father. They both had a good opinion of each other, which is probably rare.

HOPING TO CONCEIVE

"I'm trying to get pregnant" is now understood to be a way to spend an entire phase of one's life, just like "We're saving money to get married" used to be.

BLANCHE W. waited until her late 30s.

There came a point when I saw that trying to get pregnant was going to kill me. It was my first day in India, in the Lake Palace Hotel in Udaipur. I have to show you pictures of these places. I knew in the morning that I was ovulating—I was very tuned in to my mucus by then. I didn't even want to know that I was ovulating, but it was unavoidable. I had a car and driver and a guide to take me to Mount Abu, a Jain temple that was a few hours outside of Udaipur, a hill station. So, there we were in the car. There was this wonderful turbaned man who was like a classic Rajasthani: handle bar mustache, colored turban, really lively dark eyes. He was the dri-ver. And then there was this young guy who was my guide who sat in the back of the car with me making small talk for hours. We got to Mount Abu, which is filled with this incredibly elaborate symmetrical carving and a ceiling so vast that you have to lie down on the marble floor to see the whole thing. But even before I lay down, I was standing up with my head back, looking up at this great ceiling, and I started to feel faint. It was just like the woman in *A Passage to India*. I didn't know if I was having a religious experience or a sexual experience. But at the end I knew that God meant for me to have an Indian child. That's why I had not been able to conceive the previous ten years. I was the crossroads of East and West. So I got back in the car, and it was understood that this man, the one who was sitting in the back, and I would have sex. Not because I was attracted to him but because it was meant to be.

I don't know what he thought. I have no idea. But I sort of somehow knew that we would have sex. Even though I really liked the driver. The driver was gorgeous. This other man was a sort of wimpy-looking guy. I wasn't attracted to him. So we drove back, much of the time in silence sort of knowing what was to come. And we got back to the parking lot near the Lake Palace Hotel, but there was one little glitch. Which was that I was going to the driver's house for dinner. And I wasn't going to give that up because that was to be an authentic Indian experience. And how was I going to sort of sneak this guy into the Lake Palace Hotel? So it all took place in ten minutes. We got to my room, which was classic Lake Palace beauty, filigreed white marble inlaid with agates and beautiful Islamic arches, and as Ruth Prawer Jhabuala says, It Happened. He was definitely the clumsiest, least erotic sexual partner I'd ever had. I don't know that I even undressed. When it was over, which was in an instant, I had to run to meet the driver. But I stopped to tell the man—Bati—that was his name, Bati—that I might be pregnant now with his child, and if I were, I would send him a note and a picture and we would come to visit once in a while.

Of course, I spent the next three months in fear of terminal illness. And, of course, I wasn't pregnant.

CATHY D., 44, the entrepreneur who told us her family stopped worrying when she became financially secure enough to buy her house.

At first I wasn't going to try to get pregnant. I went straight to wanting to adopt, actually. It had been on my mind for a couple of years, and my final epiphany was breaking up with a guy I'd been with for about six months. He was a kind of typical Jewish neurotic and a divorced father of two. And I found I was sorrier than I had expected. Being part of a family had meant more to me than I had thought. I guess I got more scared of not doing it than of doing it when I thought of what things would look like ten years down the road.

But one of the things I felt about being a single mother is that I definitely craved the positive support and attention of my family and business associates, and somehow adopting brings you that. And getting pregnant as a single woman didn't have the same romance to it, and it would bring up more questions and seemed so complicated to me. But then when the adoption started to seem so complicated and traumatizing, I thought, *Oh, fuck, I'll try it*. And I tried to get pregnant for about six months, but I had to stop because the Pergonal drove me absolutely mad, and I was worried about the health effect of it. But other than that, it was a great experience. The guy I picked in the sperm bank was my favorite boyfriend ever.

No, you don't meet them. The bank has the pictures and keeps them, and you read the bios they give you.

No, I've never been pregnant. I had assiduously protected myself. And my mother had a tough pregnancy with my brother when I was about two years old, and that was on my mind, too. To me it was a vision of not being able to do things, so I found it very scary. Plus I had to keep running my business. I did think it would be much more of an intrusion into my life than the adoption.

JEAN I. recalls some of the many changes of heart and circumstance she went through before deciding to adopt.

I got pregnant accidentally. I don't think I ever would have felt any certainty as to whether or not I wanted to get pregnant if it hadn't been for this accident, although you may believe it wasn't an accident. The guy was awful, though, so right from the start what I was contemplating was being a single mother. When I first got pregnant, I really didn't know what to do. Then I went to a therapist—it was the first time in my life I had sought professional counsel. Then I decided that I was very happy pregnant, even though the guy was

a total asshole and I didn't want to be with him. And then I miscarried. And then I decided to keep trying.

So I got a friend to help me out. On what basis did I make the decision? That's all a little fuzzy. I remember that Willie John wasn't my
first choice. I asked a couple of people. He may have been my second
or third choice because he was so crazy. Like, he's incapable of showing up anywhere he's supposed to or doing basic things. He's completely unreliable. The whole thing was really tough. We'd always had
a great sexual relationship. It was good within the confines, but it very
quickly got to the jerking off in a jar stage, which wasn't so great. We
certainly agreed on no custodial or financial responsibility. I'm not
sure he would have been identified to the child.

Finally, it became too exasperating. He drove me crazy. So that's
when I went to the fertility doctor and the sperm bank route. And
then I got pregnant again, and then I miscarried again, and then I
adopted.

The adoption decision? No, I didn't make that decision very
cleanly, either. As far as I was concerned at this point, one of the
things that makes adoption unappealing is the idea of judgment, of
all the people who come into your life and decide whether you're fit.
I didn't want to qualify. I didn't want to explain my situation to
home-study people or case workers. I felt there was this big case-
history hurdle on adoption, and you get to audition for either an
agency or a birth mother. It felt creepy, and it felt like you would
always feel a lot less adequate if you are single. I think a lot more
single women would adopt if they didn't have in the back of their
minds that they have to justify their lives to a stranger.

And foreign adoptions are just as hard. Single women can't adopt
in South America because they're Catholic countries, and they
won't give a child to an unmarried person. In Korea, the laws are
explicitly slanted against single women. They're only allowed to
adopt older children or children with special needs. The law says
you are second-class citizens. And even in California now, Pete
Wilson is trying to get a law passed that single women can't adopt.
But around then, I just went to Romania to see what the situation
was, and how it was going to be, and whether I wanted to do it—
and I ended up with this little kid in my house.

If I'd known, I would have gone straight to adoption. Pregnancy to me is just a horrible necessary means to the end of having children. I was never interested in getting pregnant per se, or giving birth—it sounds like a horribly painful experience. I just wanted a kid.

When I look back on trying to get pregnant, though, I can see what the point was, because I guess I wouldn't have considered adoption until I was sure I wanted a child and had put myself through the other stuff. But I have a different take on some of these things, you know. My father is adopted, which I've always known. And my sister was adopted by my father, in that she had a different father. So there's sort of an adoption culture in our family.

JOAN S., 43, says that she has shelved the question for now.

I can tell you that trying to get pregnant with somebody I wasn't involved with emotionally, and wasn't lovers with, was infinitely easier than trying to get pregnant with either my lover or my husband. All we had to do was get sperm into my vagina. It didn't matter how we did it.

He was a friend I'd been having an affair with on and off again for twenty years. And then I asked, and he agreed to try to make a baby. He had performance difficulties for the first time in his whole life. But we would just laugh about it and rent porno movies, and I'd give him a glass or something to jerk off into. And then he'd proudly come out with a glass with his teaspoon full of sperm, and I'd get out my syringe and inseminate myself and then hang out with my legs up in the air for a half hour while we chatted. It wasn't very erotic. We split the cost of everything. Then we found out that he had developed sperm antibodies. I was just relieved that it wasn't me, that I didn't have hostile mucus. It always seemed like the most damning thing you can say about a woman was that she had hostile mucus. Anyway, as soon as we stopped trying to get pregnant together, we were suddenly real turned on to each other.

ADOPTION

The number of single women who adopt each year continues to climb.

CATHY D., 44, who is raising a little boy on her own.

When I first told my parents, I was worried that they would take that as some kind of failure: Oh, that means you won't get married and have your own. But when I told them, what they said was, "Oh, we thought you might do something like that." Because they had read in the *Enquirer* about single women doing that. Isabella Rossellini, Linda Ronstadt, Michelle Pfeiffer . . . Living as a single woman in New York turned me into a kind of celebrity in my family, anyway, so in their mind I fit in with that class of people.

And during the process of adopting, it got hard for them when it got hard for me, and I tried not to talk to them about it too much, but they worried about me. And they had to deal with their friends when someone would say, "What if the mother comes back and takes the baby back?" and stuff like that. My mother would say to me, "Oh, you wouldn't believe what Una said to me today. . . ."

A dream? What comes to mind is almost a daydream. About once a month something comes to me in my mind that something awful is happening to my son. And it overwhelms me, not just because something is happening to my son, but also because I stop and think, *What would I do?* I lived through a couple of deaths of guys I dated. And it's in my mind somehow. And I think, *What would I do? How would I go on?*

The daddy thing? I think he's probably worse off for not having a dad. Oh, it bothers me, and I think it's important to have men around and also for me to play a lot of different roles. And in the end a lot of kids grow up without a dad. It's not as if it's the norm anymore. I don't think it's a tragic thing, but I think it's better if there's one around.

There are hurdles you have to get past. When we were in Nantucket this summer, this little five-year-old girl, the daughter of some friends, was asking me, "Where's Kenny's father?" and I said, "In Texas," holding my breath. And she said, "Why is he in Texas and Kenny is here?" And I said, "Because he doesn't know him. I adopted Kenny." So she said, "Oh." Her mother had told her about adoption. She said, "Oh, like BamBam in the Flintstones."

Did I ever tell you the story about my nephew talking to me about adoption? He was ten at the time. He said, "Was Kenny adopted?" I said, "Yes." He said, "Does that mean his mommy didn't want him?" And I said, "No . . . she was too young and she couldn't take care of him." He said, "How old?" And I said, "Twenty-four." And he said, "That's not so young." Then he asked, "How much did you pay for him?" I said, "I didn't pay for him. I paid for his birth mother's cost at the hospital because it's expensive." And he said, "Oh, you pay money to be born?" And I said, "Yes." And he looked at Kenny and said, "I wonder what he's going to be like when he's my age. I think he's not going to be mean; he's going to be very nice."

LISA C. said she would rather not get pregnant.

There are so many children out there with terrible lives. I love the idea of taking a child out of an unwanting environment and putting it in a wanting one. It would make such a difference in someone's life.

And so adopting seems easier. You know, I always thought I wanted a child—this came out in therapy—I wanted a child because I wanted someone like me who was sensitive and good and gave her life for her parents, and doesn't care if they don't have a job. And I always thought about having a little girl, you know, that I could mother so perfectly. And then I think there's part of me that would be very resentful. I remember my mother always saying, "My mother never let me do the things that I let you do." And I could see myself saying, "My mother was never at my games or looking at my report card." You know, so I think those things have to be straightened out first.

CHRISTINE L. doesn't feel single women should adopt.

I think it's hard to raise children in this day and age, so I don't know that I regret not having to do that day in and day out. I regret not having children in my life as a regular matter. I have nieces and nephews, and that's very important to me. I sort of feel at this point that it's, like, too late for me to have children.

Adoption? I don't know. I would not do that as a single woman. I would only do it if I was with someone. I think people adopt children for a lot of the wrong reasons. They adopt children like they buy a house in the country—because that's what they need next. There's a real consumerism to it.

ANITA S., who's turning 40, talked to her lover about the fact that she was going to adopt. He has a family in another city.

I'm sort of nervous about that. I wrote to him this summer and said, "Look, I'm really thinking about adopting, and how do you want to be involved? Here's the whole range: You can kind of disappear, or you can become more involved." And I think it really troubled him because he and his wife had tried to have children; they tried to adopt once and had a miserable time with the social worker. Then he would never go into it again, but it seemed to me symptomatic of a lot of what was going on in the marriage, which is his refusing to get more involved, as though he has a ball and chain he won't get rid of. So, basically he said that he just couldn't—he felt that he had screwed up in the past and felt guilty toward his wife, and until he cleared that up, he couldn't get extremely involved in it. And I think that's right. Because it might be really confusing for the kid. In a funny way, I don't feel any pain about that. I just feel I'm going to go ahead and make my life, would be foolish to hold back because of him. I've made my peace with it, actually, so it's just what I'm going to go ahead and do. If he wants to be interested, then he'll have to do something about it. He's a responsible person, so he won't do anything weird. He'll try to be scrupulous, in his own way. So I'll see what happens.

SUSANNAH W., now in her late 40s, whose mother arranged for her to become princess for a day.

For the first time in my life, I started to think, *Well, I could adopt as a single mother if I made more money, so I've got to make more money. And then I have to decide do I really want it in my life.*

Now that I've gotten these jobs that pay enough, I'm facing that. I'm saying to myself now, *I don't think I can do it*, just to get used to the sound of the *No*, just seeing how that feels.

And I feel I could live with it; I could live with being single the rest of my life. Maybe it'll be different in three weeks—but at the moment I have an extremely interesting life.

It's a very different thing to make your decision than to have it made for you. That's something, that freedom of deciding myself, and it takes a long time. For three years I was dependent on this other person to make the decision, and now I'm facing it a different way.

If I went ahead it would be an adoption. Because given my bio-logical background, it was never really important to me to be preg-nant. I don't want to perpetuate my heredity. I thought pregnancy would be the most convenient way to have a child, and adoption would not be a second-best decision for me. I always felt that it would be ideal.

SINGLE MOTHERING

By and by, some categorical beliefs yield to new impressions.

REAH S., 35, attorney from Providence, divorced, keeps every-thing hypothetical.

I began to feel that it would be easier to have an intimate rela-tionship with a child than with a man—which is the opposite of the way I'd felt all the rest of my life.

PHILLIPA C., 50, the veteran of three marriages.

People say to me, "How can you possibly manage to make money and raise these children at the same time?" And the secret is: *I don't have a husband.* What I can't see anymore is having to bring in X amount of income and being a wife *and* being a mother. That just seems impossible. The whole single-mother thing is a crock. It's much easier to raise children by yourself than to handle children and be a wife at the same time. And to support the household.

So when people say to me, "How do you do it?" I say, "It's simple, I don't have to be a wife." In other words, it's two out of three. You can be a wife or you can be a mother or you can be a provider. You can't be all three.

One reason I didn't have children till I was thirty-nine is that I had so many husbands. There were so many men in my life, and many of them were like children. They required nurturing and feeding and socializing, empathy, authority, and so on. All the child-raising things. Children aren't like a husband, but they're all con-suming. I think that if I didn't have children, I'd probably live with a guy. But until my children are older, I just can't imagine living with a guy.

I sometimes still have a fantasy of someone to share certain things with. Particularly things that have to do with child raising. But I know that the benefits I would have from sharing those things would be far outweighed by the daunting problems of having to deal with another ego.

MARY ANN B., divorced, whose two sons are now in college.

It's different for single fathers than it is for single mothers, that is for sure. Because they have a whole society bent in the direction of help. And females live in a society with the direction of blame.

Well, you know, sociologists say that single moms are routinely less hierarchical with their kids, decisions are more consensual. And that the government of those households, either by design or by default, becomes much more democratic.

I think that was particularly useful in the adolescent years, a stage that I really loved. And I wonder if anyone has done a study about rebelling with single parents. Because I was really braced for it, and it never happened. And I don't know if it's because there was so little government by then that my kids had nothing to rebel against or because they really were part of things. I mean, I suppose the criticism would be that adult women use their teenage kids as company, so the roles have really changed. That was my social life in the suburbs: the adolescent community. At home, it was dominant adolescent culture. And because you do talk about a lot of things, they really are your social life in a lot of ways. So there's a whole lot less rebellion.

With a husband, there's the business of his authority, which as the wife and mother you've always got to relate everything to. It's impossible—just like the unannounced rules and assumptions about mealtimes, all the unannounced assumptions about having to be the co-pilot. You're sort of representing his point of view whether you know it or not if you're married. And removing that made it much easier. And Murray said the same things. He has a really close relationship with these kids, too. And our kids found they much preferred to commute between those two fiefdoms. He didn't remarry either. We just found it much easier. The kids never can figure out now why we were ever married. We're so different.

And they, who kept the eternal flame of "Someday we'll get back together," now couldn't even understand how we could take a vacation together.

JEAN I.'s daughter enters kindergarten this fall.

Work is hard for everyone, not just for single parents, but it's even worse these days because of the anxiety, the end of any kind of notion of job security, the fact that there are always threats of layoffs and cutbacks. Everyone brings that home to their family—it's not unique to single parents. If you're unhappy at work, you go home and things are really not better off if there's someone there. I think there is one less source of conflict when I get home. There's nobody saying, "My day was harder than your day—my job is harder than your job."

To be honest, I'm so depressed about my work situation, I can't think straight. I used to have no doubt at all that the children of single mothers are better off. Now I'm more tempered. I haven't changed my mind about it, but I guess I'm feeling a little stunned by my general situation right now, my work and money problems. But it's certainly true that these children often seem very, very well adapted to their situations. They live with less conflict in the home. They don't see conflict between parents, so they live in a more serene world. I think that for that reason they're often better adjusted generally.

Of course, a lot of this is if you have the luxury of good child care and it's class based. If you are working at minimum wage and have to struggle through your day and then at five have to rush back to get the kid, I'm sure that works as a source of tension. If you don't have enough adequate day care, and you don't have enough money to pay the bills, that's also a source of tension for married couples at a certain level. My comments presuppose enough disposable income to not be hysterical all the time.

But for a woman in that situation—perhaps terribly insecure financially but still able to scrape up the child-care money—there is one whole element of stress that is removed: that feeling that she is only one member in a marriage, but she does too much, carries too much of an unfair burden. Among the couples I know—a certain kind of professional two-income couple—there's such a high level of tension between mothers and fathers about responsibilities. . . . Those children certainly are exposed to a lot more family strife than those of single mothers.

But there are other little heartbreaks for children of single mothers.

JOCELYN H., 42, is sending her son to college soon.

When Thomas was born, I remember when I left the hospital, and I thought my life was over. He was colicky. He cried. I cried. My life was a total mess. It was while I was pregnant that my relationship with my husband got strained. We were married—happily—for a long time before that, and I thought it was just the pregnancy. But after I came home, the baby was just so hysterical most of the time. . . . It was really tough for me. I guess at one point I approached my husband to talk over the situation. He looked at me—and I remember the words—and he said, "Grow up. You're a mother."

And I said, "What the hell do you mean?" I was floored. I called my mother and said, "I can't handle it." My mother said, "Fine." She called everyone in our family—my sisters, my nieces. They all got together and decided that each day someone was going to come and spend the day with me. He remained colicky, and I felt my whole life was . . . it didn't belong to me any more, it belonged to this little person. I no longer had control—he had control, and I had to do what he wanted and not what I wanted.

And my husband just couldn't stand having the baby around. "You do more for the baby than you do for me," he'd say. "You used to have time to make dinner." He never understood why I was always doing something for the baby. He complained, and I told him I thought that was my job. So he was feeling more and more left out. Even if I did something for him, it wasn't good enough because it wasn't what I did before.

I think what happened was the bonding process came after my husband and I separated. Because what I was trying to do before was make both of them happy, and I was totally miserable. I have to be honest, I never really thought of myself at all. And this may sound odd, but I went to quite a few workshops, and I learned a lot about self-esteem and so on. I think I learned a lot. I used to be angry because I didn't feel I was giving my husband what he needed. At first I thought, *Why isn't this working? I can't make him or this baby happy, and why won't this come together?* And I thought, *This has got to stop, and I can't feel miserable, but I do feel miserable, I can't get things to function.* If I had been able to function better, I think I could have bonded with my son a lot earlier than I did. Though even if I had functioned better I don't think I could have made my marriage work.

This is going to sound really strange, but one of the reasons I got out of the marriage is that my mother and father had trouble in their marriage. As a kid, for a long time I didn't see it; I thought they were, like, the happiest couple in the world. But one day my mother said to me, "You know, I always stayed with your father because of you children." And I never understood. I guess my mother felt she had to take care of us, and there was just no way out for her. And so I thought about it, and I thought, *I'm not going to do that. I'm not going to do that to my child. I'm not going to stay in my marriage because he needs a father.* . . . My sister said, "Are you sure you can handle this?" And even though I didn't know I thought, *No, I'm not going to stick in a marriage just because someone will help me with my son.*

When I was in the transition of separating from my husband and, of course, I had to work but I couldn't afford a baby-sitter, I went to my mother and said, "I don't know what to do." So my mother said, "OK, we'll work it out." At that point my son was about a year and a half. And we made an arrangement that I would drop him off at her house on Monday morning and pick him up Friday afternoon.

When I brought my son back to my home, when he started school, he was one of the latchkey children, as they say, who had to hang out at school until I picked him up. Of course, you had to be there by six o'clock. But he seemed never the worse for wear and tear.

Now when his father calls, Thomas says, "I don't want to talk to him," and I say, "Just be polite." And he says, "No. I have nothing to say to him." And my ex-husband asks me and I say, "I'm not going to make him." I thought Thomas should make up his own mind. I never said, "Your father did this or that." I just said, "We didn't get along, and we had to go our separate ways." I wanted him to make his own assumptions about what his father was like.

Once, when he was in kindergarten, my son said to me, "We had to draw a picture of a family, and I drew a picture of you, me, and grandma, and that's a family, right?" And I said, "That's right, that's a family!" So he had his own perception of what a family was, you know?

CALLIE S., late 50s, who has raised a little girl on her own.

I would have liked to have had that someone to share it with. Having a kid is a very heavy trip, if you'll pardon the heavy sixties-ism. There's heavy stuff and a heavy responsibility. God, it would have been great to have had somebody to share that with. Someone to talk to about things until they'd start making sense and you'd stop obsessing over them.

ROSA M., who is raising a little girl on her own.

As far as Lilly is concerned, Daddy comes to stay over now and then, but between visits she almost forgets him. She's acted very adjusted to it, but I feel guilty that someday it's not going to be OK. But, you know, when any man stays over, I'm careful not to upset Lilly. She and I sleep together, and we spend all of our time together, and she gets upset if that routine is upset. So I have a guest room, and when a man stays over, he sleeps in the guest room, and I end up sleeping with her as usual. It works fine. Of course, at first there was hardly anyone to try it out with because, like I said, there was a year where I had sex once and the next year the same thing and the next year maybe two times.

EVELYN'S BABIES

Worth going through a miserable Wonder Woman phase.

EVELYN B. is a professor of mathematics and now the mother of two children

Am I lonely? But I have my kids. Let me tell you something. . . . When you hold a baby, and your baby looks you straight in the eye, and it trusts you and loves you, it's better than anything. It's the most wonderful thing. And, every phase of their life . . . I mean, I have a daughter who is five feet nine—*everything* I say is horrible, "I hate you, Mom!" The door slams. I love her to pieces. I think women who go through life without children are making a terrible mistake.

When I decided I wanted to have kids, I had tenure. I was thirty-five. And I said, "I want a baby." He went through the ceiling. . . . "I'm not going to . . . !!!" But it was weird, he really loved me. . . . "Needed" is a better term. He *needed* me. I was like his parent. He used to lean out the window and shout, "If you don't love me, I'll jump out the window," and I'd be scared to death. So when we finally decided, OK, we'll have a baby, we knew he was not equipped to handle me and a child himself. But I *wanted* a baby. And we got pregnant right away. And then I had fourteen miscarriages. Two dead babies delivered. I spent three and a half months, three times, flat on my back in bed, trying to save a baby. I had a miscarriage on Mother's Day. That was a good one. . . . My whole thirties decade was spent in hospitals, in doctor's offices, in bed.

And he went nuts. Partly he was worried about me, but also it was because I couldn't take care of him. I was busy . . . he must have gone crazy because he was torn between wanting me to have what I wanted and then I'm sure wishing every one of these babies would drop dead, instantly, which they did. He lost the last job that he had, and he just steadily started going downhill. And I worked. Through the whole thing. I was teaching, writing books, I'd be correcting papers in bed while I was, two days after the miscarriage, back teaching. It was a Wonder Woman phase, but a miserable one. And then we adopted my daughter.

Do I regret not having biological children? No. Are you *kidding*? You should see my kids!!! Oh, no, no. They're my kids. I've had them since they were two days old. And it was the most wonderful . . . you can see the picture. I have, objectively speaking, anyone can tell you, the two most beautiful, brightest, exquisite, beautiful, talented children in the world.

After my daughter arrived, Kevin and I were OK for about three or four years, and then I wanted another kid. And he said no, and I said yes. And he stalled and he stalled, and finally we got Tim, and Kevin freaked. I think because it was a boy, I don't know.

What I'm worried about now in my life is they'll be gone, and *that's* when I'm going to be lonely. My daughter will be gone in three years. My son will be gone in eight years. You think you can't wait for it. . . . *Oh, God, I'll have a study, I'll have* . . . But the truth is that it will be hard this summer with both of them at sleep-away camp. I'll be out at the house in the country alone. And I think, *What'll I do with my day?*

Everything will change. Right now I'm more of a mother than a single person, if you know what I mean. I think that a single woman who has a child has more in common with a woman who's married than with unmarried women. I don't feel I have very much in common with those women at all. I think I share *more* with married women whose husbands don't help. . . . We have other parts of our identity that occupy us. Maybe you'll hear different from other women. I don't mean I scorn them or I'm not friendly with them, but . . . my connections are to women with kids.

I have friends who've never been married, who are very successful in various fields. But, you know, when they want to go out for dinner, they want to go out; they don't want to come here where my son is playing basketball in the living room. People who don't have kids, they don't understand a household like this. And I'm not about to change it for them. So, in a very friendly way, I have women friends I only see outside the house. And men actually are much better about coming over and playing with the kids. I have male friends who come over, and they're great!

No, they're friends. Well, there are no men. I mean, they're gay or they're married. I mean, I could get laid every day of the month if I wanted to go out with married men, but I won't do it. And once you eliminate cowboys. . . .

I think things really changed from one generation to the other. My father was extremely worried that I would "get too smart" and no one would marry me. And he was a strong supporter of me academically . . . he was just concerned. And the very last thing he ever said to me, literally ten minutes before he died, was, "I wish you had a husband to take care of you." It's inconceivable, really, that my ex-husband would say that to my daughter. And my daughter wouldn't know what he was talking about, you know? She just would not.

The kids are now old enough to go up to his house by bus. They adore him. And my daughter says, "I know Dad's crazy, Mom, but we love him." And she absolutely gets it. She's fourteen now, and Tim is ten. And Tim especially does, I think, bear scars from all this, but he loves his Dad, and I think that's great.

Now he's a model father. Except, of course, he pays nothing for his children. But I told him he couldn't see them if he didn't stop drinking. So he stopped drinking. Has not had a drop to drink in ten years. The divorce did wonders for him. Got a job. Has had it for six years. Sees the kids every weekend. And the older they get, the better he is with them. So, compared to some of my friends, whose husbands have seventeen-year-old gay lovers, Kevin is a model father. He's become the hero of the divorced women's set. I mean . . . you've got to think of life as humorous! Because he is absolutely man of the year.

THE DADDY QUESTION

No plans for a father.

FELICIA C., 44, is the mother of one eleven-year-old girl. Her second divorce, finalized two years ago, ended in a court dispute.

As it was, Anna was too unhappy that her father wasn't at home anymore. Right after the divorce, and for a long time after, I could see that it wasn't worth it to try to introduce men into a situation that was already difficult for the two of us, especially for Anna. Because it shut the door on her dream of her father coming back, on her parents getting back together again. It was too hard for her. It just wasn't worth it for me, so I still have no social life.

Also, there's another thing. We're coming into a time where it's possible she would feel I was competing with her if I start going out on dates just when she's becoming interested in acquiring a boyfriend. And that doesn't seem to me to be worth it. It seems like it could cause more trouble and sorrow than I would want to cope with.

And I don't mind waiting. Especially since there doesn't seem to be any right person anywhere near me.

Another thing about not seeing any men or not having any men around is it seemed to temporarily or minimally assuage the anger of her father, and that made it easier for her. Especially when he came to pick her up. I'm really interested in her mental health, and it's necessary for my own health, so I really don't want to do anything that might jeopardize that.

How would I feel if Anna turned out to be single? Sad.

SOPHIA R., mother of one biological child, one adopted.

Of course it's better if there's a father. It's better if there's a cat, a grandmother. But that's not how life happens.

We all grew up thinking that the family we're going to have is a family of choice, that having children is something you can choose, how many, et cetera, but then that's not at all how it happens. It happens some other way you never imagined. We always think that you're going to have the marriage that you wish and the child that you wish, but life is full of surprises.

JEAN I. again, the one whose daughter was born in Romania.

By the time she was two, Molly started to ask me for a daddy. Did she ever resolve it? I don't know. She appointed my father. She did that the year she was three. We were in France at the time, on vacation, and she had to call him long distance. She said, "I've decided that Grandpa is going to be my daddy." And she called him up and told him. Now, a year later, she still calls him Daddy, which, when they're in public, embarrasses him a little. He feels like an Anthony Quinn character. And she tells her teacher that her daddy lives in Minnesota, as my father does. She'll confuse anyone who'll play along.

No, I haven't really tried to alter it. I always say, "Oh, right, Grandpa-Daddy." She says "Daddy," and I say "Grandpa-Daddy."

CHILDLESS/CHILDFREE/SO FAR UNDECIDED

It's not something any woman comes to lightly. But the pattern seems to be that many of those who feel they made their own decision are relieved—or at least at peace with their choice. Those who feel the decision was made for them carry their regret through life like a wound.

MONICA V. recalls what it was like, after her divorce, when it seemed as if every other woman in the world was having babies.

Oh, it was horrible, it was just horrible. You know, I was the god-mother of all these little children, and . . . nobody knew how to be or act. I *wanted* to be around children, and I was very jealous of my friends, and envious of their having children. But I was happy for them. . . . I mean, I'm not competitive with my friends like that, and, well, it was very mixed and very hard. Very hard. It was horrible, just a nightmare. And I remember thinking, *Oh . . .*

ELLEN P., the curator, has experienced the bald, astonishingly crude discrimination that many people exhibit vis-à-vis single women.

I'm a member of a country co-op where there are twenty units, almost all of which are familied. Their misconstrual of my relationship to children has been one of the greatest pains in my life, really. Because I'm childless, they assume I don't like children, and because, being childless, I wanted certain things to be observed, like a low level of noise or appreciation of different needs in this place. And all this became very embattled—to the point where I have been really in a lot of anguish up there. This idea of not liking children was conveyed to the children by their parents, so that I became the sort of witch person. Where, in fact, my entire life I've had a sort of extraordinary regard for children and a kind of gift for communicating with them. So it's a great irony for me to have that sabotaged in that particular place. And the fact that I don't have children is not entirely a choice. So there's a lot of pain around that.

I'm not even sure that the social ramifications of being a single woman don't have the most intense manifestations in the area of not having children. And men, as if there was some kind of scent, imagine that you have stopped being sexual at a certain point in your life. The relationship between fertility and sexuality is one that I find particularly destructive. And sad—for me, anyway. There was a moment when I thought the only way to get rid of some of the anguish would be to look at my choices, the ones I made and those that were made for me. In order to curate, I had to give certain things up. When I had a choice to get married and have a child, I made a different choice, even though it wasn't completely conscious at the moment.

JANIE A., who is putting herself through law school.

The DNA strand, that's what I find really repellent, and God only knows what that says about my psychological state. I think it would be painful to be reminded of myself. Somebody said to me about children, "But they're nothing like you." And you could say that is narcissistic, and maybe I've read too many science articles or something, but I think whatever comes out of you *is* you, and I imagine that would be very unpleasant. And then I also think something very awful is going to happen. You know, when the child is in fourth grade, you get that call from some policeman up in Vermont where your kid went on some skiing trip and the policeman says the bus went over the cliff.

So that's the second thing I think of. The first is, I don't want someone like me walking around, and the second is my motto, "What you don't have, you can't lose." I think of that phone call. . . .

Also I think of the time factor. And I think, *Now, wait a minute. . . . I feel completely overextended as it is. Now, how does someone do this with three children? How is this possible? Just check off the boxes of what you need to do! But get a child's lunch ready and clean them and dress them and organize a birthday party?*

Plus, this sounds horrible, but you can't get rid of them, the way you can get rid of a boyfriend or a husband. *They* can be gone in the morning. You know, "Five hours to get your stuff out"? But that kid—that kid is there; that connection just seems terrifying. It sounds so selfish.

But then my therapist says, "I don't think you can give yourself something that nice." I just can't see it that way. I can see it that way in other people but not for myself. That's right. He says it all the time. "Deprivation," he calls it. Interesting that my therapist thinks I'm depriving myself, and my sister thinks I shouldn't have children because I'm too selfish. I mean, she hasn't said it, but she thinks it, that I'm not selfless enough to have children.

But also if you really think about it, just how weird it is, to create another human being . . . you know, with someone else. . . . It's really too weird to think about it. *You mean, another person would grow in my body and form?* I mean, it's just the weirdest thing I've ever heard in my life. It's just too weird to do, in a way. I find the idea of pregnancy really interesting, but it's the emotional stuff. . . . I mean, you carry something in your body that someday is going to pay rent? It's too weird. If people thought about that, they wouldn't do it. If they thought about adolescence, they wouldn't do it, either. I don't know what they're thinking about.

Who knows, maybe I'm going to have those horrible horrible regrets everyone talks about. I was listening to a friend talking about it, and she was saying that she just can't get over the fact that she's not going to have someone there for her when she's older, and I was thinking to myself, *Who is going to stick around, necessarily, when you're in those adult diapers or Pampers . . . ? That's not part of the deal.* I think she just assumed that when she is older and can't get around, this kid is just going to be there for her. Yeah, it's nice when it works out that way, but I can't imagine having a kid and counting on that.

PAULINE A., lives on the opposite coast from her eight nieces and nephews.

When I think of being single forever, the one thing that I do feel very sad about is the idea of not having kids. It's not that I need to fulfill some sort of maternal potential that I have. It's that I always thought that I would have some sort of family, that it wouldn't be just me out there all by myself.

No, I haven't yet really thought about having a kid on my own, but having a family is something that's very important to me. I haven't gotten to the point where I'm completely happy with the idea of having to be by myself for my entire life.

EILEEN Y. looks back to the period when she took care of her dying father, then shifted her focus to her work.

Yes, there did come a time at which I became fairly convinced that I would not get married. I suppose so. And yet, I had a hysterectomy when I was about forty-seven, and I thought I had really faced the fact that I wasn't going to have children before that, but it hit me very hard all over again. And I realized that something in me had gone on imagining that somehow I would have kids.

There really was nobody I knew that I wanted a child by. I think I'm really fundamentally a very very faithful person. And there have been a few really important relationships for me. And I had *no* money. You know, I'm seventy-three. If I were of a different generation I probably would have had a child anyway, or I would have wanted to adopt a child. I wish I had done it, but I didn't. And aside from one friend, the poet Muriel Rukeyser, I didn't know any single mothers. I thought that she was terrific. I liked her son, very much. But it seemed an exception. No, I had all these old-fashioned ideas, that children should have two parents.

CAMILLE O., whose parents were artists.

Once when he was already ill, my father asked me to go fetch something for him from his work hut in the garden. And I hesitated. My whole family was in the room: my father, my mother, my step-father, my sisters. They started laughing, and saying things like, "How can you not go out there? What are you frightened of?" And I said I'm frightened that someone's going to kill me. I'm frightened of something out there. And my brother said something like, "It's pathetic." In a joking way. And nobody said, "Oh, I'll come with you. . . ."

On the outside I was the tough one. And if I have a real con-frontation, I'm extremely aggressive. You know, I've confronted purse snatchers in New York. . . . When it's real, I can yell, *Stop it!* You know, *Stop it! Drop it! Give it back!* All that kind of stuff. When it's real. But when it comes to darkness and night and the ocean, things that I can only imagine, I'm frightened. It has to do with something abstract. With being alone. With not having found the person that you could share that stuff with. That could make you feel stronger. I think when you have children you kind of become that block that you wished you could be for yourself. You show them that you're strong when they're afraid of the dark.

KATIE K., who will be 41 next week, has no children and plans on having none: She believes kids should have a father. She's very close, though, to her sister, who has three.

I talk to her daily. I see her children twice, maybe three times, a week, and if I don't, I speak with them on the phone. Plus my friends. I have very close friends. Yes, as a matter of fact, a lot of them are single. We kind of hang around together. It's not that I don't have married friends, but it's different, especially if they had children. When they have their first baby that is all they talk about for a really long time, and I love to hear about that, but I wish they would include me in their conversation in some other way, as well. That happened quite a bit with my friends, especially when my college friends got married. You'd get together at their house, and their children would be running around, and you'd say, "But I came over to visit *you*!" It's not that I don't enjoy talking about children, and I can talk about my nieces and nephews, but, you know, they're not my children. And when I talk about them, I don't think I get the same reaction as if they were my children. When my little nephew, Jimmy, was starting to walk, I remember calling a friend and talking to her about it and her saying, "Oh, well that's really nice," but in a kind of tone. . . . When one of their children is walking it's like, "Oh! Congratulations! That's wonderful!"

EX-HUSBANDS AND QUASI FATHERS

Sure, many ex-husbands are cowards and skinflints, but many men who did badly in the old role of conventional fatherhood do better in the new ones.

MARY ANN B., whose two boys are now in college.

Actually, I have more contact with my ex-husband now, and at this stage it's pleasant. The word "husband" really doesn't apply to that relationship, even with the "ex" in front of it. I actually took a vacation in Mexico with Murray last February. Without my sons. They didn't come, though they were certainly the reason why we still have this relationship—or why we went through the purgatory phase of it and were determined to come out the other end of it, both of us.

We just have become really good friends. He's the only other person on this planet who has as much invested in the two boys as I do.

No, Murray and I don't sleep together. That's the funny thing; everyone wonders, "How do you deal with the sex issue?" When Murray and I were sexual, we had totally different bodies and longed to jump in bed with each other. That was twenty-five years ago. We don't even look at each other now! It's very affectionate. I mean, we have a lot of forgiveness with each other, and it's totally strange. Mercy is the main emotion.

CALLIE S. recalls the father of her little girl.

I liked him well enough to have a child with. I didn't like him for purposes of getting married. Had he been Quasimodo I probably wouldn't have been thrilled to have gotten pregnant by him. And it could have happened. . . . I mean, there is at least one Quasimodo in all of our lives, no?

I'm not friendly with my ex-husband. I'm not unfriendly. I talk to him when occasion warrants it, but I don't call him to chat, and he doesn't call me to chat. I used to have a friend I dated before and after I was married, and he's now married and we talk. Who else? Oh, my kid's father. I have a relationship with him, and his wife and his two children. His kids come and visit and stay with me. When I'm in the Phoenix area I may or may not stay at their house. It's sort of one big happy family. It actually is.

FELICIA C., who had two nasty divorces.

My two ex-husbands are both very present in my life because I have a child by each of them. And it's a completely different experience dealing with each of them, and I have to adjust all the time. One has been outsmarting me since I was seventeen and still is very good at it. And the other one has to be placated and soothed, which takes an extremely long time, and much effort, before we can have a semblance of a rational conversation about things that he still has an important say in, such as our child—just about the only thing he still has any importance in, which happens to be an important part of my responsibility at the moment.

Do I wish he weren't involved? He's not the father I would have picked if I'd had any idea. And I may not be the equivalent right mother, either. But I am glad that she has a father because it's one less thing to worry about. It's another tent pole, however unstable.

BILLIANA M. feels that connection and love for their children enables both members of a former couple to remain parents together.

We were both at our daughter's wedding. The anticipation of it was really frightening for me. But he just couldn't stay in touch with me, so I didn't know how we were going to connect. I realized I'd become insecure that I'd gained so much weight, and was not feeling at my top game. But also to see him with someone else, and to see him with her the way we used to be. . . . But once we said our hellos, there was an underlying sense of family and connection and love and warmth, so it didn't feel weird, it felt pretty right.

EXTENDED, INTENTIONAL, AND VOLUNTARY FAMILIES

So many people are redefining family for themselves that the old norms seem less and less mandatory, or even desirable.

JEAN I. invents her family as she goes along, usually around her daughter's needs.

Part of my calculations has to do with the fact that Molly thinks there should be a dad and Molly thinks I should be married. She's started to ask my casual friends to marry me. But she also—bless her heart—when she ran into a couple of her friends she hadn't seen since spring, she said, "Why do you always have different baby-sitters?" So she also has this sense that the baby-sitter should be a part of the family, that they shouldn't come and go. Celia is family to her. Also, you invest a lot of your emotional resources in your friends that would be invested in your husband. You've got to have people you know well enough to call when you have great news or terrible news; you've got to have someone to talk about your work situation with and to talk about your kid with, you know, to fulfill all those roles. Sure, I miss having a lover, at least as a built-in audience for all my concerns. But having that kind of a role in someone else's life in that way, I don't miss that.

CATHY D., single mother of a little boy, finds herself worrying on his behalf.

Mostly I do feel a sufficient sense of family. Some of my friends are absolutely like family. And I evaluate people very differently now. Some people I hadn't thought of as close friends have responded so wonderfully to Kenny that I responded differently to them. But in principle, all of my close friends have been wonderful and are very familial, and they visit Kenny as family.

I'm so conflicted on the issue of relationships that it's hard for me to answer. I don't think I'm particularly sane about the subject. So I think the fact that I'm fine about not having a father for Kenny is probably a sign that the family we have is sufficient unto itself. But I'm worried that I am asking my son to do too much in my life, and I need to do too much in his.

But right now he's at an age when it's not particularly relevant. When he starts to feel the loss and asks me, I'm sure that I'm going to feel terrible. But I'm hoping, in my dreams, that he won't ask me at all, that he won't notice.

JANIE A., whose married lover has told her he wants her to have a child.

I'm the one who's ambivalent. But when I talk about going ahead, I've been very pleased that not once have I seen a glimmer of "I'm out of here." It's always been, "Sure, we can talk about this, if this is something you really want." I guess I like to know that, even if I don't go through with it.

CAMILLE O. says her friends are her family.

Not being with a man, all I miss at the moment is the sex. If I didn't have deep, close friendships, then I would be deeply lonely. But if there's a common denominator among single women it's that you have to be able to make relationships with other people other than your own lover.

I look at friends and my sisters who have their husbands, and I say, "I don't need that." I need to have someone be the father of my children, definitely, but for myself, I get so much of what I need from my close friends. In moments of vulnerability when I really feel needy and like I need close companionship, I have one or two women friends I can actually go and sleep in their bed with. It's not sex, but just that I want to be with somebody. It can't just be any-body, it has to be somebody I'm close with. So what I think we have in common is that we have the ability, or the strength or whatever it is. . . .

PETS

No one missed a beat when I asked about
cats and dogs as family.

NINA L. laughed when I asked her if she had pets, as if the question were code for something else.

No. And I feel sometimes that I'm going to get to be some cold, distant person because I haven't been touched enough. And every once in a while I try to be more affectionate with my friends. I think that it's kind of awkward sometimes; I don't know if it's just the way I am. But I'm thinking about getting a dog.

MEGAN L. also laughed when I asked if she had a cat.

My roommates do, so I live with cats, but none of them belong to me. And I don't have cat earrings.

I thought maybe, maybe when I get my first maternal urge I might get a dog, and then if I get the urge five or six or seven more times, I might start to think about babies.

MARTHA H., the one who has to bring her mother to her sister's each Christmas.

Does my cat see me cry? Sure. If I'm lying on the bed or on the couch crying, she comes over. She doesn't seem to have any emotional response to it. She's quite a callous little kitty. When the dog died, I came out and he was lying dead in the front hall and she was jumping across his body, completely insensitively, because she wanted her breakfast. If anything, she was glad he died because she didn't have to guard her food anymore.

Yeah, I talk directly to my cat. Sure. When I come in I say hello to her. And I greet her in the morning because she always comes into the bathroom with me. And sometimes when I'm going to feed her, I show her the can of food before I open it, the way you would show someone a wine bottle. But I don't talk baby talk to her the way some people do. I don't like anthropomorphizing her.

JENNIFER B., the one whose parents stayed together for the children.

I just lost my dog. It was extremely emotional. She still lived with my parents, and she had a seizure when they were away. I took her to the vet, and it was hopeless. She should have been put to sleep, but I didn't want to make the decision without my parents being there. When I left home, I really missed her. It was so nice to see her when I went there, and it's very lonely going home now. My birthday was yesterday, and the dog was missing.

LUCY L. is summing up what she had learned about herself in the last decade.

I can't ever live without a cat again.

MIRANDA C., 35.

The adoption was incredibly fast. And plus, it's funny, I mean it's weird, but contrasting it to five years earlier, I wanted to get a cat from the ASPCA, and they gave me an incredibly hard time about the fact that I was living alone. They give you an interview that's much worse than an adoption agency for human babies. Like, "Who's in your house? Why?" Really, it was so odd. I walked out of there, and I bought myself an expensive cat. It's going to have a nervous breakdown when I bring the baby home.

MARY ANN B. asked me if a geranium counted as a pet.

Larry said he was attracted to me because I didn't have any pets. He thinks that women substitute pets for men, and that's why they're always petting them and cooing on them.

I think it is true, actually. I think pets are good company for women. And they're cuddly, and I think human beings do need to cuddle. I am not sure what to do about the cuddle thing. Because nobody cuddles with their vibrators. I mean, orgasms are not a prob-lem, cuddling is a problem. And when I think of what I miss . . . ? I miss kissing someone I love. And you can kiss pets. I mean, you can't kiss them sexually. But you can kiss them. Someone could come up with a great list: Pets who are good kissers. I mean, it's not parakeets or goldfish, we know that. Maybe someone would come out with a breed that are really good kissers.

BLANCHE W., the endocrinologist.

I got two cats. I got rid of them. They required too much intimacy.

HOME AT LAST

*Carrying Her Own Trousseau over
the Threshold, Alone but Together*

Not long ago, I was invited to lunch at the home of an attorney,
along with someone who owns a business and a magazine editor.
Socially and economically, we were a motley group, with a wide
range of interests and incomes, but all four of us were single mothers, either divorced or never married. The children had been invited, as well—three were adopted, one was conceived by artificial
insemination. We ate in a lovely room, though I must say I found
myself wondering how often the chairs would have to be reuphol-
stered, since our hostess's son had just turned two. The furniture,
the walls, the lighting were playful but elegant. The food was delicate and delicious, served on rather remarkable, hand-painted dishes. There was a fine cloth on the table. Adjoining was a sunken
living room, which reminded me of something slightly beyond the
grasp of my memory.

When they had finished eating, the four children left the table to
play, and the women could hear one another speak. Our conversation
then wandered, as had been intended, to the subject of single motherhood. It was a congenial group and, aided, no doubt, by the delicious
lunch, the talk was merry and frank. As it happens, all three of my
companions had at one point tried to conceive via sperm banks, and
they soon fell into good-humored comparisons and reminiscences.

"At my sperm bank, the guys wrote letters for potential takers,"
said one of the women, "and mine wrote, 'Whatever you do, please,
please don't give this child a weird name!' And I thought, 'This guy
must be all right.'"

"Mine wrote something about hoping I was someone who loved life and would teach the child that above all," said the attorney. "And that this is how he would always think of us. He sounded so sweet and generous, I felt it was the best relationship I'd had in years."

"It turned out that they had pictures on file," said the entrepreneur. "And someone working at the sperm bank was willing to give me pointers."

"Oh," said the magazine editor, "I just asked them to give me whoever was the tallest Jew."

"I was much more prudent than that," said the other. "So I'd say, 'Well, how about number two-thirty-six?' And she'd say, 'Well . . . number three-thirty-eight is much cuter.'"

The talk then veered to letters written to birth mothers when one is in the process of adopting a child to ongoing relationships with birth families to wills to the perennial centerpiece of all single mothers' conversations—child care arrangements—to the question of dads and dad models, and then on to vacations, household arrangements, sheets.

"Sheets? That's funny," I said. "It's amazing, when you talk to single women about their lives, how often the subject of sheets comes up."

"Oh," said the businesswoman, " I went to a dinner last night where the women talked *endlessly* about sheets. They just wouldn't stop."

"What aspects of sheets were they talking about?" I asked. "Thread counts?"

I was joking. But within thirty seconds, all three of my companions were in a mock-serious discussion of thread count.

"The standard is by dollar amount," said the magazine editor (whom I would never have suspected of entertaining a single thought about sheets, let alone refer to a thread-count standard.) "At what point does it become ridiculous?"

"I think the standard is whether you can use a washing machine or not," said the businesswoman, who clearly had more rarefied criteria. "Above a certain count, you have to wash them by hand."

"And iron them," said the attorney. "Forget it."

The conversation eventually meandered back to the dinner the businesswoman had gone to and the diners who talked on and on about sheets. "I couldn't believe it. It was *so* boring!" she said. "I'm never going to see those women again."

The children were still playing, as uninterested in sheets as they had been by talk of sperm banks, donors, birth mothers, good child care, and other household matters. It was so all so comfortable and easy, I'm not sure I would have even have noted the conversation if it hadn't been for the jokes about sperm banks, which still seem slightly exotic to me. But it was precisely the fact that the hostess and her guests seemed so at home, so relaxed, so easy, that was—I had to remind myself—extraordinary by any but the most recent standards in America, where matters pertaining to housing have been, historically, rather rigid from the start. In colonial times, all individuals, were required to live within a family. In Puritan New England, spouses who resided apart from one another were fined. Bachelors and single women paid special taxes and were forced to enter existing households as boarders or servants.

Not counting very high-priced madams or the kind of retro maidens who wind up as eccentric hostesses, it's only recently that single women ever mention themselves in the same breath as good sheets. Of late, however, the topic seems to recur with increasing frequency. Some may see this trend as nothing more cheerful than an indication of the good health of the retail bedclothes business, but in my view it also speaks of a certain political evolution. To put it optimistically (and why not?), I suggest that bed linen chitchat is not a sign of a regression in women's discourse, but rather a paradoxical proof of how much progress has been made. Home is where the changes show up and stay on view. Bed linen offers a metaphor for the rest: what's bought, how it's exhibited, the owner's taste, degree of sensuality, a hint of her sexuality, and, certainly, her economic power. Our hostess, the well-to-do attorney, is the customer Bloomingdale's dreams of when they are setting up their Porthault duvet displays. But the fact that so many women own or rent their own homes, furnish them as they please, and feel at home in them, saying what they want, how they want, is significant even where interior decorating is absent, where the taste is offbeat or ingeniously makes up for lack of funds, or where the place is so small that it really is the proverbial room of one's own (or even just a bed of one's own).

If a home represents its proprietor, how much more intensely telling is the bed! If the home is historically the center of the family, the bed is the center of the home, and whether it had to rest on a beaten-earth floor, whether it was raised, fancy, carved, canopied, or adorned with frescoes and elegant fabrics, it was passed down through the generations. In the Middle Ages, cupboards are said to have had primacy, but if the cupboard indicates survival, the bed supports life itself and the unity of the couple—to say nothing of literally keeping the family together, since it has never been very unusual for one or more children to sleep with their progenitors. Nothing but the well-dressed bed evokes so compellingly physical comfort, bourgeois sensualism, cushy sex and offers a more intimate presentation of stature, class, and taste. And even now that it has become relatively rare to be born in one's parents' bed, the conjugal bed remains the eloquent expression of the fact that the masters of the house have sex and perpetuate their line.

What, then, are we to make of the thirty-five-year-old attorney perusing a bed-and-bath catalogue on her way home from the office, the widow well past the courtship stage replenishing her linen closet, and some young thing in Soho purchasing her first chenille or shabby chic bedcover? If there's anything we never imagined, it's the idea of single women repairing en masse to white sales. What was set in motion was the beginning of the end of the couple's monopoly on the symbolic value of the well-made bed. We can thank the English. Of course, only Anglo-Saxons could have come up with that most bizarre design innovation: the twin bed. The single bed is a hygienic and permanent solution to the problem of how to have an intimate relationship and also have one's own space to sleep in. Said to have been invented in the late eighteenth century by English furniture designer Thomas Sheraton and originally intended to keep lovers cool in the hot summer months, the twin beds gesture was taken up again with gusto by American designers around 1915, and reached its colossal neuter apogee in the 1950s.

Once the imposing marital bed was replaced by the spouses' separate and slighter accommodations, beds came to represent not union and unity, but prudish separation. The twin bed of the

American 1950s indicated an effort to keep everything high-class, intact, and undisturbed—in so far as sex can defile, alter, and disturb. Meanwhile, on TV—as we well know since this era remains particularly and peculiarly present in the retro-loving American psyche—the absurdist ascent of the twin-bed kind of life was reaching its summit. Its decline, as it happens, fully realized a mere decade later, tidily synced with the pomp and circumstance of the sexual revolution.

But the American twin bed not only failed utterly to sustain the conceit of a miraculous entente between desexualized parents, it turned out instead to herald their split. Chastity may have been the message, but separation was the reality as the twin bed divided and conquered. And once the conjugal double bed was sundered (especially on TV series), the untethered twins could now just float away from one another. And, as we know, many of them did, and they could never be put back together again with quite the same solidity. For even while Ozzie and Harriet, wearing their nicely starched pyjamas, waved good night to one another across the expanse of a bed they shared (a fact of which Ozzie Nelson was so proud that he would bring it up in later years, as a first), the American Bachelor was taking center stage, and his principal prop was the very big, obvious, irrefutable bed. It was as if the representative of the male of the species had rightfully inherited the lion's share of the erstwhile marital couch. Please note, for instance, that in the orthodox *Playboy* bachelor pad, there wasn't a narrow bed in sight.

But, still not satisfied, in the '60s many of these gentlemen got rid of their increasingly confining double beds (54" X 75") and acquired king-size beds (76" X 80"), and a mirror on the ceiling. The implication was that they needed the extra space to accommodate the company they entertained, though some maintained an elaborate pretense that it was all merely for the sake of their own aesthetic or solitary comfort. But while they were often willing to forego the telltale mirror, a surprising number nevertheless managed to get water beds, which they occasionally insisted helped their back troubles.

As for the rest, one must imagine that many were homosexuals—self-acknowledged or not—since, by many accounts, some 15 percent of American men were officially assigned to that category a couple of decades later. For them, according to their later accounts, the bachelor pad was a gilded, despair-filled, and presumably hermetically sealed cage.

But for the most part there was really very little dissimulation built into the bachelor pad concept—only the agreed-upon secret that seductions took place there. The game was how fast the bachelor could undress the girl, and for this purpose martinis were sipped, and mood music was supplied on the bachelor's fantastic sound system—a little bebop, perhaps, or a side of Montovani (depending on the degree of the bachelor's musical rigor—or possibly his estimation of what kind of concentration it would take for him to hold out until his date got sufficiently looped). The bachelor's bed often brazenly displayed satin sheets—pennants of a hedonistic credo. Anything in bad taste could be assumed to be there on purpose, meant to be jovially winked at. A cross between the English gentleman's style and that of the girlie magazine, the pad was designed to be the setting for a bacchanal, American style, and it really didn't matter all that much, ultimately, if it turned out not to actually feature very much real action. It was the attitude that counted, and the bachelor practically claimed to have invented attitude.

Trying to come up with images of a feminine equivalent to the bachelor's pad would be a disastrous enterprise, producing only a measly list of feeble question marks. The true equivalent of the 1950s bachelor was the pinup, and she had no home save the walls of every enlisted man's room, every garage, every bar's toilet. (Although Webster's dates "bachelorette" to 1938, I have never heard the term used any way but derisively, except on the *Dating Game. Bachelorette number one! Bachelorette number two!*) The dictionary does list the Americanism, "bachelor girl," but we need say no more about that once we have asked how 1950s and 1960s males would have liked to have been called bachelor *boys.*

They had no name and they had no home: Popular narrative provided almost no clue as to how single women actually lived. Characteristically, Bob Cummings, the rakish photographer who was the star of *Love That Bob,* worked and lived in quite the nice setup, and that's where the series took place, but we never went home with Shultzie—the sexless character played by Anne B. Davis who was his love-sick secretary, wore glasses and a bun, and ardently envied the cute "girls"who were in competition for his favors, though she contented herself with gazing at him eloquently, cow-eyed, and adoring.

From a decorating point of view, it would no doubt be pretty grim, with stockings drying over the bathtub or something. The home of the couple was the elemental, central, solid theater of safety and comfort. That of the bachelor, the carnival of arousal, of lascivious freedom. The home of the single woman *had* to be a diorama of melancholy, starring She Who Had Not Been Chosen. No sex per-mitted there, no fashionably sanctioned playing around, no fine martini glasses, no good sound equipment (at best a crackling radio . . .). The scene was to be set only by rejection, betrayal, and/ or abandonment. No parties. Her role was to be either ignored or betrayed.

It was this single girl to whom Helen Gurley Brown gave deco-rating tips in the 1960s. There was no ready-made decorative scheme to be found because it was the first time in history that so many women lived alone. Historically, single women have been anything but single in their living arrangements. In the nineteenth and early twentieth centuries, according to Ruth Freeman and Patricia Klaus in *The Journal of Family History*, "Although loneliness was a very great worry for spinsters, often they did not live alone. . . . Nonetheless, where to live posed a crucial question for these women, young and old." The more affluent the family of origin, the more likely the unmarried woman was to live with her parents or siblings. But, increasingly, according to the Journal, "although cen-sus material for a direct comparison is unavailable, it appears that . . . more middle-class educated young women were living with each other, not with their parents. Many of them lived not only in shared household . . . but also in settlement houses and all-female institutions such as schools, ladies' apartment buildings, and nurs-ing homes."

Shrouded in dubious status, the homes of single women did not attract much attention, good or bad. "Women living together, even for a lifetime did not occasion scandal," write Freeman and Klaus. The radical potential attracted no notice because that arrangement was thought of as declassé rather than political. By the end of the last century, young women had come to depend less on a family to protect them in their vulnerable unmarried status, and they began to feel free to live as they preferred—with friends, or in some other environment compatible with their outlook, rather than remaining a satellite to a family-centered constellation. Whatever the arrangements, the idea that a household needn't invariably be headed by a man or his widow had been established, and it became possible for a young lady to leave her parental home for reasons other than marriage without losing her class.

The late 1950s saw the normalization of many alternative arrangements and the appearance, in popular culture, of women roommates who were allowed to be both optimistic and sexy. Marilyn Monroe, Lauren Bacall, and Betty Grable, for instance, who sported astoundingly high heels, tight skirts, and very serious bouffants, shared a cute little apartment. They—the girls—were designed to seem just legit enough, but the title of the film and the eponymous television series tells the tale: *How to Marry a Millionaire*. It didn't matter what kind of bed they had. Once they had a beau, they only had to keep him out of it long enough to have him work himself up into the froth required to propel him toward proposing marriage.

As usual, we can thank the '60s for a little evolution. And what do you know, Mary Tyler Moore had her own place, featuring *a sunken living room!* The show's producers apparently felt they didn't need to say more, for no bedroom was offered. She slept on a convertible in the same room where she lived and ate and cried for the camera. Nevertheless, Mary Tyler Moore's cheerful place—everything that was taken for granted about it—was evidence of the end of something old.

The racy bachelor pad soon became a dolefully retro cliché, the incarnation of a ridiculous sexuality. Whatever could be salvaged from it was of a material nature and could now be accessed by anyone who cared to, and had the money to, purchase the products.

And, presto, three decades later, a single woman gets herself to the Wiz and buys whatever she wants or whatever some quick salesperson can talk her into. Do single women have the money? Even while we are being bombarded by invocations of shiftless women raising huge broods of violent children at the state's expense, the reality of twentieth-century life is that the single woman may well be going home to her own house (according to the U.S. Census Bureau, nearly 54 percent of single women living alone actually own their homes), from a fairly well-paying job (not as well-paying as the man's equivalent job, but still . . .), and on the way stopping at a caterer's to put together the menu for a dinner party to be held in her home that evening, of the type that only materfamilias were formerly entitled to host. Or she may be picking up pizza before going home, putting on a pair of earphones, and lighting up a joint. Or she may be sitting on the side of the bed eating her heart out, but the bed will most likely be covered by a spread, be it from Lord & Taylor's or Kmart. And in the rest of her house, there are stereo components, CDs, TVs, rugs, coffee tables, futons, good china, bad china, books, computers, CD-ROMS. Why, she is . . . a citizen of the U.S. of A.! Entitled to anything she darn pleases if she's got the dough.

There are plenty of women who don't have the dough, but they are not busy being Hester Prynne, either. The current single woman's home is no less cluttered than that of any other female citizen of the late twentieth century, with both objects and clichés. The establishment of single women as Real Americans was accomplished via their spending habits. Like the woman who told us earlier that once her business became successful and she moved into a great town house, her family suddenly had no problem with her marital status, the women who can buy are miraculously personae gratae in the American mall.

Now that to be alone at the prime of one's life—at the height of one's earning power—is no longer an odd exception, single women are an increasingly attractive target market for advertisers. According to the marketing director of *Single Living* magazine, the average single American woman has $15,300 in disposable income, compared to $11,400 for married consumers of both sexes. Single women now are coveted by advertisers for products traditionally targeted to men, like automobiles and financial services, as well as the women's magazines' mainstays, like cosmetics.

Of course, many of these women are saturated with consumer goods, potentially debtridden, or at least guiltily charging their credit cards up to the max, but they have earned it. For such a woman, the romance lies in carrying her own trousseau over the threshold, in a suitcase (bought with her paycheck) boasting her own initials. True romance is adventure and self-sufficiency.

At least now when single women now talk about their beds and mention matelassé, piqué, dotted Swill, Porthault, Egyptian cotton, English linen, chenille, or no-iron polyester blend with a nice flowery print, they don't have to pretend to be sexual wallflowers. Some may be celibate, but the morally correct sexual deprivation of the past is no longer exemplified by rough sheets, hard pillows, and a creaky mattress of old worn out springs. You don't have to have sex to rate a 208-threads-per-inch count. All you need is a Visa card.

On a day-to-day basis, what does it mean to live alone now? How do we gauge the balance between privacy and loneliness, solitude and unfettered anxiety, vulnerability and independence? For some women the relationship between home and comfort is obvious. For others, the experience is one of complex and constantly shifting contradictions, varying from day to day, sometimes from hour to hour, just the way one expects the light does in a well-known room.

Except for that small but interesting minority who viewed discomfort and incompleteness as a necessary aspect of their design scheme, the women I talked to seem so comfortable in their homes that it's very difficult to imagine that there isn't some parallel to their psychological space. One way or another, these are people who inhabit their lives. Loneliness is what detractors think of when they imagine single women's homes. But my guess is that many of the women who felt lonelier in past relationships have found solitary loneliness to be as potentially rich and useful as it may be forlorn and boring. Or, more commonly, to be sometimes lonely but to often also feel that solitude can be, simply, an opportunity for well-being.

"Sleeping alone is one of the things I love," more than one woman said. Home is where aloneness is played out, for better and for worse. Loneliness, whether intermittent or implacable, is taken for granted, and the women I talked to usually had moved beyond that to other distinctions. Indeed, their intimacy with solitude is precisely what may predispose them not to enter into a new relationship. They remember the opposite discomfort and what it's like to lie in bed next to someone when there are problems. "Especially if you wish you were elsewhere, or when you're angry, or when you're restless and would rather get up and tinker around the house."

A woman used to have to "wait" for a home until any number of elements were in place. "There was a time when you were supposed to wait around for your trousseau," one woman in her mid-forties was saying recently. "But now, at a certain point you say to yourself, *What am I waiting for?* and you just go ahead and fix the place up the way you want to, as if it was going to be permanent."

Even those young girls who have a romantic and even hopeful view of marriage tell us that they expect to live with someone before they marry him—"to make sure," they say. So, in a total reversal, cohabitation has become the responsible thing to do. At any rate, the parental home no longer serves as a holding tank in which the maiden and her maidenhead are carefully preserved until the time she is transported into her permanent marital living situation— though some former maidens get stuck there for financial reasons.

I would conjecture that the particularly striking disparity between perceived image (loneliness, bareness, rigidity, aesthetic poverty) of the single woman's home and the experienced reality (cluttered with life) is a direct result of anxieties about the spiraling impermanence of "the couple." The idea of a single woman's living in a "real" home violates not only significant tribal customs but also disrupts the process of passing property on in an orderly manner. What's more, it is blatant evidence that there is such a thing as sex outside the conjugal bed.

In a traditional home, there are traditional displays for outsiders that help to support agreed-upon lies among the insiders: A schism in the family, for instance, will probably be carefully hidden. And the bigger lies of our society are embedded there, as well—buttressed by the billion-dollar furniture industry, the commercials, and the shelter magazines, there exists a cultural subtext that almost anyone permitted into the home can read according to a tacitly agreed upon code. Single women have not stuck to the old code and its easily readable text because it doesn't account for the realities of their lives or the lies they would wish to tell. They were excluded by the mainstream, and the more idiosyncratic they were, the less readable in classical terms, the more they were marginalized. At the end of this century, therefore, unlike the more readable family home, the single woman's home is an as yet unanalyzed display, rich in multiple meanings.

After shelter and the projection of an image, the home's most intimate function is to express the fantasy of a visit. Being visited and fantasizing about being visited are two very different matters: Those probably aren't the same visitors. If the couple's home is designed to indicate completion, the single woman's home is rather an unplanned invitation to extemporize. The single woman's singular vision is the result of her own complex compendium of fantasies—her home is designed for no one gaze, save that of phantom lovers past and future. That is, the gaze she tries to please is her own, limited principally by her own imagination.

And yet these homes are quintessential late-twentieth-century places precisely because of the tremendous feeling of impermanence, the ambivalence that results from too many mixed messages. The play of new and old reflects both the incomprehensibility of the transition in the culture and the complexity of the new householder. The lessons of childhood continue to play in her mind, but now she can amend the results.

"It's really hard for me to be a grown-up and call the painters," said one successful professional woman, who also told me that decorating her house as she wished had been her most pleasurable and reassuring activity of the recent past. It was starting that had been strange—on her own, for her sake alone. Nevertheless, the place needed a paint job, and she made the call. She had the garage redone. She had the septic system snaked. She changed the screen on the back porch. She discarded the odds and ends from her parents' kitchen and purchased good pots and pans. She bought exquisite towels and sheets. Really, really good sheets.

A BED OF ONE'S OWN

For sleeping, dreaming, reading great books or trash, sex with one or two or three, talking on the phone, rolling around with a child, a place for the cat to purr or the dog to drool, a bed is truly a testimonial to how you make it.

CAMILLE O., who remembers the sound of the rain on the leaves outside her father's house.

The last time I had to share my bed with someone . . . You know, all you hear about is women feeling deprived when they don't get to have sex, when they aren't sharing with someone. But I felt very deprived when I had to share my bed the other night.

I know that when I visit friends who have children, I feel so lucky when I leave. You do little things you can't do when you have kids. I'm trying to devise ways in my head, when I think of this problem about how I would negotiate this if I do have children. . . . Because I do feel that I would go bonkers if I couldn't have some private time. And it's true that even with a partner there in bed with you, you wouldn't sleep very well. I think part of the reason one doesn't sleep well when you're not used to the person being there is that you're worried about touching them. I have to sort of lie there thinking, *Oh, if I do anything slightly mad in the night* . . . I want to be able to feel free. I'm thinking of how once there was a bunch of us, around eight people, and we went to Cape Cod and rented a house. And I shared a bed with someone I knew very well, and I found myself sort of . . . it was very nice to actually sort of snuggle with her. And it wasn't a problem. It was nice. And she's married, and she was actually affectionate back. . . . Not that affectionate, but affectionate. So I slept very well. And that's something I miss a lot, being single—the feeling of sleeping with someone who you know so well, and love, or like very much. It's completely different from having sex. And sometimes, of course, you can have sex with someone and not sleep well at all because it wasn't very good or whatever.

NINA L., who, like many of the women, expressed very few regrets for the conjugal bedroom.

Actually, my new thing is, what I really don't like about men is that they always want to put their leg on top of yours.

ANITA S. said she needs to sleep alone.

For me, it doesn't have anything to do with love. I remember being with people I was ecstatic about, and it was just always uncomfortable. In my family there was a tremendous emphasis on finding privacy. Like locking yourself in the bathroom. Or reading, which is a tremendously private thing. And that was immediately a huge relief when Hugh and I broke up, and I got to go back to living alone and sleeping alone. Even though sometimes it's lonely. But I can breathe. He won't push me off the bed or suddenly wake me up because he's swung an arm or a leg on me.

You know, it's the same thing as if you're walking down the street with a man and he puts his arm around you. . . . There's a very specific discomfort about that. And usually they're not as tall as I am. I can't walk!

ADELE U., who told us that love and dating are two entirely separate things.

What happens is that you get used to sleeping with someone, and then when they leave, it's really weird; you get really lonely and uncomfortable, and you can't sleep. I think that has something to do with being in a house—and being a woman. . . . When you're sleeping with a man, you don't really worry as much about someone coming in the window. And the minute he leaves, you suddenly have to be really afraid again and have to get your mental checklist ready: *Did I lock the door? Did I do this? Did I do that?*

But when you've been single for a while, and then you sleep with someone, it's really uncomfortable at first. You can't sleep, and you get sleep-deprived. Or you're staying up and you're in love and you're laughing and talking all the time, you know? For me, three nights a week at his house is fine, but then I'm really happy to be back home.

REAH S., the attorney.

When I got a little bit of money I think the first thing I did was get cotton sheets.

BLANCHE W., who doesn't keep up with white sales.

I don't give a shit about the sheets. I don't even know what kind I have. I'm always relieved when there's something I don't require. Do you know what I mean? I haven't figured out that Porthault sheets are infinitely better than whatever I've been using. It's not something important to me. Well, I don't really like it when the sheets completely clash, but it's not a detail that I pay that much attention to.

But as to my nightclothes . . . though I have to say it's been so long since I've slept with anybody in any kind of expectable way that my general standard of living has dramatically increased since the last time. I did start to get into underwear with Martin, just a little bit. He seemed to like it.

I used to have a water bed, and I used to have satin sheets. None of that now. The one I have now? I bought it with myself in mind, primarily. But I was certainly wondering, *Would I ever sleep with another person?* At home I have an extra magnetic mattress, which I find very comfortable—it has little magnets in it. And newcomers to the bed find it extremely uncomfortable, like a bed of nails. But there have been very few newcomers in the last several years. Also, I sleep with my rubber balls, and sometimes some crystals. Haven't done crystals in a long time, but I always do rubber balls. They're for relieving tense muscles in the neck, for keeping my knees from rolling in and banging each other. I'm sure at this point they're also transitional objects. I don't like teddy bears or stuffed animals, but the closest I've come is my collection of balls. I'm so used to all of this by now. Occasionally, though, an old boyfriend comes over who I haven't seen in years, and they're a little taken aback. "What's this!?"

ELLEN P., who wishes she went out less.

When I moved in to this loft, I built a platform . . . so I could sit at the window and work and see the river. About three feet, maybe a little more off the ground. And then it turned out that you can't legally have a bedroom without a window in it. So the bed came out of the dark room and went out onto the platform. It looks like a kind of white cloud, and it also looks also a little bit like a throne. And since it's a loft, people walk in and see it there. For me, it's a source of enormous pleasure to be in that bed on that platform where there's also actually a tree. But I sometimes feel that I have to explain to people when they come here that it wasn't initially the idea to put the bed on the platform.

ON YOUR OWN

How does it feel?

REGINA M. has found her way to phase II.

A year after I'd moved here, I realized I was *living* here and I thought, *Let's make this home.*

PAM A., who just bought herself the really good sheets, is working on formulating a vision of herself in her own home. She keeps referring to her apartment as "this place."

What do you mean "a grown-up home"? Meaning if you were married and had children? Or the kind of home where I would have people over for dinner? That's why I wanted to get more space, so that I could entertain better. It's got grown-up furniture in it.

I'm really confused about the fact that for the first time I have people come to my house to clean it. I'm uncomfortable doing all this stuff that grown-ups do. My mother was alone from the time I can even remember, yet I will have been alone longer if I stay alone. From the age of forty-one on, she never had another husband. Yet she did all this stuff, and she seemed to manage everything naturally. It's really hard for me to call the painters and say, "I want my house painted."

ABIGAIL Z., the wistful architect, is in transition from the 1950s to the millennium.

It was always hard to figure out whether to give a man the key. Because now I've learned that I'm always their transitional woman. I always used to have men who were getting away from another woman, and they would throw themselves at me and I let them. I never wanted to give them the key, but I thought I had to because I'd lose them if I didn't. And it was always wrong, I always lost them anyway.

But I'm more and more in my own life. I'm doing my house now, making it wonderful. I painted it pink! I'm doing all these things in my personal life, and my career is sort of in a place where it's fulfilling and exciting and there's all my other activities and friends. . . . I've sort of put myself together, but alone.

ELLEN P. Of course, the theme of home is rooted in one's deepest past, but being in one's own place goes a long way toward making some old questions obsolete.

I actually believe for myself that one of the reasons I am single is that my own sense of home was dismantled so early, and I didn't have a place to go home to without being essentially a visitor. So when I finally had a home, it meant I could go there and nobody would tell me to leave. I didn't have to be good or polite and could just be home for myself. . . . It took a long time for that to be the case.

BILLIANA M. On the day of the closing for the sale of the house in which she and her ex-husband had lived for twelve years.

When we got divorced, I moved to an apartment complex that felt very unmine, very unsafe. I didn't want to be there. Then I moved into a little house in the woods. A little tiny house. That was two years ago. I was forty-eight-years old. It felt like it was my place and like I was really on my own and had to call all my resources to me—and there was something really exhilarating about it.

Now that the house we shared is actually going to belong to someone else, it feels like an ending—and it's terrific. I've gotten rid of almost everything that was in my old life, so the things that I have now, even though they're shabby and second-hand, they're mine. It's for me, not for the public, and it reflects me much more. Now I don't feel as if I have to consider other people first. So I do sit down to eat, for myself. Sometimes in front of the television, sometimes at the table. I go in and out of being structured. But this is something new. I always make at least one good meal a day for myself. And I use really nice utensils, I make it really gratifying, and I buy good food. Good quality food.

My bed is nice. I have the green cotton sheets—you know the ones, the green cotton jersey sheets that are so squishy and comfortable. And a nice comforter. My bed is very much set up for comfort, for dreaming, to envelop me and give me an optimal place to rest.

REBECCA S.'s husband died about ten years ago.

Well, I was relieved because of all the agony I had when he had cancer for three and a half years; he had chemotherapy, and I was his caretaker completely. I was so physically tired and emotionally spent that when he died, I felt relief! I began to breathe. And, you know, he was always holding back. He was never stingy with his money, but if I wanted to make a change in the furniture or do something, he'd say, "Let's wait a while." And I always yielded. That's what he was always saying: "Let's wait a while."

It built up so that when he died, I made a revolution. This whole apartment looks different. Completely. And I didn't buy much. I simply threw out what he wouldn't let me touch. I threw out, threw out, threw out. . . . He was a squirrel; he collected everything—things, facts. . . . Ask him any question, it's like touching a button. He gives you the answer. He had a memory . . .

He had fifteen hundred books. Good ones, too, believe me. I'm sorry I gave some of them away. I was desperate. I wanted to have less around me, just less stuff around me. I felt cluttered. I felt so . . . claustrophobic.

And then I got new carpeting, and I got everything new, everything. . . . It looks like a new house. And my friends would say to me, "My God," they said, "a revolution here!"

EVELYN B. who told us in the preceding chapter that she occasionally dreams of having a study.

Well, yes, this is my dining room, and I got this screen so I could have a tiny bit of privacy. But as you can see, the problem is my office just sort of flows out into the rest of the apartment. I mean, nobody cares but me. My kids certainly don't care. But my male friends come over, and they say, "How can you get anything done?" And I point out to them that they don't have to stop working to fold laundry.

RENNIE N., the composer, who lives in her parents' old house by the sea.

I remember when I was moving in that I did tell people—my birthday's in the middle of summer, in August—and I did tell people that I wanted my wedding presents for my birthday because I said who knows if I'll ever get married, and by the time I do, I'll already have all this stuff. So I want these presents now.

I was turning twenty-nine, but it was because I was starting a job, finishing graduate school at last. That was my sense of becoming an adult—that I finally could have all these things. I remember my church threw a church ale for me, which they used to do for people getting married. So they gave me towels and dishes. One of my brothers said to me, "Well, if you want your wedding presents for your birthday, we think it would be a lot easier if you would register."

Oh, yes. I certainly did register.

ROSA M., whose marriage was passionate but violent.

I like things just the way they are right now. I moved into this house when I got my current position. I was hardly working when Lilly was a baby, and we were barely surviving. This job wasn't a lot of money, but it was stable, and that's what I'd been waiting for. So I found my place and signed the contract. And right after that was when I really started feeling happy. The people who come in to visit in my life are going to be the ones I want to see.

What does my mother think? She thinks it's fine. Of course, she's alone now, too.

VALENTINE J. has been widowed for thirty-five years. She says it took her family years to understand why she wanted to keep such a big place all for herself.

Yes, even after he died, I did decide to stay here. It's big but I felt . . . the rooms are all furnished. I couldn't go through a redecorating. You know, I just recently had curtains made for the living room. My God, I spent weeks trying to find the fabric and everything. I couldn't do that again.

EILEEN Y. Once the clichés are dispelled, a place very quickly seems neither right nor wrong, but just home.

I don't recall exactly when it stopped feeling temporary. I remember the first three or four months I felt I'd never adjust to this much space. Then that quickly disappeared. It's gotten prettier as time has gone on and not much shabbier, but it leaks like an old ship. It's always leaked, and now it leaks a little worse. You know, whenever you move to a new place you think, *Like the old woman with her skirts cut off, could this be ever I?*

And then it's forty years later.

NOT A FINISHED PLACE

For some to live in a finished place means acknowledging a reality that they haven't yet gotten themselves to process.

CALLIE S. has raised two children on her own, but you'll note she still refers to herself as living "without a hearth and home."

There was a point in the not too distant past where it suddenly came into focus that this probably was how I was going to live my life, and by that time . . . This gets a little complicated in my life. Are you familiar with the Cinderella syndrome? More or less? Well, you don't have to be more than that. Basically that's how I lived a lot of my life. No matter how well I was doing, or how well I was working at my work, there always was lurking someplace in the background the assumption that some nice Jewish boy was going to take me away from all this nonsense and put me back where I should be, which was home, with a couple of kids and a garden and a driveway. That's really who I was supposed to be.

I certainly would have lived another life financially if I'd known this was how it was going to be. The accents would have been on different syllables if I'd imagined that I was going to spend the rest of my life alone. Or, rather, without a male. Without a hearth and home and all that jazz. There's always been like a temporary permanence or a permanent temporariness about my home. I've got things that I love here. It's very much my home, and it's where I live, and you'd certainly recognize me if you came through the door, but it's not the finished place I would be living in if I were living in a place as a married woman.

CATHY D. expresses the fundamental ambivalence.

I did go through a stage with a guy when I had this fantasy that I would be saved because I would go live in his pool house and have a baby. And I remember thinking, *Should I buy a couch?* Because any minute I was going to move into M's pool house and not have to do this anymore. But he was one of those guys where you wake up afterward and you go, *Oh, my God, I think I loved an ass.*

Rennie N., who took over her parents' home in Cape May.

I got a little bit of money when my grandmother died, and I spent most of it getting established, getting furniture, but I had a little bit left at the end, so I got a stained-glass panel that hangs in my window and is truly beautiful. But I feel it should be an actual window and not just hanging. And sometimes I tell myself, *Oh, when I have a man to marry I want to go to his house and see where this should be installed.*

But when I really think about where it should go, it's to a church or to a convent. I do think of living in a monastery. That's the only other thing I can think of if I don't get married.

Camille O., when I asked for her sense of what home is, paused so long, eyes closed, that I began to apologize for having asked.

No, it's not really a difficult question. I'm trying to figure out if home is still my father's house. I do go down south quite often, to the house my father's had all my life. My bedroom is still my bedroom. There, it smells like home. I walk in, and I smell the tomatoes and the grapes, the smell of the garden, and I miss that. That smell after it's rained. There's a grapevine that's grown across the house; it's right outside my bedroom window. So there's the smell of the grapes and the rain on the grapes, the sound of the rain on the grapes. There's a completely different sound to rain in the summer than in the winter. In the summer I could lie awake for hours listening to the rain hit the vine leaves.

It's funny, because I left home so long ago. I went to boarding school when I was about twelve.

But, yes, I do have an apartment now, near my office. It has everything: furniture, books, a john. It's small, but fine. It does feel like home, in a way, because I bought it. Yeah, it's a condo. A friend of mine, he's a cabinetmaker. He made my kitchen for me, which is really nice. It's a small galley kitchen, not one that you sit in. That's what I miss. If I have people over, you can't sit in there, you can't fit more than two or three people in it. You know, it's hard to resell single-bedroom apartments because they're for single people, who aren't generally buying. At least in Boston, they might rent them, but they don't buy.

But when I think about it . . . yes. It does feel like home to me. It feels like home.

MARY ANN B. says her house no longer felt like home when the kids went away to school.

I was out there in Connecticut for the good public schools. And you know, quite frankly, it was a cheaper and easier way for me to be the poor member of a rich community.

Almost everyone was in couples. I had almost no social life there. My kids did, but I didn't. I commuted to my social life in the city. Which is why as soon as the kids were out of high school, I moved to New York.

AMELIA J., who expected to remarry quickly when her marriage broke up sixteen years ago.

It's like what we were saying before, I thought that this was a phase, and then it turned out to be my life. . . . My neighbors and I . . . we all thought we were going to be in these apartments for two years. And then the '80s happened, and then the recession happened, and then forget it. You can't move out. I want to live with someone.

I've gotten my house on Long Island fixed up a lot faster than my apartment. I keep trying to get my apartment all fixed up, but I can't get it right. It's nice, but there are sort of crucial things missing. Like the dining room. Sam came over and said, "I see you haven't made a proper dining room yet." And yet there is a table and there are rugs and a painting, but it needs something to sort of pull it together. And my living room . . . you know, the plants have never been put in beautiful pots. I do sometimes feel like this is not my house. I mean, I put a lot of money into it, I fixed things up, but way down deep, I feel like it's not done.

JENNIFER B., who at 32, is temporarily back in New Jersey at her parents' home.

I'd only been back here for ten hours and it was horrible. I'm not going to make it.

Why did I move back in? Money. It's cheap. The city is too expensive. I had a place for eight months in the city, but the people I sublet it from came back for the summer. I had so much work, and I didn't have time to look for another place.

Upstairs I have a bedroom and an office my parents kept for me. It was really weird; when I came back home, my mother was tiptoeing around to make sure she wasn't going to piss me off. Inevitably, though, she would come up to my office to see if there was anything she could do for me—get me something to drink or something—but she was very careful not to piss me off.

But she did piss me off when I found her outside my door listening to a telephone conversation. So she could catch up on my life, I guess. This was less than ten hours after I came back.

MONICA V., who said remembering why she lives the way she does is like tuning in and out of a radio frequency.

You can't take it too seriously, you just can't. But, it's true, I do get down.

I couldn't stay here with somebody else, it's too small. When I think of being with a guy, like this guy Kit I was talking about. . . . I'm so excited about him. Really thrilled about him. But the other day I started thinking, *Suppose we live together?*

Groan . . . You know, I don't want to live in his place, and he's not going to—It's too small, and I . . . I got really depressed thinking that I'd have to give up my place.

It's not as if when I moved here I was making a commitment to staying alone. I don't remember feeling one way or the other about it. I was just so happy to have my own home and so happy to, you know, to put all my stuff around me. I didn't have to do it his way, I could do it my way. . . . You know, it didn't seem like this is it, a this-is-where-I'm-going-to-be-till-I-die kind of thing. I don't think that. I think what's going to happen is eventually I'm going to have enough money, some way or other, to get a house outside of the city. And now I'm thinking, too, of some major change. I've just been so anxious. No, not anxious. I don't even know what the word is. . . .

I've been doing very well lately for one of my biggest clients, so I start thinking . . . maybe I'll go to Washington. Maybe I'll make a couple of great deals, and then I'll go to San Francisco and start something else. Maybe I'll go to New Orleans. Maybe I'll live in Florida. I'm just batting ideas around, I don't know if I'll do any of them. Or maybe I'll buy a house outside the city in a community, and commute into the city and keep my apartment as a pied-à-terre. . . . I'm going to stop waiting for Mr. Right to come along, so I can begin my life. I'm ready. I don't want to be on hold anymore. I'm tired of it. At the same time . . . I'm anxious to pick up and meet a guy, and, you know, do something, too. So, it's like I feel that this is a time of change. . . . I hope it works out.

Yes, maybe that's the word. Restless.

ANITA S. told us about her dream of her grandmother's home. She is turning 40.

So how do I feel about it now? Transient. I have to go find another home. I want it to be a place I can die in.

I'm not planning on going soon. I've moved too much—every two years I've moved—so I feel like right now, I'm facing a new work life, a new place to live, a new relationship perhaps, and I'm in a total state of panic. It's a good panic. I know everything's about change. The house part is not the panic; that's trauma and money. Everything's going to change, and I think the decision about the baby is part of that, too. I have to come to some definite decision very soon.

MONEY

It's the tough part.

CHRISTINE L. reminds us of a key factor.

I make as much money as people who are in the kind of couples that live very well. But it costs as much to get a home for one person as two yet you've only got the income of one. When I look at people in my professional background who are married, they're doing much better than I'm doing because I'd need another in e to do as well.

Of course, this is all in that rarefied atmosphere of that upper-middle-class. I'm not mentioning the way most people live now. . . . Whatever problems I have as a single woman financially are minimal compared to most single women—and certainly those with children.

RENNIE N., who sometimes has fantasies of moving to a monastery.

My mother had this teaching job before she got married. She was working, putting herself through school. She only got two or three hours of sleep at night, and she used to stick pins in her hands to stay awake. She said to me, although she denies it now, "If your father died, I would have lovers, but I would never get married again. Men have too much control over your money."

I'd much rather nickel and dime myself. To me, if I have my own money and I don't take someone else's, I can do anything I want. Also, though, as a single person. . . . It takes two incomes now, to actually live a comfortable life. I mean I was thirty-one years old, and I was living in a fucking basement; it was all I could afford. I'm realizing now the attraction [of a relationship], in addition to other things, like having kids. . . . There are things that become available to me through having a relationship—having a house, having a real life. All the women I know are tired. We talk about being tired. We're tired because we have to do everything ourselves.

JEAN I., Molly's mother.

I'm a one-income girl in a two-income world. But I'm not sure two-income people have it all that great, either.

I have a new shtick I've been working on, which is that in terms of New York real estate the only thing a husband gets you is a dining room. Because I look at my married friends, and the only thing they have that I don't have is a dining room. So I ask you, is it worth it?

But you know, they all have country houses and they're all going to be able to afford private school sooner than I am. Molly's education is why I can't afford anything else. She's my luxury.

ROSA M., whose first move when she got a steady job was to buy a home for herself and her daughter.

Yeah, I did have trouble getting a mortgage. But I found one where the owner—the seller—carried the contract. And they did consider me a good enough prospect. You see, this house wouldn't qualify for a mortgage through a bank, anyway—it's too run down—so he had to find somebody like me. Its a twenty-year mortgage. I'll be sixty-three or something like that when it's paid off. I'd like to pay it off early, but if I don't, I'll be sixty-three. This is the first time I've owned a home on my own. It feels like I'm comfortable now, like nobody's going to be yelling at me and tell me this or that.

JOCELYN'S PHASE III

First came marriage, then came a baby,
then—perhaps—comes Jocelyn.

JOCELYN H., the pediatric nurse, is a woman you might see sitting on a bus going to and from work, reading a paperback book, perhaps fighting to keep her eyes open. She speaks with a Brooklyn intonation—black Brooklyn—that makes everything sound jazzy and fresh.

I'm forty-two years old this month. I know mothers now are having children at older ages, but when I got married I was eighteen, and I didn't have a child until ten years later and I thought I was old! And now . . . My son is seventeen, and I can't believe I lived through it.

A lot of people who know that my son will be going to college soon will say to me, "How are you going to handle it?" And the real answer is, I'm measuring the room! Like, *Oh, and I think the hot tub is going to fit in here . . .* and other jokes I tell myself.

Yes, it was pretty tough being a single mother when my son was small. I guess I was disillusioned about how life would be. I'd think, *I have to go home and make dinner for this kid.* I guess I was tired having to come home, making a meal, going through his homework, and then trying to make time for myself. No, I had no private life, really; I was too exhausted. What I like to do in the evening, believe it or not, I like to write poetry. I did that for a number of years. But at that point I'd be so tired, I couldn't do it. And I really liked to read and couldn't, so I'd take the book on the bus because I knew after I came home I couldn't. We had to take a bath.

I was angry a lot, I have to be honest, although I never saw it within myself. It takes a lot to get me angry, it really does, and I was angry with myself because I couldn't get organized. Believe it or not I am a very organized person—*everything* has to be organized. And I had to get him to bed, and you know what it's like trying to move those toys, and I was thinking, *Why am I doing this?* But I was a neatnik. Our furniture was, forget it. When my son was ten I remember going: "Furniture time!" But until then you really don't. They take over, my son and his friends; they walk on the couch, they climb on the chairs, the walls were all nicked from their dragging the furniture around.

When we grew up, we were not wealthy by any means. But we had what we needed. My father worked nights as a doorman, and my mother used to clean people's apartments—and that's the way I remember my mother. . . . Everything that they made went into the home. We lived comfortably.

And I taught my son the way my mother taught me. We got what we needed, not what we wanted, and I taught him the same way. If you want something you have to earn it. I don't give him something for nothing. Maybe I want him to do something in the house. Clean the bathroom. Or something. He understands that. Or if he decides he wants something, he says, "Mommy, do you want me to do something this week? Do you want me to do the laundry?" And I say, "Hmm . . . what do you want?" And he says, "There are these tapes I want. . . ." I'll tell you, it wasn't easy, because he did some home plenty of times saying, "I want these jeans. . . ." Or he'd say, "I want these new Michael Jordan sneakers." And I'd say, "I'm not spending a hundred dollars on them." One thing about sneakers: When he wants new ones, I tell him to save a half and I give him the other half, and that works.

He's very . . . he's different from me. He's a very easy-going person. He's the kind of kid who'd give you the shirt off his back and think nothing of it. And I say to him, "You have got to stop letting these people walk all over you," and he says, "I'm just being nice." And I don't understand why he's like that. I'm not as easy as that. I would bend over backwards to do something for someone, but I won't let them treat me badly.

When he asks for something and I say, "I don't have the money," he says, "It's OK. Whenever you can." Sometimes I forget and I buy a blouse or something, and he doesn't even say anything about it. And when I realize it, I say, "Oh!" And he says, "Oh, don't worry about it." I get him a sheet of paper and he's happy. The kid is happy because he can draw.

Relationships? As far as that was concerned, I thought I'd never get married again; I thought it's just not something I want to do. I feel I'm not where I need to be to want to get married again. I have gotten him to the point where he's going to go to college and can decide what he wants to do with his life, but I think that now, no, I don't want to get married: I sort of want to decide what I want to do with my life first. I think it's because I like my independence. I don't want to be the housewife. I don't want to do anybody's laundry. I just want to be an independent person and do what I want when I want. I think it's the freedom. Not having to cook for anybody, not having to . . . nothing, you know. If I want to cook, fine, and if I don't. . . . I figure, *I live here, you live there, and I see you when I see you.*

I need time for myself. Because I feel every thing I've done for the past seventeen years going on eighteen years I've done for my son, doing what he needed in his life, and the ten years before that what I did was for my husband and what he needed in *his* life. And I feel now I want to go back to school, I want to do things for me.

This may sound very strange, but I want to be a paramedic. I figure going from pediatrics to paramedic is odd. But it's something I wanted to do in the beginning, and when I went to school, I guess maybe it was just luck that I did what I did. So, yes, I'm starting over in a way.

There's something else I've thought about, which is putting together a book. But it seems so difficult. Oh, poetry, because that's what I like to write. And oddly enough at the age of forty-two I still keep a diary. I've been doing this about eight years. Actually, I have several books. Can you imagine my dying and somebody reading these? I don't know what they'd think.

I have mixed feelings about my son leaving. I'm looking forward to his being independent and on his own. But I don't know; I'm trying to tell myself it'll be easier and really underneath thinking, *What am I going to do?* And I talk about enjoying it, but I don't know if that's how it's going to be for me in the beginning.

Yeah, it was scary to me at first, when I split up with my husband, to be on my own. It was upsetting and scary. Until . . . I think what changed was when I decided I had to move from there, and I decided I had to get rid of all the furniture. The furniture was just too much a reminder of us, and I felt that if I got into a relationship I couldn't have someone else come in . . . I wanted to get rid of everything because I felt, *Let's start over. I want everything to start clean.* That's how I felt. Yes, it has stayed clean for me.

No, when my son leaves, I don't really think I'd do anything different here. I guess a long time ago it became the home I wanted it to be. I always did want to have my own room. In my house, growing up, you could never find a quiet moment. Someone always invaded your space, you were never alone. I remember, in the room there was one double bed and one single bed. I had the single bed, and my sisters had the double bed. And I remember one of my sisters telling me that if I didn't sleep in the double bed and let her have the single bed, the bogeyman was going to get me, so I always went to sleep thinking of monsters. My mother would leave the light on so we could see if we had to get up and go to the bathroom, and I always remember when I would wake up at night and look at the light at the door and I would see the door to the bathroom and I'd hide—I was afraid there was a shadow, and I would hide under the covers. So every night I would hide and be scared, and finally I got into bed with my sister. And then she took my bed and I never realized that what she wanted was my bed.

When I stopped being afraid of the dark? I should say never. I still go to sleep with the night light.

OVERNIGHT GUESTS: THREAT OR MENACE

> *It's when you get to find out whether or not you're kidding yourself about wanting solitude.*

ANITA S. finds herself less and less tolerant of visitors.

My mother came to visit me. She slept in my bed, and she made more noise than anyone else I'd ever met. I took the longest showers because the shower was the only place that I could be by myself.

When my friends are there, I go and shower at my health club where they aren't allowed in. I spent a kind of reunion weekend not long ago with two of my closest friends from when I was an under-graduate. They're both married, both women who really do value being alone and they each have two small children, so it was very interesting to hear them talk about these negotiations that go on constantly between them and their husbands, about how they're going to get time alone.

The funny thing is that they were staying at my house, and I found it exhausting not to have a private place to go to at night, especially since one of them was sleeping with me while she was there. I realized I have a lot of little things I often do before I go to bed—not every night but especially at times when I'm working really hard, and I need to calm down. I couldn't do any of them while my friend was here. And it's interesting how hard that was. She told me that she sleeps well, but I noticed that when I would wake up to go to the bathroom, she would wake up, too, and go to the bathroom, too. Which is not my idea of sleeping well. I guess that for women who are married and have children, sleeping well is relative. I was joking with my two friends about this, and one of them said, "Yes, it's only when I go away that I really get a good night's sleep."

By about the third night of their stay, I started to wonder if I could ever be married. I felt this could not go on—you know, that I could never get used to this.

BLANCHE W., who lives in a duplex.

It varies. I like having guests out here at the beach; it's good for me to have house guests in the city because it forces a slight break in my routine. I especially like house guests if they're orderly, and if they like to clean. For a couple of nights, I enjoy having someone to come home to and having the next to the last half hour of the day to talk with. More than that becomes tedious.

I sometimes have couples stay over. No, I don't think they ever have sex. Or at least I haven't heard them. That would feel weird. In the country I have couples and children sleep over a lot, and I find the transition when they leave always difficult. Yes, that's when I feel lonely.

REGINA Z., who was the oldest of nine.

No, I still haven't set aside the fantasy of living with somebody. But I don't have a room, I don't have a closet for the person. For a relationship to succeed, I would have to be open to a big redecoration. If someone moved in here, it's so much my house that the person might feel as if they were living inside my head or something.

EATING

Of course people drink alcohol and use drugs behind closed doors, but the number one solo excess seems to be eating.

PHILLIPA C., whose most recent lover quickly became Mr. Last Month.

Because I'm raising children here, I'm *more* sexually inhibited than I would be if there was a man here. But when it comes to food I'm *less* inhibited than I would be if there was a man here. When I have a man here, I feel I have to keep up the side, you know what I mean? I have a whole host of expectations of myself, when there's a man here, about what it means to be a woman—most of which are completely obsolete.

For instance, tonight's dinner. Lucy had a pizza, I had a salad, and Robert had a packaged macaroni and cheese. On the table was a Lego set—the great Kahuna it's called—plastic toys, and also a complicated marble shoot that Robert's been building. And we sat there with all the lights on, no napkins, me eating with my fingers, Lucy eating with her fingers. And it was fine. Fine. Whereas if there had been a man here, it would have been intolerable. If there had been a man here I would have felt there had to be napkins, impeccable lighting. You know, all these '50s expectations.

The fewer egos there are in a house, the fewer demands are made on the head of the household, which is always a woman. So it's easier to deal with the egos of my children when I don't also have my husband's ego to deal with.

MARY ANN B. says she remembers especially stressful phases of her marriage in which eating was an inconvenient necessity.

I think couples get into a lot of rules they never meant to have. Like when I think back on it, it was never a spoken thing between Murray and me that we had to have dinner at such and such a time, or that dinner had to include all the major food groups or anything like that. But we fell under that pressure in a way. You sort of inherit those expectations from your own family in the '50s. . . . Once I said good-bye to all that—the timetables, the rules of who cooks, who cleans up afterward—for some reason, once we stopped a sort of couple hierarchy, all of that became easier.

BLANCHE W., whose duplex features a luxurious kitchen that she never cooks in. She *does* own a monogrammed caviar dish.

I might just have chips for dinner or ice cream for breakfast. Mmm-hm, literally. I make these fruit and protein powder shakes. Does that count as a square meal? Or I order in.

MARTHA H. has codified catch-as-catch-can eating.

No, I don't really have a standard food routine. I went through a phase for about two weeks recently where I ate frozen waffles every night. I mean, that's what I wanted to eat! And then—well, let's see, tonight I decided I had to eat in a more healthy way, and I went and bought a black bean burrito and some mesclun salad. But then I also got some hummus. I think I'm a little addicted to hummus.

If I can generalize . . . I eat the healthy stuff, but then I eat the stuff that I want to eat. So it's really pointless for me just to eat the healthy stuff because then I eat the hummus or the cookie. I have very little self-control that way. Tim gave me a box of Godiva chocolates, so I ate three whole ones and I bit into three other ones to see if I liked them enough to eat the whole one. . . . Which you can do if you live alone. You can leave three bitten chocolates in the box.

When I come home, I want to eat something immediately. I don't know why, I just do. That is the beauty of frozen waffles. . . . You can eat them immediately. And they're great. And they're not so bad for you. They're not steamed broccoli, but they're not Godiva chocolate, either.

Unless I invite someone over. Then I eat like a normal person.

PHILLIPA C. again.

Tonight, I'm going to read another one of these Flashman books. Flashman is like a bad James Bond from the '60s and '70s. Trash but really entertaining. I'm reading one now about Borneo. The last one I read was really great, about the charge of the Light Brigade. The thing is, there are cookies in the house. What is this thing about food talking? I bought three avocados because they were ninety-nine cents each, and I ate two of them. Then I went and looked them up, and they're four hundred calories each. So I realized I'd eaten eight hundred calories' worth of avocado. It was horrible. But now I'm lying on my bed and should be getting ready to go to sleep but that third avocado has starting calling me. And those cookies, they're just screeching.

LONELINESS VS. SOLITUDE

The first is painful, the latter can be liberating.

ADELE U. told us that she's sometimes scared in the house alone at night.

I feel, since I've been in my new apartment, I can sit at home and play on my computer and play my cassettes, and I'm like . . . Yes! All at once. I was very lonely when I was breaking up with George, and I didn't know where I was living, and I didn't have my things with me, and I was a real mess. But now I have my own apartment, I have my own things, I know where I'm going, and I'm back in my old rhythm. You feel lonely when there's someone who's supposed to be there and isn't there. You don't feel like a whole person. Now I do. I don't have time to feel lonely.

MARY ANN B. feels that living alone is the perfect answer to the eternal question: In the end, who does the dishes?

If you're single, you do have to do the whole housework, but I haven't found that to be significant. At least, you don't have to spend time arguing about who does what, you just do it. You don't have to argue about who does the laundry, you just do the laundry. It may actually save time. And in a way being single and teaching kids about housework is much easier. Like they don't have a bad example: Everybody just does it.

ELLEN P. says she is indeed lonely.

For me, the most painful part of being single is not having a companion with whom I can be in the richness of solitude. And my name for this is "intimacy," and where it takes place is silence and mute communication.

I think there are other forms of communication that are valuable and essential to our being, and they do have to do with touch and with physical presence, where your ego is not the main place of self-presentation. . . . I miss that enormously.

BLANCHE W. again.

The other night I had dinner in Easthampton with Phil and Aaron and Margo, and we all have our own houses there, and all of a sudden I thought, *Here we are, and we're each living by ourselves in our own houses.* And all of a sudden I felt so *lonely.* I mean, sometimes I just want to be kissed. You know what I mean?

BILLIANA M. again.

I was lonely in my marriage, and I would prefer to be lonely alone. There's something less lonely about that than being lonely with someone.

CAMILLE O. again.

I think, going back to your privacy question, that I didn't have a big issue with privacy, but I used to feel . . . I used to share a room with my sister, and I used to want to get into bed with her. And she wanted me out because she wanted to go to sleep. So I would talk to her and talk to her unless she let me in—and then I'd shut up, and she'd be able to go to sleep. . . . I can occasionally remember my father coming in and carrying me out of bed because my sister had made him do it. . . . But I think one of the reasons I usually read late into the night is because, otherwise, I have to be alone in my bed and not sleeping. And yet that's one of the worst things about being with somebody—that you can't do that, you can't be reading until you fall asleep or until you're really tired. My mother had this horrible habit, whenever she was unhappy with my father, of coming into my room. . . . The bathroom light was behind her, and I remember she would be furious . . . she'd come into the room, and I can just see this horrible silhouette, and she'd say, "Fucking bastard . . ." And I'd sit up bolt awake. I forgive her, of course, because I know how unhappy she was with him—I mean, crazy unhappy. So I think in one sense I feel like I had enough time to read, but I was basically lacking in privacy, not knowing when she was going to come in.

ANDREA H., whom I asked: What do you do on the days that you're miserable?

To address the loneliness, there are two or three things that I do: I tend to obsessively read the same books. Now I'm reading these Adam Phillips and Christopher Bollas books. Before I would read— this is when the loneliness was focused on that man and his marriage—I'd read things like *The Age of Innocence*—books I thought described my feelings. Sometimes I play Beethoven, and I play piano sonatas, number one-hundred-ten in particular, Schnabel. Or I play other music, depending. . . . I can't believe I'm revealing all this stuff. Sunday night I play *Into the Woods*. And once in a while I'll call somebody.

BLANCHE W., when asked the same question.

I call a friend. Exercise, go on a bike spree, try to get to work reading and writing. It's usually pretty acute, but not lasting. It's in transition, like when people leave. Sometimes it's also lonely when you leave a party. Or after you give a great talk. Like when you accomplish something and you have people around you—and then you're back by yourself. If things are bad, I sort of need other people to help me not hate myself. I have to just say, though, tonight I did something I've never done before. Which is a great step forward. I lay in my hammock during the sunset. Sometimes when I'm alone it's hard to give myself quiet pleasure. I'm very good about going to dinner by myself, or to the opera or the theater. All of that, by myself. But quiet pleasures at home are hard.

Now, do you want to talk about loneliness when you're with somebody? That's worse.

MARY ANN B.

What do I do when I am lonely by myself at home? You know what? I don't think I've been lonely. I've spent six years living like a nun, and I don't think I've been lonely. There were times when I was longing for a sexual relationship, but they were rare, I have to say. I wasn't unhappy with my prolonged celibate period. And as for lonely, you can be really lonely in a relationship with a man. Which I think is the worst kind of lonely. And I really think I've been poor in money but rich in friendships. I have really close relationships with my women friends. It's been one of the richest parts of my life.

HILLARY P. **The second time we spoke, she was in love and ready to move in with someone.**

There's the worry about what if we break up and someone has to move out and—you know. . . . But we can't stagnate here. And I want to live with him, and he wants to live with me. So it seems the thing to do.

No, I'm not worried about losing solitude and privacy. I actually will get to have more if we're living in a bigger place. And maybe I have more privacy and solitude right now than I want.

MY DREAM HOUSE

Old Fantasy, New Ending.

SARAH O. **lives with two other women.**

I used to watch Mary Tyler Moore. When I was growing up, she was my idol. In fact, when I went to buy an apartment, I wanted a sunken living room like hers. She was single. She stayed single throughout the whole series. The difference is, I just always thought there would be a lot of men out there.

REAH S., **even though she said has no plans to have a child.**

I sort of have a fantasy of myself living in that apartment by myself with a child, but it's sort of fuzzy and vague.

SUSANNAH W., **whose sense of owning anything developed long after she left her parents' house to go to school.**

I dreamed God had a sale. God was a retailer, and he had a big white sale. It was all because I had great sex last night, and afterward Evan was reciting scriptures to me. He's Catholic, and he keeps telling me I'm a heretic. He keeps telling me about church stuff like unnatural motions of the flesh. So I dreamed God had a white sale. Yes, I guess the white was cleansing. I think any shopping is redemptive.

MARTHA H., who talks to her cat and is addicted to hummus.
I had a dream recently about my mother. We went back to the house I grew up in. And it was much smaller and quite tatty—you know, worn at the heels, run down—but my mother didn't see it. I saw it. We went through the whole house . . . even though the people who were living there were not there. We started with the kitchen, and she saw it as a place of achievement, I think—this is where she had her finest hours—and she picked up a tea tray— which was just a little rickety tea tray, a piece of junk, really—and she said, "Oh, here's the tea tray. I used to pretend it was an antique from Aunt Lilly."
And then we went through the other rooms, and they all looked the same—shopworn—and when we got to the living room, she sat down on the sofa and she ripped it, and she got very upset, and she tried to cover up the rip, and I said, "You've got to tell them that you ripped it. You'll feel much better." And she said, "I couldn't possibly, I couldn't possibly." And then she turned to me, and she said, "I assume that when you're in your own house, you're practicing to be a woman." And I said, "What are you talking about? I'm not practicing to be anything. It's my house; it's where I live, and it's who I am." Which I thought was a pretty good response for a dream.

ANTONIA O. now lives in a studio above a garage.
Yes, sometimes I get scared that I'll end up homeless. Well, a little. That's why I'm thinking of taking all the money I've saved and building a small log house from a kit. So that I have something of my own, because my situation is precarious. My father just sold our place, an eighty-six-acre farmland with an old farmhouse on it. He sold the whole thing to my brother-in-law, to guarantee that it will stay there in one piece and be there for everyone, and we're all wel-

come, and we can all have land if we want to build a house. But it's very precarious for me now because that might not work out, and I have to make sure I have a place to go. I wonder about that. I don't own any property. I own a car, and a small word processor. . . .

Well, you can buy these log-cabin kit houses, tiny ones for about $17,000, so you could get a cellar dug and a foundation put in and get the house put up. So I was thinking of that, anyway.

RENNIE N. had given some thought to her dream house.

What I think about is Scotland, or some wonderful rugged place in Great Britain, but not England, and it would have one of these wonderful gardens that I understand are in the west country. It's stone, it's something that's been around for a long time that's sort of fallen down but been pieced together. I imagine the man who goes with the house is Scottish. It's his house and property; the house has been in the family for a long time. But the family doesn't have a lot of money. Sometimes they turn out to be Catholic. And because they were recusants, they had a lot of taxes and that sort of stuff. But this house . . . He will have headed off as a very young man and had to have persevered—you know, had some big crisis and been all over the world, coming to himself, coming to God, all the rest of it. And then he finally decides that he's got to go home, and that he's got to make a go of this house—this falling-down place that's the family property. So he's back there working on that for maybe a year or two. And it's hard. And he's always wanted to marry and have children, and he doesn't see how this is going to happen, but he feels called on to go back and get this house in order. And by the time I show up, he's got the house set up pretty well—for him to live in it, anyway. He's managing to get the farming going. He's learned a lot about innovative agricultural methods in his travels. But the thing that he's really put time into ever since he got back is getting the rose garden back. So I imagine this wonderful man I would meet who would have this wonderful rose garden. That he made. Although again the rose garden would also have been there a long time but then become so overgrown. So he's really a husband, a house-man. He's making the house. He's making the earth fruitful again. What I would have to offer—since I don't have savings—but I could offer my income. I have qualifications that I can carry with me. I couldn't get right into an established position in Scotland, but I could figure out various ways to get an income out of the various things I can do.

The wallpaper? Roses. No, not any particular varieties of roses. Just lots of them, all different kinds. My grandmother loved roses. They were immigrants to the Northwest, but they finally got a duplex with a backyard, and my grandmother had about thirty varieties of roses by the end and a wonderful vegetable garden.

The house is stone. It's almost . . . there's something there that could have been a medieval keep. That stone has been used over and over again. And this man I have in mind, I also almost think he would want ecological, or energy-efficient, ways of doing things. And so he would have this very efficient yet old, full-of-history house. And he would actually be from there. I've never actually felt that I was from anywhere because there are so many generations of immigrants in my family. In every generation that I know of, there was always someone who'd emigrated. This man would be very rooted, but he would also have seen the world.

And the roses . . . I remember there was a place that I'd walk to in New Haven, a rose garden that used to be part of somebody's estate, but it was public, and there was also an herb garden. A couple of summers ago I was traveling in northern Connecticut in July, and it was a wonderful rainy July, and there were lots of rose bushes planted next to rosemary. And in the rain, together, that smell is just incredible. So I imagine this as a very damp, lush place, not hot though, and the scents—the scents are more vivid to me than anything. There are the roses, but also other scents would be there too: lilacs . . .

Now? I live on the second floor of a triplex. In Cambridge. One of those clapboard houses. It's new. It has this porch, and from the second floor you really get a view over on two streets and over toward the park. Oh, yeah, I just love it.

REGINA M. said her apartment is so small that if someone moved in, it would be like they were living inside her head.

I have this one dream that I was in my house and all of a sudden there was a room that I'd never seen before. And it had beautiful high ceilings and gorgeous brickwork and glistening paint and beautiful bookshelves. And there I was. And I thought, *How come I've never seen this room before?* A kind of inviting, larger room.

THE LAST TIME I HAD SEX

*Cybererotica, Vague Dating, and
Psychosexual Bugaboos*

I read in *Web Magazine* recently that the number one term keyed into the Yahoo search engine is "sex," occurring four times more frequently than number two, which is "chat." And, what do you know, "XXX" and "Playboy" are number three and number four.

"Masturbation" alone, when I did a search on Yahoo—not even counting "masturbate" or "masturbating"—yielded twenty-two websites. They range from Bianca's Good Vibration Masturbation Guide to Steps in Overcoming Masturbation, via the Miami University Masturbation Society, Melbourne Wankers, and New York Jacks. Skipping over Masturbation:Injuries and Fatalities and the mysterious Masturbation Mistake, you finally get down to Business and Economy:Companies:Entertainment: Video:Tape Sales:Adult Videos and CD-ROMS:A Little of Everything.

I didn't go much further. It might have been fun to browse, hopping from link to link. I'm not so sure, considering the exasperatingly slow speed of the Internet in these overcrowded times. (Isn't it odd that the lag time between promise and delivery seems to maintain a steadfast ratio, no matter how far we progress?) In any event, for research purposes, Internet sex was out of the question. Already, I found myself experiencing the beginning of one of those Age of Information blowouts that disables your linear thinking functions no matter how compelled you may have been by the idea that originated the process.

"Oh," said my friend, dismissive of my naive frustration, "after a while you hone in on interesting stuff. I myself have gotten heavily into Tantric sex. But it's very hard to do alone. I can't seem to find my own G-spot."

Aside from the stray women's magazine article now and then, I hadn't heard Tantric sex mentioned much since my college days, when it had been characterized for me as intercourse in which the man doesn't ejaculate. There was a point in the '60s at which everyone one knew seemed to be reading *The Kama Sutra* and talking not about dating, but about "paths" to this and that; not about screwing, but about the spiritual; not about penises and vaginas, but about "lingams" and "yonis." It had been a long time since I'd heard any attractive public pet names for genitals, let alone ancient Far Eastern ones.

How big a resurgence could Tantric sex be having in this country? I programmed the Yahoo search engine to look up "Tantra," "Tantric," and "G-spot." But as soon as the *first twenty* matches came up I realized that the Tantric rendezvous ancient rites had acquired a large community of new fans. Here was TantraWorks™, a gigantic interactive Tantra guide and data base. There was Tantra: The Path of Ecstasy featuring a satisfied-looking blond person in an off-the-shoulder dress (old sex, new sex, they're always blond). There were offers for private sessions and "delightful weekend workshops" in places like Palo Alto. "Visualizations" were available at Tantra.org, and under The Church of Tantra's listing, you could find a site called Everything you ever wanted to know about Tantra but didn't know how/who to ask. At that point I gave up. (Well, OK, I did try to peruse Tantra Resources in Croatia but found this site just too impossibly slow. Could it have been *crowded*?)

Mainstream talk about what's happening on the Internet, if not about pornography, minors, and accessibility, is mostly about money. True, cybersex is a growth industry (at the end of the Tantra.org page, there are links to Breath Control, Tibet, and Gift Shop), but that's not the story. The proliferation of communication about sex on the Web—Tantric or otherwise—is far less remarkable for its financial implications than for its revelation of the American hunger for, of all things, talk. Sex is just one of the many neglected subjects being revisited on the Internet. For the first time since the advent of the telephone, there is a medium that enables communication to flow both ways.

Real, engaging dialogue has become so rare that it seems sexy all by itself. In a way, chat itself is cybersex. What else is cybersex? Make up your own definition; everybody else does. Some people use "Internet sex" as a term referring specifically to a chat exchange consciously directed toward a culmination in which one or both (or several) parties reach orgasm (privately, or so one assumes). But it's bigger than that. Exhibitionism and voyeurism (of the audio, visual, and logo variety), gender switching, gender bending, hide-and-seek, flirtation, dirty words (all the more salacious because they are expressed silently)—these add up to some sort of electronic foreplay, that's for sure.

Maybe the question really shouldn't be "What is cybersex?" but, once you're (un)safely away from the Internet again and back in the real world, "What *is* sex?" or "What is sex now?" or "*Where* is sex?" or simply, as one of the women I spoke to put it,"*What* sex?"

We live in a world of inadequate explanations. One thing should be said about sex in the '90s: It's weird. It's mighty weird. But we don't know just how weird it is because in the "regular" agora, the old media such as newspapers, magazines, and television, nobody's talking about *it*. And by "it" I mean something that has to do with pleasure and connection. We talk about illness, death, condoms, marital infidelity, teen-age pregnancies, rape, harassment. What else? Child abuse, pedophiliac pornography, menopause, breast implants, impotence, anything negatively ancillary or frighteningly adjacent, everything but the aspects of sex that could make it seem attractive. Are we talking about these things because we're not talking about sex, or are we talking about these things so as not to talk about sex? We hardly ever talk about sex as *sexy*.

We're left with only sketchy notions of the vaguely good or vaguely bad, (e.g. safe and unsafe). If there is such a thing as erotic specificity, it is the domain of niche marketing. Even to talk of "sex on the Internet" is too broad. Instead, speak of XXX-rated film fans, Tantric sex aficionados, lesbian S&M practitioners who wear red socks and their hair up in curlers and stick to Windows 95 for an operating system. But be specific because the "lovers" of yore are now only one more subcategory, a relatively small niche.

I know what you're thinking: AIDS, AIDS, AIDS, AIDS. That's what we all think of now when we think about sex. AIDS is given as an explanation for everything that's wrong, a metaphor for all that's dark and dangerous, obliterating all the healthful, charming, playful, sweet ardor that unencumbered human beings might have been capable of. Indeed, fear is the only true organizing principle in the sex lives of unmarried Americans.

The fear is not principally a result of personal losses. While so many of us now have friends who have died of AIDS, and it's clear that their disappearance has caused us pain and grief, it does not follow that this should lead to callousness or desexed erotic automatism. The logical consequence of bereavement resolved is not numbness; it is, on the contrary, the permission—the imperative—to have more heart. Yes, we want to protect our friends and our children and ourselves. But must we also protect ourselves from the very idea of desire? It's not that we are too grief stricken or too prudent to allow ourselves desire. It's that we are too grim, too macabre, too paranoid, too often careening between empty and overwhelmed, too confused, and too busy.

That there's less sex is certain; we know because "frequency" and "quantity" of sexual contact are frequent topics of discussion—but detached from any details that might distinguish the act from any other. We hear plenty of facts about sexually active gay men, hemophiliacs, heroin users, and, occasionally, married Americans. Single women, who knows? There's not just less sex in bed, there's less in our conversations, in our interactions, in the air. There's a thinning of the erotic discourse to levels of such low audibility that many people have simply forgotten about it. Sex jokes and double entendres are everywhere, but those divide us from the erotic as surely as news of the latest sexual harassment case—all of these are the detritus of a cultures's sexual feast, not a main course. This is something of a spiritual disaster for the women in their thirties and early forties, who expected their sexual life to be all gold, no dross, as well as for those now in their late forties, fifties, sixties, who earned their psychosexual stripes during the so-called sexual revolution. As for women in their twenties, many of them never imagined a life of sexual freedom. If they came of age in the AIDS era, there was never any question of being free on any level about anything sexual whatsoever, except to live dangerously. The only allusion to enthusiastic intercourse is the much deplored quantity of teenagers insisting on continuing to do it. It's as if they were voting with their bodies, poor teens of the '90s, to let us know that they're still sexually alive. But in our culture, teenage sex exists in the context of the risks of AIDS or unwanted pregnancy, hormonal inevitability, and viral vulnerability—sexual encounter as seen from the lab. If the erotic is a text, our current text is barred by a skull and crossbones. Just as pirates used to bury a corpse near their treasure so that a potential thief, coming upon the skeleton, would get scared off, we see the signs of death everywhere whenever we allow ourselves to feel lust. In brief, let's just say that the happy and free sex once promised to consenting adults seems to have vanished back into myth.

Have you noticed that there is no one we can take seriously speaking up for sex? Women's magazines cover sex perhaps more than anyone, but based on the headlines—which from time immemorial have read something like: HOW TO REALLY PLEASE A MAN!—this coverage is not exactly cutting edge. For the most part, the way women's magazines cover sex now is within columns where therapists answer readers' questions about sex problems.

Well, yes, sure, we have sexual problems. But why is sex connected to illness with such insistence? From fundamentalist homophobes who invoke AIDS as a disease of promiscuity to the Tantric specialists who remind us that we can use sex to heal our spirit, sex is pathologized, medicalized, and coupled with either illness or cure. Flipping through a catalog of medical supplies the other day—sandwiched between sheepskin slippers, Breathe EZ nostril devices, braces that straighten out stooped shoulders, melatonin, fat absorbers, and vitamins—there was one of those "personal massagers," which came in four sizes: 4 inch, 7 inch, 9-1/2 inch, and 12 inch (the 7 inch and 9-1/2 inch massagers are multispeed models). It's as if to even think about sex, we need the excuse of treatment. "It's a sick world," we say to one another, as if we knew what we meant by that beyond the evocation of unfathomable malignancy.

In addition to the sexual healing crowd, pornographers are willing to be pro-sex on the record, but perhaps because of its isolation at one extreme of a continuum whose middle has fallen out of view, pornography seems to become raunchier, cruder, and more comical by the day, as if it has been mutating in the background while our attention has been focused instead on the debate about pornography, which by contrast has become static, rigidly defined, and its resolution hopelessly inaccessible. On the Robyn Bird show at midnight or one in the morning, for instance, young men and women strip down to G-strings or designer-labeled jockey shorts and beyond, and pose and "dance." The women make their breasts jiggle. The men flap their flaccid, decorated penises against their thighs. As a pièce de résistance, both sexes exhibit their rectums. These audio-visual performance pieces are qualifiedly funny (in the way that watching milk shoot out of a classmate's nose in the school cafeteria was), and sometimes actually compelling, but nothing one feels especially tempted to emulate.

The network shows, on the other hand, specialize in the Faux Sexy syndrome, though there is nothing actually racy on network television, except, perhaps for the ads, car commercials in particular—all that phallic action, those fast, powerful cars careening around those voluptuous mountains. At least by comparison.

Lately, single people are popular central characters for these shows, and their affairs or sexual fantasies story-line mainstays. But inevitably, the denouement, the jokes, the double entendres, the very costumes end up serving as a kind of sermon to us all: Think about sex and you'll be ridiculous, you'll be humiliated, you'll be laughable. There is no sensual act, no lewd fantasy, not reduced to a predictable routine buttressed by laugh tracks. With very few exceptions, the viewer winds up being drawn into a kind of antisex pact with the show, because network television assumes—correctly—that we are much more desperate for a laugh than for a lustful frisson. There is no carnal sensation, no set of concupiscent circumstances that have not been diminished, distorted, derided or—most antierotic of all—trivialized.

"Yes! I want a roll in the hay with her again!" the patient says to his therapist (Richard Benjamin) about his ex-wife. This is one of the wittier series. "What should I do?"

"Right now what you're going to do is go, because we're out of time," says the therapist. Big, big laugh track.

In the series that fills the following half hour, a woman says to her friend (Cybill Shepard),

"And if he's a good boy, I'm willing to let him jump up on my bed and do tricks."

"Wait a minute," says the friend. "Last week you were ready to dump him. . . . And now you're ready to do the monkey dance with him?"

And so unfolds the official map of Erotic America: No sex at one end, X-rated/ludicrous at the other. Suppressed or lurid: Take your pick. Unofficially, who knows? The Internet, of course, provides a very big chunk of evidence that there may still *be* an Erotic America. And so does just about any bookstore, where the number of interesting dirty books has been expanding, a good deal of them in the new women's sections. There is also the unbelievable success of the sexy undergarment industry—Victoria's Secret et al.—but I feel we must take the position that if women can go out and buy themselves nice sheets, it's a small and not necessarily sexual step to buying themselves some satiny brassieres.

In spite of all the extra underwear, an astonishing number of women find themselves placing sex on the back burner, most with regret, some with a sort of dazed, dull acceptance, others with incredulity. "It's just going off the map of my consciousness," someone told me. "I've started to take its absence for granted. I had to catch myself suddenly and start paying attention to the way I dress. I was starting to veer on the dowdy." Oddly enough—or not—this was a woman who had provided me in a preceding interview, about three years earlier, with a fairly explicit account of what sounded like an extremely high-quality sex life. But of all the topics I discussed with single women over the course of the last several years, none underwent as dramatic a change as sex. In my first round of interviews, some of the women told me about the last time they had sex as something that had occurred days or weeks or, occasionally, a few months before we spoke. But when I revisited these women several years later, quite a few of them told me that the incident they had originally described to me was still the last time they had had sex. There had been no intervening encounters.

The celibacy phenomenon is the most linear consequence of our sexual confusion. Many women told me that they hadn't intended to become chaste, that it didn't match their image of themselves—they simply hadn't found anyone they wanted to go to bed with. No one, by the way—*no one*—said it was because they couldn't find someone who would want to have sex with them. Perhaps there's a woman alive somewhere who couldn't get *anyone* to have sex with her, but I didn't meet her. True, some women still talk about wishing they could find "someone." But they also said that none of the people they meet tempt them enough to overcome the social and medical obstacles. If you're picky enough—and more and more women are—you can't even find a match for an evening.

In the early to mid-'90s, there was plenty that seemed wrong in women's sexual lives but it could be defined with some specificity. It wasn't enjoyable with this guy, who should have been right. Or it was too enjoyable with that guy, who was certainly wrong. Or it was an interesting decision to make about other women, younger men, married men, threesomes. But by the late '90s I was hearing an increasing number of ritual jokes. Most Frequent Joke number two is the one about vibrators: "Finally, a decent sexual relationship . . ." Most Frequent Joke number one, the winner by a long shot, is the quip that women make when the subject of sex is brought up: *"Wait! It's been so long, I don't know if I can even remember."*

The most popular strategy seems to come down to waiting for better times. Most of the women I spoke with did not to have a special policy, or at least not an organized one, about their sexual activity, just simply wished there was more of it and of a different sort, and they refer to their sexual past with wry nostalgia. One woman put a novel—but probably accurate—twist to this quandary when she said, "It used to be that you would sleep with someone just to get to know them. It really was effective." One woman told me that the part of a relationship with a man that would once have been considered to be a prologue to sex had become "too much trouble, too much work." If you have to play both parts, what's the point? Another said, "It's really an irony that it's become as difficult to find someone to have sex with as to find someone to love, when the one thing that always seemed plentiful was guys to have sex with." Many women say they don't meet anyone they want to have sex with. "Not seriously."

If there were a climate in which women could articulate it, I surmise that what women want is, well, perhaps something not quite so defined, some mode of sexual consciousness that is more polyvalent, offers them more options, suits a wider variety of moods, comprises sex as well as romance, the comfort of closeness as well as the excitement of independence, is more playful. Women in the so-called sexual arena do not particularly want to become the hunters. Many of them do want to have the option of being the lovers—of being allowed to desire rather than act as if merely the object of desire or lack of desire—but that's not the same thing.

Now all the varieties of seduction have been cast aside. We're not interested in these distinctions. We're too focused on the other side of the spectrum. Sexual harassment—that's the buzz phrase that makes our minds keep sliding off of sex. On the one hand there are plenty of Neanderthals still walking around, men who would feel more comfortable clubbing mastodons on the prairies than adjusting to a coed work environment with restraint or grace, and they are well-known (especially after the habits of drill sergeants of the U.S. Army became front page news). On the other hand, the sexual harassment issue hides the general unhappiness and embarrassment at disinhibited women. It's easier to parody the old roles than to understand the new and mysterious nuances of what sex and/or romance might be among men and women liberated of oppressive clichés. Too bad. And so inelegant. It's as if men and women had a chance to dance a tango together, and they got so scared they did a slam dance instead.

The issue of sexual harassment is a sort of cousin to the issue of AIDS: a problem so dreadful in itself that it's impossible to think about it dispassionately, which makes it a perfect hiding place for other dysfunctions, other injustices of man or nature.

Can we really believe that if it weren't for AIDS we would be sexually liberated right now? It wasn't *after* the advent of AIDS, it was in the mid to late '70s that the realm of the erotic became buried in all the chatter about the Intimacy Crisis, the New Sensitive Man, the jokes about quiche. The (perhaps vulgar and empty but nevertheless outwardly generous) promise of sexual fun of the disco era was descending into macabre sludge: snuff films, cocaine-induced impotence, guys who would strangle women in the park with their own bras, genital warts. Otto Kernberg was writing about his patients' inability to fall in love, Ethel Person was writing about the inhibitions of women in an environment of changing roles. Marriage went on the rise, and people suddenly became interested in baby carriage brands. There was already a spiraling panic about sexually transmitted diseases—or STDs as they're known. In 1982, an *Esquire* magazine cover announced "The Death of Sex."

Clearly, before AIDS was fully defined something was definitely amiss, different, changing, wrong. Some pundits complacently pigeonholed the downward turn as the historically necessary reversal from sexual freedom to restraint, the counterbalance of excess. Others took the opportunity to ax the reputation of the women's movement into perhaps irretrievable splinters. Meanwhile the whole Gender Theory Biz was gearing up to become the big cultural analysis machine of the '80s and '90s. All of a sudden, we not only had gender to account for, we also needed theory—either to explicate or obscure it but, in any event, to secure its importance. All of these were among the first indications that the widely anticipated backlash to the '60s, the necessity of "returning" to old "values," had been bypassed, and we had waded into unexpected territory.

Essentially, once the women no longer had sex principally with men they thought they would "end up with," many other givens toppled, and everything else had to change. Everything had to get scary. The women I talked to who were having sex (or those who remembered having had it) told me that there were men they wanted to have sex with and men they wanted to live with or have a family with, and often there was little or no overlap. Could society tolerate such behavior? Apparently not.

It is no longer the male's sexuality that serves as the sole tool to conceptualize what is erotic. As—finally—more or less equal contributors to the collective sexuality, women can be seen to have led us into subtler, more complex, issues—as befits their sexuality, some might point out. And your average American male reaction has been of unbelievable oddness. Men didn't have a clue of how to collaborate. Women, meanwhile, were not prepared for the fact that their hard-earned and still incomplete liberation would have earned them so few privileges in the real world of the senses. Women finally relaxed, and they happened upon their sexual primes in the midst of an expansive sexual doldrums. They were free women, but free to do nothing, free in name only. When it comes to sex, nominal freedom isn't in and of itself all that interesting.

But in the meanwhile, at the other end of the spectrum from the mastodon-clubbing sort, there are young men in their twenties whose own confusion, I am told by their female peers, reflects a colossal version of the Heisenberg effect. "They've been convinced that they are dogs," says a young woman. "It's not that they're afraid of women, it's that they're conditioned to think it's bad to be aggressive." Essentially, as male sexuality was criticized more severely, many of the men stopped playing. Indeed, many women in their forties told me that, having been badgered for sex for many years, they were dismayed to realize that once they decided to be interested in a certain kind of sex, men were no longer ready.

"It used to be a problem," says Abigail Z., a female attorney, thirty-five years old, "that men would have the kind of sex in which they would come and just be pleasing themselves. It seems to me that's what used to happen. But now, I find that I'm not having sex, and I want to, but there *isn't* anybody. The fact is that now I'm the one who would like that kind of sex, and it seems to have vanished."

And then something happens to women's desire. Perhaps because a woman's desire is not biologically necessary, it depends on, and sometimes principally exists as, a reflection of the other's desire. It is delicate, gossamer. A woman's desire may be thought of as filigree—starting out as a thin gold thread, easily broken at the beginning. Men's desire, on the other hand, has variously been compared to fires, rivers, and storms, and irresistible momentum is the metaphor. I once heard a man say that for him the need to have sex was like feeling his pipes fill up with foam. If there is too much foam build-up, said this person, a man will feel as if he will

explode unless he immediately has sex. Leaving aside any com-
ment one might make on the sensitivity, grace, and generosity
toward women of this analogy, looking around me, my guess is that
if someone figured out how to get all the loose, discarded gold
thread that's just lying around these days into skeins, she'd be
rich—especially if someone figured out some industrial cleaning
device for all the piles of gold put away for good, encrusted by left-
over old foam. A woman who has been brutalized by an especially
insensitive, graceless, and selfish foam producer, foam withholder,
or what-have-you will often take a very long time to allow her body
to weave the gossamer of desire once again. If repeatedly torn, it
may be that the production halts entirely, that she ceases even to
desire desire.

When left to their own gender devices, men—it turns out—are
not all foam-production machines. Their metaphors have gotten
more complex—more delicate, as well—leaving the fires, rivers, and
mountains of yore behind. And so the sexual landscape of the 1990s
could be seen as a vast junkyard of broken metaphors, which only
the most utilitarian of us, the most doggedly romantic or sexually
gifted, can still salvage.

Several women told me they were staying in relationships they
found just barely adequate (or not quite) because they do not want
to get to know any number of other people. "I'm too tired," one
woman told me in a very straightforward way. Then there are affairs
that rage with sexual passion for three weeks, only to end abruptly.
"The phone calls stop," says someone who has had this experience
and is unable to say who initiated the beginning of the end. "You
give each other tiny, tiny clues that you need to drift. And if you're
lucky, both people get it." But numerous relationships fit into no
known category and seem to serve no purpose one can imagine. One
woman calls this "vague dating." "For a long time," she said, "I went
out with people I was sort of vaguely attracted to, and I felt that they
were attracted to me. It was kind of like . . . vague dating." She said
she became more and more alienated and feels much better since
she stopped. These oddball connections have in common only the
detritus of all the rewards that should have been reaped from the so-
called sexual revolution. Of course, there are some extremely peculiar relationships that work wonderfully well. Thank God for those.

But very few, very, very few. There's no doubt that it was a good thing to get rid of the crushing old structures, whether or not we find good replacements. The '60s may have been the Anything Goes era, but the '90s are the Everything Went era, and we seem to just be waiting around for the next act.

Of course, my sample is limited. There is probably more than one woman out there having a satisfactory sexual relationship with one or more lovers, happy and pleased and with no complaints. She asks her partners to use condoms, and they do. She likes her body. She likes their bodies. They like her body. The men are well educated in the sensual needs of women. They are not too passive, not too aggressive, not too randy. But they are excited and filled with desire and so is she, and the encounters are intense, blissful, and metaphysically enhancing. She senses that soon she will want to select one of the men with whom to conceive a child, which will be reared with the help of a staff of ten or twenty. I didn't meet this woman, but I am sure she exists somewhere out there. And you will have noted that I have also excluded from this discussion those freshly in love, who are in the throes of one of those magical-seeming states in which every molecule of the self is awake and radiant with lust or love. People in this situation are, as they have been for all time, simply besotted with the wonders of sex with the loved one and/or the lusted-after one, and there is no having of any kind of a reasonable conversation with them about anything.

How far the single woman's sexuality might evolve is anybody's guess. What seemed significant to me was that most women I talked to, including the ones who'd had a number of tedious relationships or those who had had no relationships at all for some time, continued to have an interior erotic life. Almost no one said she had just forgotten about sex all together. Almost no one told me she thought this state of things was permanent—though, no doubt, some of the women fear this will be so. Celibacy after all, does not lead to frigidity. It doesn't preclude a rich and intricate fantasy life, nor does it turn women into prudes. "Women don't need men anymore," say the disgusted traditionalists. Well, they do need men for sex—at least some of the time. "I really would like sexual intercourse, you know. It's one of the ordinary miracles of life," said one woman.

Still, one does hear the occasional clear chime of whimsey and erotic vitality. "Love is good and sex is good and together they're great," one woman said to me. "But good sex without love is still great. I can't help it. I think that."

Perhaps it will all turn around, women occasionally point out to one another. "I heard of two separate women who hadn't had sex in seven years who are now in great affairs," one of my subjects said to me the other day. As an added fillip, she said: "And they didn't even know one another."

But whatever we may go back, or go on, to, we surely will have changed and perhaps profited from this strange transition. And for all that the times seem dreary in some way, there's often a jauntiness that belies the recent ponderousness of male/female interactions.

"Well, you're writing about sex and single women?" said someone I know. "You can do the next chapter on me and just leave ten blank pages."

"Oh," said one of my subjects when I asked her what I suppose was a particularly intrusive question, "I prefer my vibrator to my hand because I don't like to get that involved with myself."

It's just too bad, some might say, that most of the playfulness has to go on in women's heads only. In that sense, cybersex is authentic fin de siècle sex because sex is now mostly in our minds, anyway. By the old standards, a lot of it seems really stupid—viz, the absurdity of the woman who has Tantric sex with herself and has to keep alternating lingam-symbols and yoni-symbols on her own.

True, all the New Age stuff, whether it's about sex or not, is in a way old stuff, inherently reactionary—or eternal, its proponents might say, as relevant to the past as to the future. And it's easy to laugh at Internet sex. It's a *really* cheap date: sex between one part of your mind and another. And that escape from the literal is something both very old and very new in conjunction with sex. This is not to discount the general desire for more literal sex. It just would be nice to have some of both. But at present this is merely something to think about when considering the popularity of, for instance, Tantric sex on the Internet, having to do with age-old desires, longing, lust, tedium, the play of the senses, the fatigue of the spirit, and the perennial searching, no matter how bizarre, for sexual life in inner space. These days, at least, all the rest is anticlimax.

PENISES

Back to lo-tech, starting with the eternal givens.

RENNIE N., of the Scottish dream house and the monastery fantasy.

I think about any man I have anything to do with; I think about what he would be like naked with his penis hanging out. Before you get into bed, you sort of know it's there because you can feel it, but when I actually am with a man and I see it, I'm always sort of amazed. It's amazing what they will do.

SOPHIE K., 61, widowed a year and a half ago.

I really so much want a penis, and not a faceless one. This is a battle I'm fighting with myself because I could go to sleep with somebody walking down the street, and I could go to sleep with one of my students, and I don't, because I'm frightened of myself.

ABIGAIL Z., who just painted her house pink.

I don't care what size it is; in fact, really big ones can be uncomfortable for me, especially with anal sex, but I do care about the color. It has to be nice and pink and healthy looking, not purply and sickly looking. Or, you know, sort of brownish and not pink and fluffy.

HILLARY P. invokes a classic consideration.

My biggest fear is that I'm going to run across a guy with a gargantuan dick, and I'm not going to know what to do. Because my sister told me a story once when I was twelve or thirteen, and she was like, "It was like *this!*"

ELIZABETH P., 23 years old.

Lately I've become so much more attracted to women that I can no longer really relate to the fascination of a penis or how intriguing it is. I'm much more into women and their sexual organs than a man's. But if I were going to fantasize about a penis, it would definitely be big and black.

NINA L., 28 years old.
They can have a little nose and a big penis. . . .

REAH S., 35 years old.
Erections, let's not even talk about it. I'm sick of that problem.

JUDITH R., 62 years old.
I have an oral fixation toward them.

I'M TRYING TO REMEMBER

*In recalling the last time they had sex, women
didn't usually talk about the act itself.*

ROSA M., 37, in Tucson, the one who was so thrilled to get a
mortgage and have a home.
Yes, it happens that I do remember. It was only last weekend. It
was Lilly's dad. His name is Tom. But if I tell you that it was only
last week, it's going to tip the scale in the wrong direction. Because
in the last few years . . . well, I went for a whole year with no sex.
And then the next year only one or two times, and maybe one of the
times was with him. And then for the next couple of years, maybe
three or four times in the whole year. So the fact that I was with him
just last weekend is unusual.
No, I didn't actually marry him. He wanted to get married desperately, and in a way that was kind of fun. But I just wouldn't
do it because it was sick, our relationship was sick—and very violent. But I still love having sex with him. That's the one thing
that was OK, that was always good. In fact, he' s the only one
that I like to have sex with. Basically, that is our relationship
now. Well, I guess it has two sides to it. It has that side, and then
it has the side where about every six months he checks in with
Lilly.
But now, it's picking up a little bit, and I've had sex a couple of
times with men other than Tom. It's been okay for Lilly, but, actually, not all that great for me sexually. Maybe my standards are too
high. It's like, if you're going to have sex with somebody that you're

not having a relationship with and you're not in love with them, then the actual sexual act has to be pretty good because what else are they there for?

Yes, Tom and I still have sex, even though he's now married to someone else. Except for Lilly, it's really the only part of our relationship that survived.

AMELIA J., in her late 40s, the researcher and feminist activist.
I'm trying to remember! You wanted sex with someone else, right? Not masturbation? Well, OK, I have been having a strange sort of connection for some time with someone in my field we can call John. He lives in another country, and he comes here occasionally for conferences.

Oh, now it's beginning to come back to me—because I start thinking about his kiss, which I actually really like . . . I like the feel of his moustache and the sort of wet of his lips. Not of his lips but of the inside of the lip and the teeth, and I was always surprised that I liked it. I don't know why I was surprised. I went to meet him at his hotel, and I had to wait for a little while downstairs, so I was sort of anxious. . . . Then he came down, and we went out in the street to get something to eat, and then he just grabbed me and kissed me, and I was surprised because he usually isn't so impulsive. . . . We got into a taxi, and we went to eat at this Caribbean place, and I sort of didn't want to go there because it's too fattening, but he always likes trying different American restaurants. And right he was. It was the perfect place.

I must have suggested that we go home afterward because he never suggests it. And I can't remember if we took a taxi or we walked. One time when we took a taxi, the driver said, "Will that be two stops?" And it was just shocking because he could tell how non-coupled we were and not in a good way, not healthily independent lives. But anyway. . . .

So then I guess we came back here and . . . I can't remember the transition. I can't get us into bed. But it's not hard to come up with the generic scene because he's pretty predictable, which I don't really mind if it's the only sex I get all year. . . . There's kissing, and it's very good kissing, but probably by this time we're acting like we're an old married couple, so probably we go into the bedroom and take off our clothes. Probably there was listening to some music and maybe more bourbon.

And then, what the hell happens, let me see. . . . Groping for genitals. He likes his nipples pinched. A lot. And I'm trying to remember if this was the time he was really good to my vagina. I mean, he's not bad. But there was one time that he was extremely erotic with it. So it was very, very hot.

And so if this is the time when he did come . . . it really takes a while but that's really wonderful. Then I can really have long orgasms. And I think that when he comes he has to go into some fantasy in himself for it to happen. But I sort of don't mind, you know? That feels separate in a very good way. On the other hand, as I say, it is only annually.

Do I expect to see him again? Don't know. I did. But the last time he was in town, something was off. He just wasn't treating me well in a relational way. You know what I mean? And I just decided the sex wasn't worth it.

SUSANNAH W., late 40s, the one with the world's worst boyfriend.

He was competitive, intellectually. Midway through the relationship he started saying things like, "Oh, you're much smarter than I am." Now, you'd think that might be flattering, but knowing the person I was living with, the ante had been upped. He had to prove himself. To be worthier than me.

And he constantly complained about sex. After the first night we made love—this he claims to have forgotten—I remember waking up the morning after, and he said something to me like, "Well, that really wasn't very great, was it?" And I remember taking a long deep breath. I mean, what am I going to say at this moment? So I came up with something pretty standard, like "Well, we'll get to know each other better. And we'll please each other more." Which is totally insane for me to have said, anyway, and I think it was the setup, the microcosm of the years we spent together.

Nothing had gone wrong in particular, just unfamiliarity. The desire was there, the energy, the eroticism was there; I think he felt that he didn't please me enough. He's very competitive. But he also didn't understand that I didn't have the expectation that sex should be very good all the time. Sex was a lot of different things to me I guess. There's something I really don't understand.

Maybe there was something he wanted that I didn't give him. I don't know because that was something that we never talked about. In that very first moment, sex became a problem between us. And it wasn't . . . I feel like laughing, I don't know why, I guess it makes me nervous to think about this.

So I spent ten years with him, and sex was a problem, and it wasn't until afterward that I understood that what he basically wanted was a blow-up doll. He wanted someone to make him feel better. But he didn't want to give me anything I wanted. Even, let's just say, a very simple thing like kissing. I knew from the very beginning that we kissed in different ways and I found his way of kissing . . . well, I don't know. Unpleasant. At first I thought it's just the throes of passion. He was a lip sucker. I know, it's funny. He would first suck the upper lip and then the lower lip and then alternate. Now, I'm a tongue person. He's not a tongue person. I would feel like I was in free fall when I was kissing him. There was nothing there. It was like, no *there* there, no mouth there. . . . And then after I met his mother, the horrible thought occurred to me that what he's really doing is nursing while he's making love with me. So in my view, sex for him had something to do with a lapse in his mother-child connection. He could never really please his mother, in fact, and therefore he could never please me. Well, so no wonder he had trouble getting an erection. But that was never really talked about. I couldn't even allow myself to completely think about it.

And so our last night was like our first night. Everything was wrong, but we didn't talk about it.

REAH S. points out that when things go wrong, sex is often the first casualty.

After my chemo, he was impotent. And then that was it. It never happened again for us.

ADELE U., who recently discovered that her boyfriend was actually living with someone else in Washington.

So the last sex I had was with him. A night of bad sex when he must have already been thinking "How can I get rid of her?"

ANDREA H., 48, one of the social workers.

The person who will always be the last person I had sex with is Anthony. The others, in a way, don't matter. I met him on a blind date, and that was it. I was twenty-one at the time. It was my first big romance. Or my first big sexual romance. And we stayed in touch for years. We had an affair for years, even when he got married, when I wasn't with anyone. Or when I was having difficulties with someone.

I remember the last time I had sex with him because I was desperately unhappy about breaking up with Jordan. And Anthony had called me, and he wanted to come over, and I said, "All right." I was feeling really sad and awful, and he came in and said how thin I looked—I had lost a ton of weight; I was a rail because I was so unhappy—and how worried he was. He was very sweet. And then I said I didn't want to sleep with him because I was too upset about Jordan. Which was really the first time that I had said I didn't want to sleep with him. There was never a time when I didn't want to sleep with him in the entire relationship.

He was upset and he left, and I was upset that he had left. And then about fifteen minutes later the doorbell rang, and it was Anthony. . . . He came back up to the apartment and said that he had cared about me too much, and he had known me too long and loved me too long to leave just because I wouldn't sleep with him. Then he sat down and put his arms around me. And then we did. Then I did want to. And that was that.

We knew each other so well, and we were so suited for each other, that all the kind of pain of the breakup with Jordan sort of got released, but then—it's really embarrassing to say this—at the moment when you have an orgasm and you cry. . . . You know, it was this kind of flood of tears. And he was very tender. He was a wonderful lover, he really was. He was wonderful that way. No ego involved at all; I don't know why. Or maybe it was my naïveté, and it was just a different kind of ego.

Why did it end? His wife had a second child, and I think, I *think*, he actually felt guilty. Although I'm not sure.

ABIGAIL Z., the architect who likes pink, finds the trade-offs harder as time goes on.

What worries me now is that I'm attracted to much younger men. When I see them walking down the street, I want them!

I got this guy to come to my house to build the closets and now the bookshelves, and he is . . . gorgeous. I'm gonna fix him up with someone else! He's too dumb; he is *too* dumb. I don't want to fuck him, but this is the first time I've *not* fucked someone in that situation.

It's the nonsex aspects that turn me off. There's just not enough there. As much as I want to have sex, it's not enough.

What would I do if I wanted to have sex tonight? Even though it seems pathetic to me . . . I would masturbate. . . . I wouldn't have this guy come over, I wouldn't go to a bar and pick someone up. I'd organize the closet.

It's strange because I used to be so promiscuous. I can't believe how much I've changed. I don' t know when it started to change. Maybe around ten years ago. I remember that winter I went to a sale to buy a Christmas present and ran into the wife of a friend. I knew her through her husband. And we were standing there talking, and I realized I had slept with him. And that in fact I had slept with everybody! Everybody I run into, all the men I know . . .

I really don't do that anymore. . . . Because I think it probably was, frankly, my way of resisting intimacy, both by seducing them and because of the desire—whatever that means. But also there was a desire to have nonintimate sex, and maybe—I think, but I don't know—to destroy the possibility of ever getting intimate. Even though I like to have sex, and I wish I were having sex, I can't keep doing that, I just can't. I haven't ended up where I wanted to, with respect to men and such. Even though I like my life a lot, that's just not something I want to keep doing.

Yes, I do enjoy the sex. I love it. But there are so many reasons. And there's AIDS. We have to get into that, don't we? AIDS is number one. And number two, pretty recently I had an experience of harassment on the phone with somebody I had worked with and slept with but just had not been involved with. . . . I haven't had sex since. I mean, anger. . . . It made me so angry that this thing happened to me with someone who had control over my job—a really disgusting, perverting experience with somebody who just sickened me—and I wasn't in a position to sacrifice everything to bring him to justice. It was also a case of: Were they going to believe me, or were they going to believe him, and how far was I going to push it? If all these men in the firm that I work for were going to think, "Oh, God, she's just making trouble."

And so that did turn me off to sex. I wouldn't have said that at the time, but when I think back on what was happening in my life . . . And there was a man I was sleeping with, and I just stopped. We didn't break up. That's another thing that's happened to me, in my recent connections with men. I wouldn't call them relationships. Maybe they were dates, whatever that is, but they seem to evanesce, then just stop. By mutual assent, somehow. I might see them again and think, *Oh, God, there's another person I slept with.*

CONDOMS

Condoms have become the artifacts of sex in the '90s as they never were in the '50s. Prophylaxis is is no longer just a means of protection, it's become an indicator of character.

MARTHA H., corner office.

How does AIDS interact with my life? Not at all. You mean how do I conduct myself? Oh, yes, I do ask someone I'm sleeping with to put on a condom. But it isn't as if there are people I avoid specifically because of the fear of AIDS. There are so many other reasons to avoid other people. No, I mean, seriously, if you thought somebody had AIDS, wouldn't there be other reasons to put him on the no list?

BLANCHE W., who says she sometimes finds herself just wanting to be kissed.

There are condoms in the drawer. I should probably replace them because they're about three years old by now.

I don't know. I think some have an expiration date. But I have attention deficit disorder, so I find them everywhere in the house. I keep finding some behind the cosmetics or in a travel bag—from when I was optimistic.

In other words, if in fact I ever got to the point of needing a condom with a man, it would take probably half an hour to find one.

GINGER G. discovered that her lover occasionally visited prostitutes.

And even in the dream we used condoms, but he put me at risk, and I was throwing a fit and screaming at him.

ABIGAIL Z., who really enjoyed playing fast and loose through her twenties now finds she no longer has a sense of what a normal affair would feel like.

Well, I was with someone in a high-risk group of people, and I stopped that. And then I was with a man who was much younger, about ten years, and we didn't use condoms. . . . I can't remember how many years ago it was—six or something—and I got tested, and when I was HIV negative, I said, "You're either going to have to get tested, too, or you have to start using condoms." And he wouldn't do either, and we broke up.

ALICIA D., in her early 20s, takes condoms for granted, but she lives in a kind of psychological wilderness that makes anything having to do with men unsafe, including sex.

My senior class was the first class for which they put the condom on the banana. Afterward, we talked about it all the time. There were these church steps by the high school that we would always go and smoke cigarettes on, and I remember once we had all just come back from a French trip, and one girl was hysterical because she met some guy there and gave him a blow job and she was terrified he'd given her AIDS. We knew everyone and knew all the gossip, so we'd go, "Oh, if he slept with her, he has AIDS, and then if he slept with *her*, she has AIDS. . . ." We were a very incestuous group.

So we knew about AIDS, but it didn't affect us so much. I don't think the smell of AIDS was in the air so much. I don't believe that people were together because they were afraid to be promiscuous. And at Oberlin, everyone was hyper-AIDS aware. I've never since been in such a condom-respectful sexual community. Even if you were having a one-night stand, it was very AIDS protocol-y. No matter what, everybody used a condom, but in terms of one-night stands, it never stopped anyone. You'd go to the disco, and there was a party bowl full of condoms. There were condoms everywhere. I think it changed the way people had sex, but it didn't change who they had it with or how many people they had it with. It's just that as soon as your clothes got off, the condom was on.

But with some of the sleazebags I've been with . . . You're there, and it's the first time, and you don't want to act like a jerk, and the condom won't go on until they think they're going to come. They use it more like a prophylactic. . . . They put it in you, and they take it out and put the condom on. Or they say, "Are you on the pill?" You could say, "Well it has nothing to do with that if it's for AIDS." But you wouldn't say that.

MARY ANN B., the one whose two sons recently went away to college, takes the same safe-sex behavior for granted but has no trouble observing the rules. It's what's beyond those increasingly established conventions that confuse her.

Yeah, AIDS is a moot point right now. AIDS is not at all a deterrent for me to go out there and have sexual relationships because I deal with it, I deal with the condom issue. The big issue that affects the sexual relationship is that I don't meet men in my line of work. The other big deterrent is I hardly ever feel like getting to know somebody new and I'm not eager to have sex with someone I don't know.

JOCELYN H., who works as a nurse, and has a relationship that she has kept going but somewhat at bay for the last fifteen years.

AIDS disturbs me only in the sense that I do have some gay friends. I lost one who I was very close with, a coworker of mine. It's hard. My son's guidance counselor, we're very close and he's gay, and we go out to lunch. Thank God he's well and healthy, and I hope he's around for a long time. But it's scary.

It does have an impact on my relationships with men, and that's one of the reasons I'm with this one guy. That's one of the reasons why I'm not eager to have relationships. I think anything new would have to be a very abstentious relationship. And it does scare me because, as I say, people are not up front with you, and it scares me because I'd like to live a long time.

VIBRATORS AND VEGETABLES

The principle problem with masturbation appears
to be making room in the schedule

LINDA P., 31, near Seattle, sighs and shakes her head.

I'd much rather masturbate than go to bed with an idiot. I don't need this shit. I don't need to sleep with a man like it was that last time. I said to him, "That last time I slept with you it just made me feel terrible, and I'd rather masturbate than do that."

I think of my ex-boyfriend when I masturbate, I must admit. Of course, that may be less because he was so sexy and more because he was away so much of the time that most of the sex I had was with myself even when I was with him. But normally I get home so late, even if I think of it I don't have time.

Yes, I have one. In the locked drawer in my bedroom are vibrators and lubricants and drugs.

GINGER G. in San Francisco, landscaper.

It's more of a turn-on to be with someone else. And I have more fun with someone else, but only if it's someone I want to be with. I can't stand having sex just to have sex. I've done that a couple of times and end up not liking it afterward.

Yeah. I usually do it regularly every week, but there're times when I just don't. I'm busy and I just don't have time for it.

REGINA M., who had the dream about finding a big new room in her house.

Oh, such long periods of chastity!

I do have a relationship with a vibrator though, a Panasonic, a rather large phallic-looking thing, which I'm terribly grateful for. Yes, I did buy it myself. It was very hard. I mean, I couldn't just go and get one anywhere near where I live. I bought it at Bigelow's pharmacy, a long time ago. I also use it for my stiff back.

The thought of it breaking down hadn't occurred to me. Oh, God, that would be terrifying. I'm always telling people, "Oh, go buy a vibrator." I prefer my vibrator to my hand because I don't like to get that involved with myself. It's almost more important than a house. A sort of commitment to self-sufficiency.

Sometimes the plug doesn't work with the extension cord, and that's upsetting. And then sometimes I've left it on my bedside table and I'm terribly afraid that there will be a burglary and the police will come and find it. I once used a carrot, but that was in my youth—my earlier youth, before I had the vibrator.

REAH S. asked me to be particularly sure not to identify her in a way that would be recognizable to her office colleagues.

Sometimes carrots. Sometimes cucumbers. Sometimes bananas. And sometimes shabbas candles. But that was when I was younger. The problem with vegetables is that they have all these quirks in their shape. I'm thinking of carrots, for instance—you'd have to use the end you cut the greens off of. But even then it's hard to get it smooth. Yes, I would try to use a grater. Cucumbers are usually too big. It was sort of frustrating. Bananas are better. But then there's the problem of the point. Oh, you keep the peel on, otherwise it would get all mushy. And with the cucumber, the dilemma is, do you take off the waxed green stuff? But then it sort of feels as if it could start falling apart. I would sometimes put condoms on them because of the pesticide. I actually tried once using one of those soaps that gets rid of the pesticides. But then I decided that since I had condoms anyway that I wasn't using for anything else, I might as well use them for that. I tried hairbrush handles. I think I graduated from shabbas candles.

Water. I realized I could lie under the faucet and move in relation to the stream of water, so I'd be getting fucked by the stream of water. . . . Now I have an elaborate Jacuzzi. The jets are great, and they all have their own personalities. Even when they're on maximum, they all have different strengths. And the position you can be in is different So some are best when they're behind you, and some are best when you're flat out against them with your pelvis tilted forward, and others are best with your legs up. Oh, but then I'd get panicked that I was doing something to harm myself. Like, maybe the water pressure was too hard and could it burst my uterus by forcing its way in. And, of course, there's no one you could ask these things.

A friend of mine used to use coke bottles and got really nervous that they would break. I kept telling her it wasn't a good idea.

It never occurred to me that I could use fingers until a guy did that.

The worst thing though about masturbating is that you can't kiss.

None of these methods was very good. It wasn't until much later when a vibrator got added to the whole equation that it got good. Until then I didn't understand it. I just didn't get it.

Yes, I did keep my vibrator while I was married. I got to a point with Harry where we would use it sometimes because I could come with it. I didn't like doing that, though. Why not? A combination of this feeling of cheating and also because it was all part of sex when I was married, that it was all about getting off. It was all about him getting off. He had this theory that he had to release toxins. So I started feeling like a toxic waste dump.

NINA L. was embarrassed but emphatic.

I've only discovered recently that sometimes I can put my arm around myself and feel comforted. I very rarely do. Like, I'm a lousy lover to myself. I don't do to myself what I do when I'm with somebody. Then it suddenly dawns on me, *Well, why am I doing this? I could treat myself better than this.* I think all this might be because what ever remaining sex life I might have might be just with me, so I better get better at exploring it or something.

No, it's *less* sad. It seems like a positive thing that I find myself touching a part of my body with the pleasure of both touching and being touched. I'm liking the touch. I'm liking myself as opposed to just getting off. I think masturbating always felt like the latter to me. Lately I've been taking much more pleasure in the way my body feels—in the morning, stretching, and just being in my body, feeling it. . . . And that doesn't feel sad at all. That feels great. I think what feels sad is the numerous years wasted.

OTHER WOMEN

At least some erotic feelings about other women were
pretty much universal.

REAH S. again.

Affairs with women? Wish I could. It would make life easier. There are so many nice women and so few nice men now. But I'm really very decidedly heterosexual. . . .

Oh, yes, women are often in my masturbation fantasies. I check out women all the time, always have.

ABIGAIL Z., in her late 30s.

I think about other women. I look at them in the gym. I have really powerful erotic feelings, but I've never been in a situation when I could act on it. I think I'm of too old a generation. I always wondered about why I never did and how much culture was a factor, because certainly my emotional life is and always has been with females.

I don't know about now. I certainly would be open to it.

SOPHIE K., 61 years old.

I find women very erotically attractive—so much so that when I was younger and in analysis, this came up as a significant issue because it was culturally such a taboo in those days, and it worried me a lot about my own sexual orientation and preferences. I'm much more comfortable with that feeling now, but they never appear in my fantasies.

Many more women I know are now going both ways, and I've been approached, but I'm not able to. Because somehow I think it would be like I failed. . . . Because I want a man, and I think it would be like a second choice. Out of a kind of sexual desperation.

ELIZABETH P., 23 years old.

I was traveling and I met an older man who was thirty-five, and he had an eighteen-year-old lover, a woman. I stayed with them for almost two weeks. We had this wonderful affair. . . .

What did I like best? I would say maybe having the man behind me. I'm lying on my side and have the man inside me and the woman is facing me, touching me or whatever. She's in my presence, as opposed to the man being out of sight, out of mind. I feel him but I don't really see him.

GINNY O., 29, has had sex in a threesome a number of times.

It was the man I really wanted, but the woman made it more

exciting. In most triangles, I am definitely the new party, the new entertainment. Often they were a couple, so I was the novel thing. Once there was a woman, one in particular, who really wanted me, and that's the first time that ever happened. It was incredibly exciting, but the only reason I could do it was because the man was there. So it made it OK, but the whole part with *her*, I'll never forget it. That whole feeling of being with her and what that felt like and somehow making it OK in my mind . . . But the other thing that happens, too, is when you're with a couple, it's a lot about power. It seems as though it's *all* about power.

CELIBACY

None of the women I talked to planned to become abstinent. Nearly everyone assumes it is temporary.

PAM A. Not everyone remembers sex with longing and regret.

I was with someone who wanted to have sex all the time. The worse the relationship was . . . I mean, he was unrelenting. And, in fact, for me, it's been a great relief not to have to have sex when I don't want to. . . . It's that simple. And at the end of the marriage, I just wanted to sleep.

ANTONIA O., who's been thinking of building a house from a kit.

I think I'm not a very sexual person. Not long ago I thought, maybe I should read a book on androgyny. I think I'm feminine but only slightly. My sexual feelings are slight. . . . I've never met anyone I've wanted to marry, I have no lesbian feelings, I'm not . . . I don't wish for intimacy, physical intimacy, with any women I've met and been friends with, and I like men, and I have crushes on men, but I've never had a really raging sexual desire that would tie me up with boyfriend after boyfriend. So I'm not on that end of the scale. I'm really close to neutral.

I think it's just biology, though. I think I've always been this way. So when other people were really derailed or bent out of shape with sexual desire, I wasn't. I've had chances. I think it's just in me. I don't know why—how much of it is psychological, how much of it is character. . . .

CALLIE S. tells me the last time she had sex was not long after her ten-year-old was born.

There's a kind of an unhappy realization that creeps forward. At some point in your life, you have to start wondering, *Gee whiz, have I gotten laid for the last time in my whole life?!* You understand, I'm not walking around horny and waiting to get laid. It's just the sheer fact of the matter that it's a possibility. Sometimes it's hard to believe. Somebody's been playing with the script! Somebody skipped pages here!

LUCY L., a midwesterner, broke up a few months ago with someone she describes as an absolute creep she couldn't fall out of love with. She works as a bartender and tells me her customers hit on her all the time. She used to go home with someone every once in a while, but she hasn't in a long time.

If you've felt a certain way about someone, and you haven't managed to allow anybody else to hook you, you're still sort of possessed. I think people's bodies get possessed. You know, like there are frozen moments. You come out of one relationship, and you're not able . . . I'd go out with people and really get close to them, and they'd get close to me, and then just about the time for any regular thing to happen, instead, the creepy guy I'd been involved with was between us. I'd go to bed with someone, and I'd see him instead—not imagining myself having sex with him instead of the person I was with, but just seeing him there in my mind. Finally I stopped. I couldn't even move.

EILEEN Y., in her 70s. There are still the classic dramas to contend with, too.

I had just seen him again for the first time since our affair, and we probably felt the same way, and then six months later he was killed. That . . . made it hard to go on after that, to have other affairs. I was actually in another affair when he was killed, and it really was difficult after that. I felt that that was the most important relationship for me, and it sounds like a very old-fashioned, romantic story, but I think it's not that simple.

No, I didn't ever again, no, which I rather regret. But then, I'm choosy. Nobody came along whom I wanted to have an affair with. . . . I probably stopped falling in love in the same way.

CAMILLE O.'s dilemma is more typically contemporary.

I want to have sex. I think about it all the time. It's just that there isn't anyone I want to sleep with. There are plenty of people I could go to bed with, but it just started to seem less and less appealing. I don't know what I'm going to do, to tell you the truth.

THE LAY OF THE LAND

Everyone agrees on one thing: It's weird.

GINNY O., 29, whose marriage lasted three months.

So wait, is there any information on the incredible amount of time and patience required to masturbate on Prozac?

SOPHIE K. said her acquaintances expected her to be a long-suffering widow.

I was married for thirty-six years, so I have spent most of my life going to bed every night with one man. Now I meet people whose spouses have died, or a lot of men who are divorced or married but unhappy, and many of the men, they have medical problems. . . . So there's a lot of mutual masturbation. But what they want most is intimacy. Sex is not necessarily the issue. What they say is, "So you go to bed with this one, with that one, but you're bored or you're still alone." And what they want is intimacy that takes away the loneliness. For people my age, sex alone is unsatisfying.

SUSANNAH W. says that hardly anyone she knows seems to even have sex, anymore.

I don't even want to have desire because then the next step is, who would I have sex with? I do try sometimes. But I'm so bored. I'm just incredibly bored.

I just broke up with someone. I had sex with this guy three times, and it went progressively downhill. The third night he came over, he did something and he held me, and I thought I was choking, and it reminded me of being with Joe. So shortly after that I broke up with him.

The thing is that at our age, the guys we sleep with are imprinted with their last relationship. No matter how much they say they hated sex with their wives, if they get divorced after twenty years, that's the sex they're imprinted with—the sex they had for twenty years. And it's bad sex . . . or at least incompatible sex. But they still really just want to do it that one way.

And that prevents them from really being intimate. Or from being sexually creative. Men claim they're all looking for something unique, but really they just want white bread. And women aren't like that.

So, it's back to the vibrator.

ABIGAIL Z. catches herself speaking in a very loud voice and continues at a volume just above whispering.

And why? Why am I going to the gym? No one is going to see me naked except the other women in the locker room. I mean, who cares. There's no one left in the entire city of Boston I would want to sleep with. I've run out! Should I move?

And also I have found, as I get older and the men get older, that the men just aren't into sex so much. It used to be a problem that they would have the kind of sex in which they would come and just be pleasing themselves. It seems to me that's what used to happen. But now, I find that I'm not having sex and I want to, but there *isn't* anybody. The fact is that now I'm the one who would like that kind of sex, and it seems to have vanished. I'm sure I haven't had sex for at least six months, though I can't pinpoint a date. But it seems to me that in the last couple of years before I stopped, the men were much more interested in *my* having a good time, in pleasing me, and I don't know why. Maybe they're finally more insecure.

MEGAN L., 26. This was her answer to my question about the last time she had sex.

And at this point we're living in such a chaste age. It's been ten years [sic] of living with AIDS. I would never think of sleeping around without using a condom. Although, as a perversion—a very nihilistic one—it becomes interesting, the whole idea of sleeping with someone without a condom, the risk of getting AIDS. I think underneath most conversations of safety and protection and people reminding one another to stay protected there lies a tiny bit of that. But I think living with that . . . I know it's a cliché, but it does really weigh on how you behave with men. This turn of the century I think we're living in a framed Victorian age. I'm considering putting on white gloves to go down into the subway. And I wouldn't mind the sort of blandness and unexciting sexuality. . . . I wouldn't mind going the whole way and dressing up and wearing pearls to dinner and going through the full rituals of chastity. It's interesting to see how far repression can go, the whole priesthood of it. You don't even see kissing in the movies anymore. At some point in the '80s some cultural critic said there's too much kissing in movies. And then a couple of years later then there just wasn't any more. The only stuff about sex is about fidelity and marriage and love and religion and so forth and so on, and there's absolutely no action in any of the scenes. People talk dirtier. The language is raunchier, but that's it.

THE LAST OF THE RED HOT MINUTES

I asked, "Can you tell me about the last time you had great sex?"

REAH S., 35, the attorney.

It was on the sand. It was in Mexico, an archaeologist. I'm not kidding. It was kind of unbelievable, actually. It was just great. It was very hot, and we were sweating, and we were behind a great boulder that cast a shadow so that the sand was a little bit cooler there. My behind was on a backpack. He's called me a couple of times, but I don't know if I should call him. I mean, maybe it would ruin it. Maybe if he came here, I couldn't stand him, you know?

But I catch myself daydreaming about it. I'm sitting there in my office and thinking, *God, on the sand. . . .*

VALENTINE J. tells me about "when I was your age."

That's right, it's breaking the rules that we're all scared of. But when I was first married, it used to be so much more. . . .

You know, I remember in those days they had the afternoon tea, where there was music, and one day I met a friend accidentally, on Fifty-seventh Street. I was coming home, and he lived in the neighborhood. He said, "We've been friends for so many years. What's the harm if we go over to, let's say, the Essex House?" It was early afternoon, and he said to me, "Have you got time?" And I said, "Of course." He was a friend. And we went into the Essex House, we had champagne, we danced, it was a wonderful afternoon. And I never told my husband about it.

BLANCHE W., who wishes she'd get kissed more.

I can have casual sex more than I used to. Like the time I slept with the Tibetan lama, just so I could have sex with a lama. It was in a palace in Mysore. That was like an old style '60s thing that I would have done then, but, actually, I had never had sex with a lama. So, I figured I should do it. Of course, I was also psychotic at the time, and I thought that maybe he had some sort of fast track on wisdom and peace. I mean, he's supposed to have a fast track on wisdom and peace, but I thought if I slept with him, he'd give me some of that. I was at that time just getting over someone. It was this grand room with a canopied double bed. It was the main front room in the center of the second floor of the palace. In front of all these rooms there was a sort of porch-hallway kind of thing, and since I was in the center, I was right where all the carriages would come in, so I was like queen for a day.

He had burgundy robes—because he was a Tibetan lama—and underneath he had a T-shirt that had some kind of American something on it. It was sort of funny, that whole way you can't get away from American commercial imperialism. He did have an absolutely wonderful body that looked like those Cambodian Buddhists. He knew how to use condoms. I had some. And there was a ceiling fan.

Now, you don't have to print this, but it was boring. Why? Well, for one thing it was the afternoon, I wasn't drunk, I wasn't stoned. It was more like a self-conscious adventure than a reckless adventure, you know?

ROSA M., 37, she who scraped together money for her mortgage, needed help maintaining the fairly rundown house.

Well, I just couldn't keep up with the repairs so everything was slightly in shambles. And then I met Harry, who was working at someone else's house in the neighborhood, and he said he would help me out, too, with some of the things that needed painting and repairing and so forth. And he did. And we got caught up more or less with the things that just had to be done, but he'd come over every once in a while for the odds and ends. And I could see he liked me and that he was looking at me, you know—I could tell he liked me.

So one night I said to him, "I don't want to live with anyone or marry anyone right now, but I wish I had a lover, someone who would come over every few weeks and spend the night with me and then who would leave again in the morning. Someone who would be my lover and my friend. I don't think it would be too tough a job." He was smiling. So then I said, "I am screening applicants now for this job. Do you want to interview?"

EROS EVOLVES

Now and then there is something new under the sun.

MARY ANN B.'s kids recently went away to college.

After I ended my last live-in relationship six years ago, I really wasn't interested in dating. Plus, I wasn't sure how. I worked at home, and I worked with mostly women, and actually my life had assumed a kind of order and calm that was kind of compelling. I had no motivation to change that. Romance and sex came *at* me.

It's probably no coincidence that it happened when my nest emptied because I think having children around was a great barrier to sex, especially adolescent children. If we remember how hard it is to take partners home to meet our parents, it's a hundred times more difficult to take partners home to meet your grown children because they're much more interfering and critical. Plus I find that a critical adolescent son can unglue a man faster than anything else. If you want to take anybody with an inflated ego and see who he is without it, just take him home to meet the teenagers.

So then. . . . When did this happen? I guess after that long period of chastity, it happened first with Zack, who did turn out to be a kind of manipulator and a womanizer, but I'll say this: it did get me interested in sex again. So then once I decided I was interested it did open me up to the possibilities, and they are certainly there. Am I sure they're there? Yeah, I am.

Actually, you know what, it didn't take long at all to stop worrying about my body. I got around that by not undressing until I'd said, "Look, I have really small breasts. If that's a problem . . ." I didn't want to think about it. I wanted it to be full-throttle into lust. Once I got into bed, I decided not to worry about it. Maybe I worried for six years, but once I had an actual partner where the question came up, it went away. And it really did help to say something beforehand. No, I never did it when I was a kid—I would never have announced what I would have worried about as a kid. But now I just find it nice to get the worries out of the way before we get the clothes off. First we have to discuss sexually transmitted diseases; then I have to talk about my breast size.

How does it occur? Very naturally. We explore who's been tested and why and what and determine whether and how sex will proceed, usually with a condom. With Zack, once it was clear that neither of us had any reason to believe we might have a sexually transmitted disease, we started having unprotected sex. But then when I moved to Oregon, because we were about to begin a long distance relationship—and it is clear that he is a very attractive man—I said, "I don't have to hear about everything, but if you have sex with someone else, you should use a condom with them if we are going to continue having unprotected sex. And then I don't have to know." These are not exclusive relationships, or at least I don't make that assumption. And with M. we use condoms.

I know I'm not the first person you'd think of as having this incredibly active sex life. And I have to say my major appeal has never been the body; I have never had a great body. So maybe that's the benefit at this age, because I have never thought of myself as having a great body. But sex has never been better. Yeah, better than married sex. Or better even than young sex. Or sex that is trying to be fabulous forever. I guess at this age you realize that nothing is fabulous forever.

Yes, this is the first time I've been seeing more than one person at a time. I've always been a serial monogamist, and all my friends say, "Oh, my God, you're in a typical guy relationship—you have a lover in every city."

REAH S. spoke about seeing two men.

They do know about each other, yes, and that hasn't been a problem. Is one better in bed than the other? Yeah. One is better in bed than the other, but the other is better at conversation. And it's a new sexual relationship, so maybe it will improve. Things get better all the time.

ANNETTE F., 34, divorced two years ago, who had described herself as "off the grid."

Since we talked, I've gotten involved with someone. I'm having a wild affair, believe it or not! Sex is unbelievably great! How can it be anything but great after two years! That's right, yes, that's where I'm calling from! I'm here, at his house! He's Chinese. He's a Chinese molecular physicist. I've realized you have to tap markets outside the U.S. Chinese men are just wonderfully affectionate and demonstrative; they're not afraid to show emotion, they're not afraid to be romantic.

I know, I'm amazed! First time in two years! I've been having a really good time. I'm shocked! I really am just in bliss. I adore him. Unfortunately, he is here with a special team of Chinese scientists, and he has to go back to Shanghai in a couple of years. . . . But then I don't know if it will last that long. No, I don't expect it to lead to marriage. He's a confirmed bachelor. And I have children. I mean, he may decide he wants to have children someday, but he's thirty-six, and he's never been married.

No, it's not always that easy for me because I'm not so great at being cool and dispassionate, I get emotionally involved. But in a way it's working out nicely because I have the children, whom I have to be with most days—my ex-husband has them for two days on the weekend—and he has his work. He's very ambitious, and he works like a dog; there's no such thing as quitting time for him, so the way it works so far is we have the weekend together, we have a couple of days a week, and I go home and I'm with the children all week. So far it's really been ideal. I mean I've only been seeing him for two weeks, but so far it's just absolutely wonderful. I'm having such a great time. I just feel really lucky. It's just been ideal. It may all end in tears, but right now I'm really enjoying myself.

PHILLIPA C., 50, recently—completely by accident, she points out—fell in love (with someone she met at an AA meeting).

That's nothing new for her. What's new is that she has no intention of turning this into Marriage #4.

It can happen. I just can't believe it, but it really can happen. For the last five years I've been totally in the mother thing. I'm a mother . . . my children . . . I'm chaste, and so on and so on. Yes, of course being chaste is part of it because that's what a mother is: She's someone who turns off her sex. That's how I can roll around on the bed with Bobby, even now that he's five and a full-fledged boy. A mother turns off her sex so she can have sexy physical contact with her children.

I think about this man all the time. It's thrilling, but I don't know if it's good for me. I think about him fifty minutes out of every hour. But he's so delicious. It's so delicious. But I've stopped working. I've stopped sleeping. The only good thing is I've stopped eating. I can't concentrate on anything. I feel out of control. I feel schizophrenic. I can't do this to my kids.

The fact is that it's wonderful and thrilling, but it's a disaster in terms of my life. I mean, what am I going to do? What do I want out of this? I don't want a ménage with him and the kids, and I certainly don't want to get married, and I'm too old to have another child. What would be great is if it could be just three hours a week, but it's not like that. And yet, what else can it be?

AMELIA J.'s dream.

I was on my porch and even though it was autumn in the northeast, there were passion flowers and bananas on the trees, and my peculiar cousin was there, and she explained to me that the bananas weren't edible.

Oh, Lord, edible-oedipal . . . As I say this to you, meanings become clearer. . . .

VALENTINE'S ROMANCE .

It all depends on if you know and if you want to.

VALENTINE J., 94 years old, asked at first to show her age as 85 instead, "because it doesn't sound as old," but then relented. We speak across a table covered with a wonderful cloth. "Quaker lace," she tells me. Leaning over, I happened to notice that she is wearing knockout shoes, with fairly high heels. Very, very elegant legs and feet. Her hair and makeup are perfect. She only recently changed the color.

. . . getting back to my friend. I call him my lover. Well, yes, I guess he is a younger man, he's in his mid-eighties now. The way I met him was on a trip. Two friends and I were going on a trip to the Berkshires, a five-day music festival. These are friends I've had for years. And we went down to the bus stop on Thirty-third Street, and there was this man standing in front of me. And the driver said to him, "Are you traveling alone?" and the man said, "Yes." I had never seen the man before in my life. But me, I've got sort of a flip tongue sometimes, and I pushed forward and said, "Oh, how much nicer would it be to travel with a young chick?"

And he turned around, and if looks could kill. . . . Well, we got on the bus, and there were three men and about forty women. I said to my friends, "Stay away from this guy." But he was sitting behind us on the bus, and he heard us talking about living on the East Side because one of these friends lived on the East Side, and he was born on the East Side. So he leaned over the seat and said, "Well, gee, I was born on the East Side," and then we became a foursome. The next day one of the women said that she was inviting him into the room to have a drink. This friend of mine, who is also widowed— they were both widows—she attached herself to him. He's a very good-looking man, very well dressed, handsome, very fine man. And whenever we got on the bus, she had a seat for him; whenever we stopped for lunch, she had a seat for him. I didn't pay any attention to it. We went to Chesterwood, to French's, the sculptor's place. It was a beautiful, beautiful trip. My friend is very hip on classical music. He sings, he's a classical singer. Just a beautiful trip. So the last day came, and the bus took us back to Thirty-third Street. He lived in Queens, and she lived in Brooklyn. He had hired a car to pick him up. So he took her home. And I took my suitcase and I called a cab and I went home. I opened the door and the telephone is ringing. It was this man. He said, "What are you doing tomorrow?" "Tomorrow, I'm going to the beauty parlor," I said. He said, "Well, I'm on vacation. I'd like to come over." I said, "Well, not tomorrow."

He said, "I've looked at you for five days with your hair the way it is; I can look at you for six."

So I told her that I had met him by accident in Bloomingdale's. And we went for lunch, she and I. And she said, "Did you make a date?" and I said, "Yes." And that was it.

So we started going out together, and, of course, like all men he would have liked to get in my bed. Which is normal. You go out with a person, you start to care about a person, he was very fine. And I said, "Not until I'm ready." I said, "I'm not ready yet. I may never be, but this is too soon for me." Actually we went together for six months before I felt comfortable. And we've been going together since.

My lover is quite different from my husband. Except in a lot of ways he's like my husband was. He's stubborn, like my husband was. In a lot of ways. When he sleeps . . . he likes the covers not to be tight. And his foot sticks out of the bed. My husband slept that way, too.

Yes, it's the funniest thing. The first time I saw it I said, "My God . . . I've got to tell you something very funny." I said to him, "You're like my husband's clone."

Oh, no. That didn't upset him. No. And we've really had a wonderful relationship all these years. He always reminds me . . . I said to him one day, I said, "The day I decide that you're going to share my bed, you're going to take me out to dinner to a very fine restaurant, and then you'll book a suite in the hotel." He said, "Okay." Then he told me later that he got home and thought, *She must be a nut!! This woman's got five beds in her apartment! Five beds, there's no one here, and she wants me to take her a hotel!*

No, in the end, he didn't take me to a hotel. No. But by that time it was just one of those things, a spur of the moment.

I think he must be retired for about eight or nine years. He still lives in Queens. You'll have to change some of this in your book. Yes, put him in another borough.

He comes in on Saturday, and he goes home Monday morning. Now he takes a limo. He says it's too difficult for him to travel by subway. Because by subway you have to change two, three trains, and you have to wait. He used to come in by subway. It was no problem.

Well, yes. It is a romantic story. He's a romantic. He said to me

the other day, "Do you miss me?" I said, "Well I miss your flowers."
He always walks in with flowers, every Saturday. He's a natural
romantic.

Am I a romantic? Yes and no.

But it's true I would never consider living with him. No way. I
think any woman who reaches a mature age is very foolish to do
something like that. If the woman has to marry for financial security, I can understand it. But if you don't need any financial help,
we're too set in our ways. I always say, "You know, we would've been
divorced in six months." You know, your husband did things around
the house, you did things around the house. One likes to leave the
closet door open, another likes the closet door shut, and constant
twenty-four-hour-a-day living wears away the romance of it.

At the beginning he said to me, "If you insist on marriage in order
for our relationship to go forward, I will get married." I said, "Oh,
boy, you're safe." And he said, "Is it for financial reasons?" I said,
"No. If I were to get married, I would see to it that my children get
the money their father left." I said, "I wouldn't get married under
any circumstances." And I had a happy marriage. But why should I
give up my independence? Why should I give up my privacy?

When I open my door, it's a wonderful feeling. And I don't have
to prepare any meals for anybody, I do as I please. And I've done
more for him than I think a lot of women do who are married.
'Cause he was ill a few times in the hospital, and I went every day
to see him just as though he were my husband. Because I have that
feeling for him. He would do the same for me, no question.

And he *loves* to travel. The drop of a hat. Call him tonight, if
there's something special, he's ready, he's all packed and ready to go.
We've traveled a lot in Europe. We travel under separate names, but
we share one room. I travel under my own name, I feel that's the
way I want to travel. How is it sharing a room? I have no problem
with him. It's a change, you're only going someplace for two weeks,
you're going on a cruise. I mean, it isn't like living with him. Yes, it's
like a little honeymoon, but after so many years of marriage I don't
want anyone underfoot.

Yes, in many ways it's a better sex life than what I had with my
husband. My husband was not as experienced as this man. Let me
see. . . . I would say my husband was a virgin when we got married.

I was, too. Well, of course, those days most everybody was. But this man has been with a lot of women. A *lot* of women. He was married a couple of times. He had a good marriage, but she was sick. They were only married for two years. The other one he married before he went into the service, and he was thirty-two. When he came home, he was thirty-five, she was a different woman, he was a different man. But I can picture him, he must have been a very good lover. A very good lover and an active lover. And he still is.

Yes. There's no reason *not* to have an active sex life. No, nothing very acrobatic. In your eighties there are certain things you can't do. . . . No. But if you have a man—I happen to have a man who's a lover—there are ways—I'm talking very frankly to you—that a man can satisfy a woman. It all depends if you know and if you want to.

NO CAT FOOD, THANK YOU

The Poor Old Thing vs.
the Ball Buster

"What I wonder is what all these single women will be like in old age," one of my friends was recently musing. "One thing's for sure: Women who have had the guts and initiative to remain independent now certainly aren't suddenly going to become passive in old age and sit around in SROs eating cat food out of cans."

Yet old age has become one of the more bizarre arenas of subrosa ideological struggle in the recent past, in which an unseemly battle is waged between those who maintain a perception of old unmarried women as witch-victims and those who don't. At the moment, no one would deny that the very concept of old age has a serious PR problem. The economics of aging are determined by image, and older individuals in America have become increasingly invisible, even while the *topic* of old age is invoked with increasing frequency. Every once in a while social security or Medicare is "saved" by congress, but that's about the extent of the homage paid to our older citizens.

We know that a huge cohort will soon be hitting retirement age, with perhaps catastrophic results. And of that cohort, an unprecedented number will be women with little or no family. What climate they will be spending their last years in is unimaginable. Clearly, they are not in a position to do very much to buttress themselves against the trials of the future. One category in which single women do appallingly bad is saving for retirement, and by many estimates, older women are going to be in really bad shape. According to a 1993 Merrill Lynch study, fewer than half of women approaching retirement age had begun saving for their retirement before they turned forty (compared to 67 percent for men). "There are ways in which I guess I still think a man is going to rescue me," the single mother of three children recently said to me. "I haven't saved anything. I'm waiting for the man in shining armor." She pulls down a high salary, but finds it evaporates on children's expenses. Some women who haven't even thought of starting to save perhaps simply *have* nothing to save. Others may be gambling that they will be walking down the street and find a wad of money wrapped in a rag. They may as well hope for this since the possibility of being supported by their pensions from work or Social Security is almost as far-fetched. Of course, retirement will be much shorter than might have been expected since, even if things go moderately well with Social Security, many of us will in any event not be able to retire until at least seventy-five.

Nevertheless, the generation coming up has already altered many other American traditions, and old age will certainly not be an exception. Perhaps we are already feeling the effect of the shifts, for while frightening past images of what "old" means to women continue to wash nightmarishly into the margins of consciousness, several promising new models are already emerging. Of these new, improved visions of aging, two are especially popular: On the one hand, the "Elegiac option"; on the other, the "Hey, Buster option"— the lyrical vs. the proclamatory, the flute vs. the trombone, the lily vs. the giant sequoia, the old pussycat vs. the gray panther, the Poor Old Thing vs. the Ball Buster.

Superficially, the Elegiac option appears more in line with the traditionally feminine, the kind of romantic, pretty acceptance of approaching death one used to expect of bosomy lady poets and other incipient poor old things. But far from resigning themselves to devolving, the proponents of the contemporary Elegiac mode celebrate their last years, albeit with wistful elegance. "Oh, so you think that it's a terrible fate to be a woman growing old? We will turn away from the pragmatic everyday world and toward the ineffable beauty of the sensual world. We love the earth and all its cycles, and the earth loves us in all of ours. We will embrace our future and even the thought of its conclusion." When published in magazines, essays expressing this kind of thinking are often illustrated with soft, blurry landscapes, overcast skies, subdued autumn colors. The mood is invariably referred to as "bittersweet."

On the contrary, the hard-won, aggressive (phallic, some would say), Hey Buster option dispenses with the details, as in: "Hey, buster, you don't know what you're talking about if you think you're going to count me out. I'm in the game, steadier than ever. So watch out." In magazine articles, this position is almost invariably accompanied by a sharply focused black-and-white photograph of women in power suits seated around a glass or pale-wood table of corporate design. The women and/or the conversation are nearly always referred to as "highly energized."

The Elegiac seems cornier, yet is in its way as radical a departure, a remarkable evolution in women's thinking as to what ought to be seen as beautiful. This is a crucial exploration because losing a connection to beauty is one of the purest sources of pain in a woman's aging. And the truth is that aging—more than dying—seems to be the trouble. It is aging that seems the most charged, laden with dread—not just the aging that robs a woman of the sexual primacy that belongs to the nubile, but also the aging that leads to despair.

"What is it that you are most afraid will happen?" I asked one of my subjects, a woman who just hit fifty and had not yet come to terms with this event, whether Elegiac or not.

"A total loss of dignity," she said. "Other people's eyes. I fear the look on people's faces when they see how hopeless I am. The eyes of people who know me. You know, like my children."

But enhanced by the Elegiac vision, aging can be seen to be precious, suffused with loss yet also filled with a profound sense of the meaning of each moment, not damaged but adorned by reflection and transcendent acceptance. The Elegiac idea is to package the sense of loss with a reveling in one's last sunsets. The trick here is to make sure, while engaging in gracefully sad acceptance of the subtly beautiful later years, not to fall into a deep depression.

Entering the ring from the opposite corner, however, the increasingly powerful counterpoint to the Elegiac promotes the energetic rehabilitation of postmenopausal women from their former status as poor old things and into a new role as powerful citizens. In a recent *New York Times* op-ed piece entitled "Mighty Menopause," this point of view is perfectly exemplified by Helen Fisher, author of *The Anatomy of Love: The Natural History of Monogamy, Adultery, and*

Divorce. Her theory is that as women pass menopause, their hormonal balance shifts toward testosterone and they therefore become better able to engage in forward motion of every kind, including the desire for power. Fisher also points out that "as middle-aged women display more assertiveness, middle-aged men display less of it. Men's testosterone levels peak when they're in their 20s; then the amount of the hormone steadily declines. This helps explain why men become more nurturing as they age." Well, not all men, but let's not be sticklers. And the issue of testosterone is a brand new one, replete with controversies yet to come. But in the end, the content doesn't matter all that much. The message that has been clearly and powerfully lobbed into the discourse has already been expressed by the time you have read the headline: Pairing the two words "Mighty" and "Menopause" in thirty-point type on the op-ed page of the *New York Times* is more convincing than any number of hormonal analyses of men and women in middle age.

It wasn't so long ago that the word "menopause" all by itself was invoked mostly with the utmost discretion. And then all of a sudden, there was Gail Sheehy publishing *The Silent Passage*, a *fashionable* book about the dreadful subject. The floodgates were opened. There was a sort of menopause-fest in all the women's magazines and radio and TV talk shows. It became clear: menopause sells. Soon, the erstwhile hidden change of life was casually brought up in conversation, and discussions of hot flashes, flushes, and estrogen replacement became acceptable dinner-table fare. And, paradoxically, once they had taken to airing their symptoms, these women became somehow more . . . dignified.

Recently, the very notion that menopausal women are depressed has been challenged. In a paper entitled "Depression and the Empty Nest," published in the journal *Sex Roles*, Lenore Radloff found that women are no more depressed at menopause that at other times. Researchers tell us that, on the contrary, there is a great deal of evidence that women past menopause experience greater satisfaction and self-confidence

In any event, menopausal women did not restrict themselves to purchasing literature describing their condition, and what will hasten the older single woman's promotion to the rank of full citizen in the culture is not estrogen replacement (though that may help) but buying power. Just a few years ago, the *New York Times*, in its media column, reported that an advertising campaign for *Ladies Home Journal* has been launched with the goal of changing advertisers' perception of women of the ages thirty to forty-nine—about forty million of them. This was news: women in their forties are described as experimental, discerning, and well funded: the "biggest, smartest, most powerful" group ever. And these are women who consume the products: Indeed, market surveys show that women thirty to forty-nine are twice as likely to be heavy users of cosmetics than younger women. A *Ladies' Home Journal* editor is quoted as saying that "people who would've turned their noses up at us five years ago, now see us."

Just a few years later, by a strange coincidence, my local Barnes and Noble features twenty-four books on menopause, sandwiched between PMS and fertility—quite an interesting lineup. Indeed, much of the research we have been hearing of adds the pleasantly credible aura of science to a perspective that has been gaining ground on its own, which is that women have many more options than had been supposed, in every domain. This makes reaching fifty look very different. Fifty can never look like fifty used to look when it is sported by a collection of strong women who have managed to survive the hard years, those who have managed to shatter the glass ceiling or at least keep pressing against it, those who are holding steady at the helm of their jobs as politicians, theoreticians, social scientists, firefighters, truck drivers, and so on, those who survived bad marriages (or bad endings of good marriages) or life long solitude in fighting shape, those who see no reason whatsoever to become rejects just because they no longer menstruate.

And yet when I asked women, "What is your fantasy of old age?" I received an almost unending melody of groans, moans, and *oys*. Most women said they didn't have a clue, though many feared the worst. Many of the women I interviewed confided a fantasy that they (at least intermittently) considered to be realistic: ending up as a bag woman. True, married women I know have the same fantasy. But single women seem to utter this thought with especially authentic dread. Perhaps they are particularly susceptible to the sting of the old stereotypes, and these seem to ring with special resonance in an unforgiving economy, when the homeless and forgotten are all around us. But, also, the idea of homelessness—true homeless-ness—stands as a metaphor for all that is unknown and frightening, for spiritual rootlessness as well an incapacity to feel at home in one's own expectations.

An ominous blankness laden with denial is a framework for the future that is hardly exclusive to single women. But the improvised nature of single womanhood adds a dollop of extra anxiety to this late-twentieth-century malady—or lends an advantage, depending on your point of view. Whereas a proper nineteenth century person, if asked, would have reeled off the program for several decades to come, an average citizen of the late twentieth century will only answer, "Old age? I don't even know where I'll be five years from now." Among the various uncertainties of our highly ambiguous era, none is as bizarre and even impossible to grasp as our drifting con-cept of what's to come. There are glimpses, glimmers of contradic-tory futures, but none has any more credibility than the others.

Even the women who actually are in the phase of life we call old age have problems thinking five years ahead and seemed to be vaguely hoping for the best and/or fearing the worst—which is pret-ty much what women thirty, forty, and fifty years younger are saying. "It's impossible to think about," said one woman in her fifties, "because we don't look like what we thought we were going to look like." And appearance, as we know, matters. It's the bedeviling result of some amazing cocktail comprising women's advances, higher life expectancy, better nutrition, medical progress, hormone replace-ment, lower birth rate, dwindling religious beliefs. When did a woman of fifty cease to have much of a relationship to the quin-quagenarians of the past? Hard to place exactly, but certainly it was well established by the time of Gloria Steinem's notorious retort in May 1984, when told by a journalist on her birthday that she didn't look fifty: "This is what fifty looks like." I remember staring at an accompanying photo of Steinem waving (or hailing) and thinking, *Great arms.*

Better equipped to confront old age physically, mentally, and financially than our predecessors, many of us are nonetheless more afraid than they were. The lack of certitudes (even bad ones we could resign ourselves to) invites every anxiety to march in so that we stop being able to envision or plan anything. "An image of the future is something I can't get except in terms of panic," said one woman. "And I can't plan because the planning is opposite to what I have in my head." What is it that we can't plan for? What is it that we fear, exactly? Well, what everyone else fears: poverty, pain, humiliation. But combining women, helplessness, solitude, and death yields an especially potent bouquet of horrors, and we have been primed to be receptive to it.

We all know the lonely old unmarried women of the past, and they are among our most tragic shared fantasies. There's Dickens's great, ghostly Miss Haversham, living half-crazed in her big, spooky mansion, in the company of cobwebs, tarnished candelabrum, and all the macabre debris of a former splendor, scaring the bejeezus out of our Pip. And there's Hepzibah—"Our miserable old Hepzibah," as Hawthorne put it. He then copiously apologized to the reader for introducing "not a young and lovely woman, nor even the stately remains of beauty, storm-shattered by affliction—but a gaunt, sallow, rusty-jointed maiden, in a long-waisted gown, and with the strange horror of a turban on her head!"

And then there's Nabokov's brilliantly diabolical invention, "the Haze woman" (widowed, but she could only exist in the age of divorcées), blowsy, clinging, hungry hearted, pathetically concupiscent, headed fast to nowhere, whom Humbert runs into and then actually marries, but only to remain in voyeuristic proximity to her young daughter, Lolita.

But these characters at least benefit from the wonderful brush strokes of their talented creators. In real life, we are only one degree of separation away from the rawest form of anxiety and archaic fears, images fit for romance fiction, bad films, comedy sketches, and common parlance—even though they have been around for several hundred years: the desiccated spinster; the silly widow; the bitter witch; the ever-suffering woman who sacrificed her life for others; the empty woman who has lived on just to preserve her dead husband's memory and status; the grotesque old coquette with her gigolos in tow; the poignant former belle who once turned down many offers and who is now each day more devastated, given to tippling in her increasingly shabby digs; the ridiculous romance novelist as well as her lonely, sentimental, foolish, neurasthenic, chocolate-eating reader. And these are followed by the parade of the swooning, the masculine, the oversexed, the hot-and-bothered, the frenzied, the numb, the frustrated, the inhibited, the too respectable, the disreputable, the unacceptable, the crazy, the desperate, the thrown over, the useless, or the merely useful.

And this sort of woman gets the death she deserves, the end befitting the purposeful, dark and childish fairy tale she seems to serve. It's not just a bad way to die, it's the result of a curse, a vision of death replete with archaic terrors of the specter of the old woman dying alone in a miserable hovel, perhaps of starvation, with no one to care for her or even realize that she died. She's buried in a pauper's grave, presuming there still are such things, while maybe somewhere in the lovely, swaying cornfields of Kansas, her sisters' grandchildren and their children frolic joyfully.

When the horror-movie mists clear, one does wonder why this specter business so tenaciously adheres to the old single-woman image, as opposed to the fantasies regarding old married people, which seem to shift according to cultural and economic conditions and even individuals. These dreadful visions seem especially absurd since most people end up single—and everyone dies. There's no chance of noting any of the glitches in logic, however, since this is one of these things that almost everyone is thinking but no one says aloud. Whatever it is that can't be said, this is certainly another instance in which the threat of punishment is commensurate with the perceived threat of the socio-cultural transgression.

Hundreds of thousands of elderly women are living now without the benefit of either the Elegiac or the Hey Buster option, in conditions that are at best spiritually impoverished, at worst—and all too common—inhumane and debased. There are exceptions, of course, a significant number of them. And it is precisely that increasing number of resolutely independent female citizens of a certain age that augurs change to come. Therefore, image—which translates into motivation or the lack of it, then into governmental support or the lack of it, and into popular acceptance or the lack of it—is crucial.

As silly as they may sometimes seem, the new constructs for aging offer a hope of escape. Whether it is the Elegiac or the Mighty Menopause faction that prevails at any one time, single women have a great deal to gain. And, taken together, they provide a dialectic that can provide both a spiritual dimension (the beautiful autumn prism) and a way to stay in the world (the Mighty, Mighty stance). If you combine them, you're covered. But either one can be put to good use when taken up by women with sufficient initiative to act on them, women who are eloquent enough for others to identify with. And it is this identification that provides the possibility for a self-image women can live with.

To many women, the choices seem mighty skimpy. *The Elegiac? Is that the best you can do for us? So passive. So sad. The Mighty Menopause option? So undignified. So unsexy. You don't mean Hey Buster, you mean Ball Buster.* While we are not prepared for a feminine ideal that's not sexy, or at least trying to be sexy, a woman who tries to preserve her sexual attractiveness beyond its natural life is precisely the sort that soon seems pathetic. And a woman who puts a quick end to the waning of desirability by taking herself out of the running is not only seen as desexualized, but also defeminized and, as a matter of course, an honorary enemy of romance in general and men in particular.

Will there be a point when women become willing to publicly acknowledge the insulting nature of these stereotypes by joining together in indicating more realistic, complex, and palatable visions of aging? It seems obvious that their political and economic future will depend upon this. If there is anything more palatable ahead, if older women are to be released from the realm of the invisible, it is surely by veering toward action. And then it is clearly a matter of collective action, which is to say political activism.

There have always been strong, influential women who promoted the idea of an important role in the society for the post-childbearing female. Margaret Mead wrote about this as early as 1949, in *Male and Female: A Study of the Sexes in a Changing World.* Her thinking about menopause, for instance, was that its function was to curtail the period in which women are subject to the hazards of childbearing, thus prolonging their lives. The experience of women would thereby be made available to the group, providing them with the benefits of a genuine social function. She speculates:

We may ask to what evolutionary use we can put this great body of healthy post-menopausal women, free from a narrowing and engrossing attention to young children. . . . Faced, as her ancient predecessors may have been, with a period of survival beyond her mate, she may find a special role and special usefulness in working for a larger body of mankind. A few preliminary case studies suggest that the knowledge that she will have no children, or no more children, also releases in a woman a kind of wholehearted commitment to art or science or religion, which was previously bound, unavailable, waiting for the specific motherhood that did not come.

Mead's arguments still seem pertinent, referring us to battles not yet won. Economically, politically, and professionally, age discrimination hits older women with more vengeance than any other group, even younger women. Since, even now, women only make 75 percent of what men make for equivalent work, women who are now retired not only had significantly lower earnings, even if they worked, but have much lower pensions.

But despite the economic realities, the day-to-day lives of older women are evolving so quickly for the middle class that change for all seems inevitable. Consider, for instance, that even with much less money, elderly single women do better than elderly single men. WHAT? ME MARRY? WIDOWS SAY NO, you may recall, is what the headline read. They live longer and better and more independently. Their adaptation is often phenomenal.

Like Steinem, most women do not look the way they thought they would at fifty—and up. But the difference begins decades earlier, in the rescrambling of age-appropriate functions. Women in their late forties are giving birth or adopting. Women in their fifties can be grandmothers or new mothers or, having opted not to be mothers, choose to stay free of any obligations having to do with children at all. Ultimately, of course, there is the profound reality of aging: the deterioration of the body. But so many women seem to be absolutely insane on the subject of the visible signs of their bodies' aging that it really doesn't seem fair to stake a claim for any particular advantage or disadvantage for single women.

What to do, then, with the sexuality of a woman with more years? Here's Helen Gurley Brown in 1962, in *Sex and the Single Girl*:

Men *adore* young women, it's true, it's true! . . . their honeyed skins, muscle secured firmly to the bone . . . even their innocence. . . . But you have some *new* things going for you which the children haven't—your total chic, poise, professional standing, warmth, true friendliness born of compassion, charm, and experience. Don't underestimate these qualities—they are surprisingly attractive to men. Nevertheless, as long as youth is made a cult of in our country I don't think you can afford *not* to try to *look* as young as you can. . . . What is so tsk-tsk-tsk about it?

Brown then informs us, however, that it's easier for a man to "bring off" this attractiveness late in life. While "the lined craggy look" that becomes a man's features in later years is *not* so entrancing on a woman, women—with effort—can achieve late-life attractiveness. And she then neatly segues to the idea that:

bodies are easier than faces to keep taut and lovely (although the face machine I mentioned in Chapter 11 can do a lot of good), you should be making the maximum effort with *them*. After all, your body is what you make love with!

Almost forty years later, we still haven't reconciled our contradictions about older women as sexual beings. One day we read in Newsday that feminist writer and activist Jane O'Reilly proudly proclaims that, at fifty-seven, she's "'fat, aging, and libido-less—and finally liberated'" and announcing that there is a life after sex. But the next, we hear Jane Fonda quoted as saying that "if you have to build a butt, it might as well be high and hard."

"What really gets me is the age thing," I was recently told by a very attractive, very successful woman in her late forties. "How come," she asked rhetorically, "when men turn forty or fifty or whatever, they get to get new puppies, like Donald Trump?"

"I don't know," I answered, wondering if there was any reason whatsoever why we would *want* to acquire Donald Trump's mating habits.

"I know my body is still fuckable," she said. "I may not look good every single day—that's what aging is about—but I know I'm still very hot."

On the other hand, another woman, no less attractive, confided in me shortly after her fiftieth birthday, "I feel as if something terrible were over." So perhaps not all women feel desperate to retain their sexual attractiveness in the original form.

Will medical advances continue at the same pace and will we be allowed to take advantage of them? How will the relationships between children and parents have evolved? Where will we live? These are some of the questions that would be posed if we weren't too dismayed, bewildered, and busy to consider them. Will many of us end up living with friends or with siblings? Will there be institutional collective housing, and will it be centralized and run by the U.S. government (Muzak piped in everywhere, K-rations)? Or by the cities (Los Angeles—new age; Detroit—soul; New York—dilapidated and ironic; suburbs—no personality but nice trees)?

Or will there still be privately run "old-age homes"? (Will we still call it "old age?") If so, will they be overcrowded, grim, barren, and dangerous, or will they be humane, pleasant, and filled with amenities? One's fear regarding the latter option is having to listen to piped in Beatles music over, over, over, and over again. "Yesterday, all my troubles were so far away. . . ." Or perhaps a medley of more obscure items: "They call me Mellow Yellow. . . ." "Young girl, get out of my mind. . . ." On the other hand, perhaps it would be a better use of one's thinking energy to feel compassion for those who will come later and will be stuck with Metallica. It's not an idle query, for who can predict how pop culture will manifest itself then? And will it still pop for us, or will we feel as neglected and irrelevant as many of the American elderly do now?

There are hints of possible good fortune to come I realized as older—*much* older—women talked with me about traveling, the pleasures of friendship, the complications of octo- and even nonagenarian romantic relationships. Of all the women I spoke with about being uncoupled, they expressed the fewest regrets. Men have come and gone, died, been good, been bad, early ambitions have been fulfilled or not, illusions have been mostly lost. It seems to even out. "We all end up in the same place," said one elderly woman.

The confusion about aging is perhaps no deeper for unmarried women. Once we get past the years in which our biological role is still ahead of us, the future's only predictable resolution is death. And even death, without the markers of religion to guide us before and after, has become more unfathomable than ever.

Cheerfulness and the proponents of the *new* death (the New Age new death—thought through, lived as an experience in and of itself, and probably videotaped) are no match against the terror of the unfathomable end, the fear that one sometimes forgets but never stops experiencing, that which all but the most mystical among us are doomed to experience when we really allow ourselves to drift down in the place where we contemplate death and are obliged to see how we feel stuck with so many regrets that we can't look back, so much fear that we can't look forward. Or so we think for now.

"I've had a good life," says one of my subjects, close to ninety. Her hands tremble quite a bit, but she's wearing nail polish. She's carefully attired, and she has lipstick on, albeit a bit smeared. Her cane leans against the back of her chair. Her arthritis is so painful that she cannot walk unassisted. But it's plain that she is telling the truth as she confidently understands it. "I've had a good life," she repeats. "I've been loved."

That is the traditional last curtain of a fine show—historically, the best we can do. But for many, many of us now, a good, well-lived life can no longer be defined by how much love has come one's way. No chance of summing up that easily. And for the younger women, there may be no categories in place yet to sum up and, anyway, no one to sum up to. The purpose of summing up is to ease the way to the next phase. But, for us, what is there to prepare for? Who shall we meet but ourselves, who have been our own makers?

Have we done our best? If there is only one life—with no before or after—have we missed crucial opportunities to love, to procreate or to create, to be good, to be great, to be free of the need to be anything? Have we wasted our days, or is there no such thing as waste but only a life and its encounter with history and then its end? Are we ready, we who haven't been ready for anything? Maybe so. Who is to prevent it but ourselves?

THE END

"Do you have a will?" I asked.

BLANCHE W., 50, has the apartment in town and the house at the beach.

I have to say that, being single, writing wills is a pain in the ass.

As my friend Lou says, his attorney always knows when he gets a new boyfriend or girlfriend because there's always a new will. And that's me, too. What I do now is, when somebody and I break up, they will stay in my will during my single period and during the next boyfriend. But if there is such a thing as the next boyfriend after that, then they're out.

Do I want to have other people there when I die? . . . Oh, I hope so. It's so wonderfully intimate.

No, I don't make it humorous because it's too frightening. I really still hold suicide as an option, and that's part of what makes it not too frightening. Like my friend Katie—who is always worried about things like that. When Katie worries about money and worries about what will happen if she gets sick, I say, "So what? If the money runs out you kill yourself." It's true that some of this is in the context of having a grandmother who was widowed before fifty-five and is now ninety-four, and has stockpiled sleeping pills all her life. She always wanted to have the option.

The one thing I do worry about is . . . I've given somebody medical power of attorney, and I have a living will, because the thing that I most fear is being in the hospital and having nobody to do what I would do. Nobody who would be an ombudsman, who would do it for me. Some people I'm really good friends with, but they would be lousy in that capacity, so I think that's really important because you know you need someone to psych the hospital bureaucracy for you.

ANDREA H., the social worker, is 48. We talk after work hours, which, for her office is around 10 p.m. She has her feet up on a shabby desk.

No, I don't have a will. No. And I should.

I don't think about death; no, not really, not too much. I think more of the moment leading up to death, I suppose. I hope that I die immediately of whatever I'm going to die of and that I'm not in pain. But more than pain—that I don't die in a terror, on some plane or in some horrible car accident.

Just tonight I was thinking, *If I had cancer, who would be at my bedside when I had lost seventy pounds and was dying?* And then I tried to keep a sense of humor about it. But today I was thinking,

Would my inamorato be there? Wait, you can't say that, it's too ridiculous. And, anyway, he'd probably be with his wife.

RENNIE N., 34, who dreams of the Scottish house.

There's a little life insurance policy that the school has, that three-quarters of your salary when you die goes to some beneficiary. And when I had to figure that out at the age of twenty-nine, I put down my mother. But she doesn't need it, and there's no one in my immediate family who needs it, so even though I haven't changed it, I think if I did, I would change it to my church. Also, I worship at a monastery, and they run a camp, and I might leave it to them, to their camp.

IDA R., soon to be 85, is almost completely blind.

It doesn't upset me to talk about passing away, no, although I sometimes get upset because I have a lot of papers that should be cleared out that have accumulated over the years. And I know that it will be an injustice to leave a stack of mess. But it really can't be bothering me that much that it's an injustice I guess because I don't make the time to clean up.

I haven't thought of who might be with me on my last day. I don't know if I'll have a last day. I will, but I don't think about a last day.

I do have a will. I have one. I wrote a will. Now, when did I write my will? I wrote it way back. Let's see. I didn't have a will in the '50s, because I really didn't have any assets. . . .

I wrote a will in the '70s. Yes, it was around then that I first became aware of the importance of having a will. Let's see, I was born in 1914, so I was in my sixties at the time. Between marriages. But I have changed it, due to the aging process of my siblings. What was for my siblings is now for my niece and nephew.

When I was younger, I wasn't afraid of getting older. I just didn't imagine older. But I do want to say something about being older: that it's wonderful because you have the capacity to be younger in your mind and in your heart.

As far as what I feel about being older without a mate is concerned, the independence is marvelous. And it's true that I can see less and less, but I don't have a problem accepting that now.

Lucy L., the bartender, in her 30s.

I don't know what I would have been like about death, who I would have been if I hadn't seen so many of my friends die. Now many of the people I work with are walking around who have tested positive. What am I supposed to think all the time: *You're going to die, you're going to die, you're going to die . . .?* That just reminds you that you're going to die, too. And then that reminds me that if I suddenly got fatally sick, I'd have to die alone. My gay friends always have someone. So what am I going to do, think about that? So what I say is: Live well. And most of the time that works.

Rosa M., back in Tucson.

All I can think about is, *Will my kid be all right?* I haven't even paid up my mortgage yet. And where would she go if something happened to me? My mother's too old. None of my sisters are options. I don't want it to be my ex. It's too scary.

Mary Ann B., 45, has devoted a fair amount of thought to the subject.

I keep saying that if I can't take care of myself, I want somebody to shoot me. But I have to write that down and have it notarized because no one will believe you. They'll just keep you hanging on there. I think what's interesting about this is that as elderly women, most of us are going to end up alone, anyway. For the women who have been single for long decades before we hit our seventies and eighties, there will be a healthy, thriving culture of women already existing.

I think for single women, your status is not whom you're married to that matters, it's totally yourself. So it's not like you're going to have to be rebuilding an identity for yourself. It's really weird. For example, at this age people don't fix me up just to get me married off. My friends—I don't mean society but my friends—they wouldn't fix me up with anybody who wasn't extraordinary. Which is why I haven't had a date in six years, I guess. But that's the point. They know I don't see any reason to really compromise.

REGRETS

No one mentioned money, no one mentioned career.

JEAN I., 48, has noticed that her friends no longer introduce her to new men. She sighs.

Do I expect to fall in love any time soon? No, I guess. I don't think about it too much. No, no. Regrets are silly.

IDA R.

I did always regret that I don't have the capacity of expressing myself fully and easily. It's because of the lack of formal education. When I grope for a word . . . And because of this, I use very simple language. My brothers had an education, my sisters had one.

I don't really know why I didn't. It's hard to say. I blamed it on my eyesight because I had poor eyesight since the age of six. But in reality I think it was the fear of competition. Now I don't look for competition or comparison because I'm myself, but I have done a lot of work on myself.

SIS N., 61, is a poet and translator.

Well, I very much wanted to have children biologically, and friends trying to console me would tell me that my books will live on, which I never found very consoling. I just think that's poppycock. Books are not children. . . . For me, that is my regret. That is the one thing I really . . . I think I regret that more than the lack of a man, frankly, or the lack of a sexual life in older years, or all those things. I regret not having kids. I've brought up a lot of other people's kids, God knows, in a rather limited range.

I'm willing to allow my books the importance they have. But I just don't think they're a substitute for children. I don't want to run the poems down. It's a comfort to me that I have those poems.

ABIGAIL Z., 37, the architect who was widowed in her early 30s.

It's true that I didn't figure out until years later that I had really loved my husband. I've always been bad at figuring it out. Like years later, I discovered how much I loved my grandfather. Years after he was dead I realized I had all these memories. . . .

So I guess it was like that during my marriage, and when my husband died . . . I was just sort of numb and shocked for a lot of it when he was sick, but when I think back on it . . . I mean, I've never had a relationship where there were pet names. . . . You know? Ever. Except with him. And I thought it was sort of phony and ridiculous that we had pet names for each other, but we did, and we made a little family, and we probably were going to *be* a family.

Yet I don't think I would've stuck with it, to tell you the truth. That's my feeling about it, that I would've cut loose at the first handsome face, frankly. I was twenty-seven. I wasn't—You know, you don't realize what it's about when you're together, and you're going through things, and then you end up with a shared history. I don't know how.

MARINA'S SENSE OF TIME

A sense of rushing, as if to fill a great emptiness.

MARINA T., a woman of a certain age, veteran of a long, happy marriage, actress and a drama teacher, mother of a grown daughter. Her husband died about a year ago.

When I was about seven, I used to cut out pictures in magazines and put them in scrapbooks, and they would be me in different stages in my grown up life. There would be me as an actress. There would be me as a wife—those pages showed a handsome man and a beautiful woman. There would be me with my children. But they were always in equal combinations. This will be my house, and this my career. There would be this doubleness. There would always be the career, and also I would work out the timing so I wouldn't have any children before I was thirty, and then I would have many children—four or five or more. The actress thing in particular—I don't know where this came from. But it seemed very clear in my mind, both those things to be attainable and to be wished for.

When I was a young woman in New York, my theory was that you found boyfriends when you weren't paying attention to it, when you were doing what you loved, doing your work. And then you would find them, sort of alongside of you. There was a certain point—I was a little bored with my work, and I was starting to feel this time thing, and there was this man I shouldn't have been involved with, and the breakup almost killed me. . . . It seemed to me at once impossible to have a baby, but also that it was very important, that I wouldn't feel all right about myself if I didn't. I always had a very strong feeling that I wanted to have children; that went way back to the scrapbook. It was at that point that I went off on my fake ocean voyage, because I couldn't afford a real one, to an island off the coast of Canada. And the very first day I went for a walk, and I looked—I was up high and I looked down—and way down below near the water was a man sitting on a rock, and I said to myself, *I'll step off this path and climb down and meet this man sitting on the rock.* And I had always been someone who, if I went to a party and I saw a man across the room who looked particularly attractive, I would kind of turn and go in the other direction. I did not know how to go toward what I wanted. And on this particular day, I stepped off the path. I think it was the first time in my life I ever did that. And I went down and met this man. He had just arrived on this island. And I remember he had wonderful blue eyes, and we had a conversation and exchanged addresses and arranged to meet the next day. And we ended up getting married.

I think there are probably as many kinds of marriage as there are people—but for me, having chosen the person I chose, he made it possible for me to become *more* independent, to do more work, to be more . . . in a funny way, more autonomous. Because in some very deep fashion, he gave me a kind of permission that I somehow didn't have before. Despite arguing and fighting and all other things that two people coming together who each wanted their own way would endure. And when I got too emotional about something, I would sort of have this sane voice that cared about me saying, "I don't think you need to concern yourself with that. . . ." And that kind of support made me freer in the world. In some very deep way he made many things possible for me.

I can imagine others, particularly looking back to some of the relationships I had before I was married, where one person sort of overpowered the other, and then there was no freedom; there was this sort of obsession and no air and a kind of desperate feeling. It seemed to push all the air out of me. I seemed to be so obsessed with the person that I couldn't pay attention to my work. And when I finally found someone to be with who allowed me to pay attention to what I was doing, who allowed me to somehow be separate within this circle, that was an enormously powerful thing. And now I can be . . . I think I'm a fairly independent person who functions pretty well, but I miss terribly the closeness of the person who knew me for so long and knew me in all my worst forms and accepted me nevertheless.

And now there is this coming around to being single again, to being a widow. . . . Yes, it's quite a word. . . . There's a kind of deep loneliness. I don't really think that we were meant to be alone, we human beings. But one of the things that's happened is we all live much longer, we women are living longer than the men—and I think maybe the women are better able to handle it than the men.

Whatever I do now, I am left fairly comfortable with a nice house in the country and a nice apartment in town, which give me some pleasure. . . . But I do think, *What's the point?* There is something about sharing these things with someone else, even when you and the someone else disagree over whatever the approach is. . . . I realize now I was inclined to go shopping and buy certain things, partly to hear a certain response when I got home, which was, "What in God's name have you gone and bought?!" There's no zest now. Only if I conjure up the voice do I feel the certain thrill of it.

Would I remarry? I really don't know. It's only been a year. I don't just mean about finding somebody else. I feel very at sea and confused. And I've lost my sense of time—which was never too strong. But it's like there's a kind of sense of rushing—rushing to fill in a great emptiness. And I think about my moving back and forth from the city to the country every weekend . . . it seems fine to me even though it's five hours each way. What I think is that it gives me the impression that I'm going somewhere. If I were in one spot, I would be even more in pain. But who knows. I don't understand it all. I have no idea exactly what is going on. But everybody gets through. Well, and I think that curiosity saves one. And friends . . . Yes, it does matter. We all wind up in the place where it doesn't matter, but I do feel supported; I'm glad to see them, and they're glad to see me, and I can't imagine what it would be without that. And I seem to get interested in work. In the last year I felt distant from it, but now the distance is breaking down. I don't know how people go through this, I really don't.

There's a real contradiction in the whole business of being single and being able to have a baby by yourself, to be independent and autonomous, and do your work, yet at the same time avoid being isolated and learn the thing that you learn by living in proximity and friction with another person. Or just being part of a great big family that fights and carries on and so on, but you're still part of it.

Now there are all these people living and dying by themselves, and we don't even hear about them. The dying process . . . Obviously, it is going to happen to every one of us, and we just don't know how to do it or even just how to get it into our head that this is what happens, and you try to find a way to go through it with the people you're close to. All the people now who are living alone—how are they going to go through it? I mean, in the old days, people were part of families—the aunt who never married, the uncle who was a bachelor, they were part of big families. When they were old and sick, they lived with the family in the house. I don't know how this is working now. How about the people who don't have anybody very close, who are living far away, or who only have two or three relatives and they're old, too, and can't be of much help? Something strange has happened along with advances for women. I don't know. Maybe in the end everybody dies alone, so maybe it doesn't matter. . . . But it's astonishing to me that we all . . . it's going to happen to all of us and we don't have any sense of how to deal with it, or what to do. We don't even talk about it.

And yet I think about my grandmother, and it was very clear to her she was going to die. She didn't make anybody around her feel guilty that she was going to die. She took the responsibility for herself. And my husband did that, too. People can do it if they are strong in their lives. There are people who are lucky enough to be so strong in their lives—some people are not in the position to be strong—that they can handle their dying, their own dying.

SEX AND AGING

For most women, desire doesn't disappear.
It doesn't even transmute.

LETITIA R., 47, takes pride in a bad-girl past.

What really gets me is the age thing. Because I know my body is still fuckable. I may not look good every single day—I guess that's what aging is about—but I know I'm still very hot. How come when men turn forty . . . they get to get new puppies like Donald Trump or something and we don't?

GINGER G., interviewed on her 34th birthday.

My big fear in life is becoming that clichéd unmarried woman. I've never felt like a beauty, and what I do have by way of looks I feel like I could be losing, so it's kind of like I better act now. I'm just not sure how I'm going to be. I'm going to start to look at younger women and their innocence and their full hair and think I'm past my prime. Well, OK, not yet, but if I look into the future I see that as a problem.

My sexual prime . . . I've always had in mind for myself that mid-thirties would be the time of my life, but now it's coming and then it's going to be going. And I guess I'm not worried about the next couple of years, but I do worry down the line. I worry about that forties to fifties period. That's where I worry most.

ABIGAIL Z., the one who realized she's run through all the husbands.

You were supposed to take care of yourself, do what you were supposed to do. And then you see that doesn't work well in the real world one or two or three decades later. Like, I used to play volleyball a lot, and I'd play as hard as I could. I wasn't going to bat my eyes and make mistakes I didn't need to make, just to make the men respond. But a few months ago I decided I was going to try playing again, so I joined this gym. And there were these young stud guys in their early thirties and then there were the forty-five-year-old guys. And there's me and then there's the little, cute girls in their twenties who can't do shit and who are just giggly—like in an "Oh, my goodness" kind of state. And they just got all kinds of attention paid to them. And I find that infuriating.

MONICA V., 48, who described this period of her life as "restless."
I do feel my body has really let me down in major ways, and that I've had to reach a sort of new agreement with my body. I got a personal trainer, and I lost some weight, and I mean it *is* in pretty good shape for a forty-eight-year-old.

But not sexually. I went through menopause, you know, about a year or two after my marriage broke up. And I found when I had this affair that sex is so incredibly painful. *Incredibly painful.* You know what they say about menopause: Use it or lose it. I mean, you read all the books, and they say that. I didn't quite understand what they were talking about. You've got to have sex on a regular basis. It's like a muscle or something. And if you don't for a long period of time, things happen so that when you do, the liquidity and all that, it dries up and it doesn't come back. And so sex for me now is a real painful affair. So, you know, what do you do about it . . . ? Well, if I was in a regular relationship there are certain things I can do. . . . But I can't take estrogen because of the cancer, so no estrogen creams, which is what really helps you, so I have very mixed feelings about sex. It's not really something I want to do because it hurts! And I no longer have that kind of thing inside—that kind of . . . sexual pull, which I used to always have.

ELLEN P., who told us she had problems in her summer community as a result of her not having children.
But being a woman of a certain age—which is an anathema for most men—I feel completely inhibited by the circumstances, by the society.

No, I don't really know precisely when it happened. It was very gradual. And I don't think that my success has helped. I feel that I have become increasingly sexually invisible. And the more I have become articulate and interesting as a person, the less I am sexually attractive. There's some kind of dismal equation of that sort.

Yes, my body is probably aging, but that's not the way I think about it. I refuse to. . . . No, wait a minute, that's probably a lie. It's probably not true.

I had a relationship recently with a younger man, and it was totally marvelous for me on many levels. And then he ended this relationship very abruptly when he met another woman at a party. . . . He came in and told me this had happened and that he wanted to continue being a good friend of mine. The only thing he didn't want to do was sleep with me. I found this a true agony. And I haven't had the courage to ask him whether the actual sexual relationship had something to do with this rather than the terror of being involved with someone so much older than him. You know what I mean? It seems to me we had a very good time in bed. For me personally, I felt incredibly rejected in this one place. . . . It was very bruising. And for weeks afterward I would imagine him with this young woman and how different her body must be from mine.

But usually I don't obsess about what is happening to my body. I mean, it's not that I'm indifferent. Hardly. But my obsession with my looks I think is pretty much generated by my extensive vanity rather than my concerns about aging.

ANITA S., the academic who's turning 40.

I think it's funny where the vanity comes in. The hair really got to me. It was the hair going gray that was just awful. And then my mother corrupted me. She said, "Oh, you have too much gray; let's dye it." I keep thinking there'll be some time when I'll stop dying my hair, but instead, lately all I've been thinking about is dying my hair really blond. For the first time in my life I want to just go hog wild.

CALLIE S., 57, the real estate agent. I asked her whether she thought her age had any effect on her social life.

Only when I was very young and freshly divorced did I feel any nastiness coming from married women. I can only assume that for these many years that I've been divorced, all these dinner parties I wasn't invited to may have had something to do with being the predatory, dangerous woman at the dinner table. That may be wrong, but I've always assumed that a single woman under a certain age can be a threat in that kind of situation. But I haven't felt that in a long time. And I haven't felt the male version in a long time either because I guess I haven't thought of myself as cute as a button anymore.

As a matter of fact, that *was* hard. And it happened very very abruptly at some point in my early thirties. And what I'm talking about is having gone from being—gee, it's hard to put together without sounding like a horse's ass—from being very visible and very . . . I was never anyplace where somebody wasn't making eye contact with me. And in a lot of instances it felt more flattering than intrusive. There was always somebody making goo-goo eyes in the next car or in the bus or subway or what have you. And then very abruptly it stopped. I had loved it and hated it as a young person. And it's not that I missed it; I was just devastated it wasn't there anymore when the blush was off the rose, or whatever state you go into. And I think I mean early thirties. But you look up in the bus and everybody's got their face in their newspapers; there isn't one pair of eyes. Overnight, the *Wall Street Journal* is more interesting than you are.

God, I don't know, I don't really know whether it's different for married women. I would assume that it's different, but why? Maybe that abrupt change isn't quite as abrupt for them. Or maybe they don't even notice it anymore. No, I guess that's not universally true.

BILLIANA M., 52.

I had a hysterectomy when I was . . . I think I was thirty-six. I really feel that that was a violent act, that I had to work through having something plucked from me. I agreed to it. I had some severe fibroids, and my bleeding was totally out of control, and one ovary was the size of a grapefruit. They were going to take everything, but I told them to leave the ovary that was healthy. I did advocate for myself to that degree. But I didn't get a second opinion; I was debilitated by all the bleeding, and hormonal. With what I know now, I would get a second opinion. But that's what I needed to do at the time. The surgeon who did it was not at all sympathetic or compassionate or understanding of women, so it didn't have a wholesome energy around it. And I also did have to have the second ovary out years later. In some sense I'm glad to have had the surgery because it was affecting my emotional life all the time, and there's been a stabilization since then. And I have to say that I have really enjoyed not having the bleeding and the leaking and the whole smell associated with all those things. I have a shame thing associated with those. I felt dirty, or offensive, and felt I couldn't be out with other people. I didn't have to be perfumed or anything like that, but I was sensitive to it. I don't expect that from other people, I don't expect *them* not to be human beings.

I put on weight, and I won't diet at all because I won't do that to myself. I know the changes have to come from the inside. But I'm not comfortable at this weight because physically it's prohibitive, and I do think other people must mind, and I really shouldn't look this way. The crux of it is—and I just came to this last week—what really bothers me is the fact that it is visible to other people that I didn't love myself enough to take care of myself.

I turned fifty-two in October. When I turned fifty it was a little bit of a future shock because to me, fifty had a totally different sound of seniorhood than forty-nine did. But when I asked myself what fifty meant to me, I realized that I could let go of some of the stale and obsolete feelings of what I needed to accomplish as a young person. I could accept the fact that I didn't keep a twenty-two inch waist. I don't need tight skin. My life shows up in my body. When I look at footage of some of these old whales that have scars and bites and nips taken out of their tail flukes . . . they're wearing their histories on themselves. When I can think of me that way, I can really embrace this body and how I am now and say, *This is okay, this is my life, this has happened to me and it's where I've been,* and I can look at it as character or as uniqueness.

Most of my life was set up to be appealing to the public, and probably men in particular, to try to look as flawless as possible. So partly the age thing is a relief. It's wonderful to know I don't have to compete with high-breasted, high-butted girls with young skin. It's not in the realm of possibility, so it's nice not to have to focus on that.

Growing up, I really found both Golda Meir and later Margaret Mead—they were ideals of mine and neither of them was considered a beauty by any means. At that time two of the beauty standards were Marilyn Monroe and Elizabeth Taylor. Of course, I didn't look like either one of them. And I always would have liked to have had it all, certainly, but I always aspired to be brilliant, have a social impact, be a creator rather than a bright beauty.

MARY ANN B., 45, the journalist. Before . . .

Yes, for the first time in my life I'm dealing with that rejection thing, and it probably has to do with aging and being single at the same time. I guess I'm something of an anomaly because I have not flung myself out there looking for anybody. And mostly maybe it's fear of rejection, but I haven't had time, and I haven't had the inclination.

I wasn't lonely. Until now there were the kids. I didn't need to do anything to beef up my social life. Now I do. I haven't had to do anything about the romance thing, and now I do—and the fear of rejection thing is big because I'll probably have to deal with it for the first time at age fifty. But, of course, self-esteemwise, you're a solid, sturdier self at age fifty.

Except in the physical. That's where I notice that it could really hurt.

MARY ANN B., 49, the journalist. After . . .

Women critique their bodies relentlessly at this age, and men's bodies change, too, and when I was back in the dating scene again after not being in the courtship scene for twenty-five years, the territory had changed considerably, and I was now looking for romantic partners among a population that looked like my father when I first started dating. I certainly wasn't attracted to younger men, partly because I was raising two. But, anyway, now I find men my age attractive. But, you know, they probably have to worry about hairlines as much as we worry about the shape of our thighs. We all worry. Undressing at our age is a trial. But it's surprising how fast you forget all that once you get into bed.

The commitment is different at this age. I love what comedian Rita Rudner says: "Watch out for the guy who says, 'You're everything I'll ever need,' because he'll suck everything right out of you." So you don't have a relationship with everything. . . . At this age, you're never going to be someone's one and only. That desire to be exclusively yours or to have somebody exclusively to yourself, I suppose that no woman gives up that idea voluntarily; most of us merely outlive it because the reality is that no man you are going to meet at this point hasn't been with at least one other woman. If that's what you're waiting for, you'll wear yourself out. Plus I suppose I got there, too, because I still have a relationship with my former husband, and it's a really close one. It's not sexual, but it's twenty-five years of history. So if any new love interest is going to be jealous of that, it would be a problem.

But what's nice about these relationships is . . . I am absolutely amazed at how juicy romance and sex are at this age and how goofily we can fall in love again, still. Not having been obsessed with sex for six years, now I find myself thinking about it all the time again. I find this just astonishing. And, you know, guys at this age do bring a kind of knowledge to sex that they didn't as youngsters, and that's not an entirely mournful situation. So it's nice. It's just nice.

It's just as well to have a sense of humor about it, though. We get these patronizing looks, when M. and I are out to dinner and he reaches over to touch my hand to touch my cheek, and the little baby waitresses think it's so charming. They thought you only died at this age.

BY THE WAY, IT'S *OLDER* AGE. NOT OLD—OLDER.

I asked, "Do you feel old? Are you scared?"

EILEEN Y., in her 70s, still gets offers to teach.

I've lived with not very good health for many years, but the failure of energy is scary. And the forgetting. I now belong to a group of women over sixty. They have all been professional women, and I guess all but me have been married. Almost all of them have had one child, one of them has two children, but they're mostly people who've had the experience of marriage and motherhood. And, in point of fact, except for the one, all but one are single women.

We talk about their ex-husbands, sure. On the whole, they were all devoted I would say, they were all quite monogamous. Or if they had one early marriage, they were monogamous once they got into the second marriage. We really started this group, which has now been going for five or six years, because there were no examples for us—our mothers and grandmothers did not live the life that we've lived. And they didn't have the old age that we have.

Yes, I guess things do even out in the end. They probably do. I certainly don't feel that they regard me as different. The one thing that's different is that I have an art, and I'm still able to be active, while most of them are retired. And that is a huge, and happy, difference. Maybe that's what needs to be said: The best way to grow old is to be an artist. Because you do not give it up, and so something new continues to happen in your life. Several of these women really mourn the fact that they can't, for instance, take a part-time job. They either would have to take a full-time job, which they can no longer do, or they just have to figure that the working part of their life is over—their professional career, their contact with the working world. And that's not true for me. I could at any point say, I'll teach for a semester, go here or there and get a job, but I don't even want to do that because I'm now in the thick of my own work.

RENEE G., 90, knows that she may soon have to live as a couple again. This time with an aide companion.

I fell, in the kitchen. I don't know, I may have slipped. But I couldn't get up. I tried and just couldn't. My cane was next to me, but I wasn't strong enough to hoist myself up. So when I saw I just couldn't get up, I thought, *Well, I'll just sit here until I can. There's nothing broken, so I'll wait until I'm able to.* And then, bit by bit, I was able to drag myself over to the refrigerator, and that's how I got myself up. Although I was very afraid that the refrigerator was going to fall on top of me. So I just kept telling myself, *It can't fall on me, it's much too heavy.* And then I was able to get up. Luckily, I had fallen on my behind, so at least this time there was nothing broken.

IDA R., who's in her early 80s, sounds fuzzy when I call her one evening, at her request, at 10:30.

No, I still never go to sleep that early. But today I guess I was bucking the wind, so when I came home, I didn't have my brain juice. . . . I woke up and I thought it was morning, and then realized it was night. But I know now that what I eat has a great reflection on my thoughts and my vitality and my actions.

By the way, it's older age. Not old age, *older* age. Aging is beautiful, depending on attitude. Life is beautiful, depending on attitude. And my attitude has been one day at a time. Even when I was younger I may have been taking it one day at a time. I never looked ahead. I never thought of dying. I was told recently that I was born a healer. I was not aware of it until I was seventy-nine. And I remember when I was younger and living for the moment, and now I know that people try for years and years and years to attain that status.

Looking back, when I had to do something and just didn't do it, I would say, "Well, I just didn't get to it." And everyone would make fun of that. They'd be sarcastic. "Oh, she just didn't get to it." And looking back on that, I feel that this may have part of that gift, that I didn't know how to handle. But I still have that feeling of not having gotten to it—since adolescence and on. All these years. Sixty-odd years.

I'm still very active in my women's organization. I'm a good leader. I have leadership qualities. I don't know whether to describe myself as a passive-aggressive. I may be domineering in a passive way. But I'm learning to let go of control. I'm succeeding.

It's true that there are things that I would like to be able to do. But whether I could . . . how could you say? I would like to be able to sing and carry a tune. But I don't know if I could accomplish that or not. That's what I mean about accomplishing. And nice things happen to me almost every day.

At the present, I do have a gentleman friend. We're not thinking of living together yet. It started a couple of months ago, so I don't know whether to bring that in at the moment or not. It may be a little premature. But I can tell you that there is this great feeling of being young again. Of being like a teenager. Of rediscovering the beauty of having someone say "I love you" and mean it.

WHEN I'M OLD? CAN'T EVEN THINK ABOUT IT.

Everybody has at least one fantasy, but a number of women told me they had never really articulated these to themselves.

ANTONIA O., 38, a secetary.

When I think about old age, my fears are being alone, like my grandfather is, and being an asshole, being a real bitchy old person, like my grandfather. That's what my fear is. What I would want is to be a nice, interesting old person.

I have this great aunt, my aunt Helena. And she's absolutely . . . she's the one who raised me. She never got married, and she died at the age of ninety-one. She was in charge of everyone, and she was, you know, the matriarch. And she was just wonderful. She'd tell you stories and take care of you. And she never would be a burden, she never would be sick. In her whole life, she only went to the hospital twice. Once for a hemorrhoid operation when she was, like, 50 and once for heart palpitations when she was about 89. She was a lovely person to be around.

But my grandfather, he's alone in that house, with nothing to stop him from being so mean, so he's getting to be lonelier and nastier. I don't mind being alone, but I don't want to be like him. People don't want to be around him. There's an image of people who have families, that those people ending up in the bosom of their families, being taken care of by adoring grandchildren, but of course that's not the way it works. Now, people who've had families are as alone as people who haven't had families.

MONICA V., 48, whose ex-husband became impotent while she was undergoing chemotherapy.

Well, let's say I guess I don't see myself surrounded by grandchildren. I don't really think very much about old age. I don't let myself. I think I have more fantasies about the next week than I have about the next twenty years. I can't imagine what ten years from now will be like. I also know that five years ago I would never have imagined I'd be doing what I'm doing now, so in a way, if there's any fantasy, I think that things are going to be okay, which is a lot for me. It's not that I have anything specific in mind, just I think it's going to be okay. I certainly hope I'm not on the street walking around with a hump on my back.

Well, I guess that is a fantasy, since it just occurred to me. So I guess that's the horror of old age.

My friend Marguerite and I have already promised that when we're old biddies, even if we have old husbands, we're going to dump them, and we're going to live with each other because we're not going to let either one of us do that by ourselves. I think that every single woman should have another single friend that they've made that pledge with. Maybe that's why I don't worry about it.

FELICA C., 49, dreads old age.

I find it impossible to think about because we don't look like what we thought we were going to look like. In terms of the future, which I can't get except from panic, I can't plan because the planning is opposite to what I have inside my head.

The end result that I fear is a total loss of dignity. And the thing that I fear is the consuming embarrassment that I normally have would be increased so enormously, and I would still be able to feel every bit of it. I fear everyone else's eyes. It'll be obvious that I need help. I fear the look on people's faces when they see how hopeless I am. In the eyes of people who know me. You know, like my children. Friends I've been able to keep up with who realize I've been a fraud all along. I couldn't go to the movies because I wouldn't have the money.

No, I don't think my friends will be in the same situation. I think they're all smarter, and they've all figured out how to protect themselves.

MEGAN L., 26.

Feminism was successful in this way: Living alone is not one of those things that I particularly think about as an issue. My fantasies of old age? I change them every day. Really, every day. One day it could be getting totally successful on my own and never have to consider the possibility of depending on someone else and having other people come to me because I deal in power, and at other times I have a really '50s fantasy of having married the rich doctor and being a happy homemaker, which would be a nice, quiet life compared to the one I lead.

MARTHA H., said that her picture of old age differed a lot, depending on whether she included money in the equation.

I've always thought that I would live to a very, very old age—if I don't die of any rapidly wasting disease within the next six months. Other family members have gone that way—like my great aunt. But, otherwise, I think I'm going to live well, well into my nineties. And I don't think that I'm going to be seriously ill at all. I imagine myself being like my paternal grandmother, who was extremely active, played bridge, was very acerbic. She was better than I am at a lot of things. She made money in the stock market. But she died of food poisoning after eating a creampuff at a bridge game. All this is completely true. It was the spoiled creampuff.

She had been widowed. My father was born in '26, so she must have been maybe fifty when her husband went. We found a poem recently that she wrote when he died, about how the light had gone out of her life. She had gone to Emerson College and studied elocution and then went to Europe on a grand tour. Her brothers were lawyers and doctors. I used to call her Lala.

I think I'll be exactly like her. But she lived with my parents. At a certain point my mother brought her home; I guess it was when we discovered that she was eating cereal for dinner every night. Though, of course, now we know it doesn't hurt anybody—and may even be good for you. But, anyway, there she was. She was very independent, and she liked to walk to town, so the neighbors were always criticizing my mother for not driving her.

That's the problem, that I don't have children who'll take me in. This identification with my grandma is not possible since I won't have anyone to take me in. Although I can eat cereal, and since I'm never going to live outside a city, I don't have to drive or anything. Either that or I see myself living maybe in my uncle's house with my cousins because my uncle lives in a big house in Maine, and he's obviously not going to stay alive—he's eighty-seven now. I think my cousins and I will wind up living together on the property. You know, Soviet style, with everybody sharing.

And then there's also money. This is where I depart totally from my grandmother's lead because she was very frugal and thrifty and really amassed a modest fortune—enough to leave us something. And I have nothing. I have no retirement. Every penny I have is in the apartment and a few pieces of clothing. I've always had this kind of Scarlet O'Hara attitude, which has been that it's OK as long as I have a job. But now that I'm about to lose mine, I want to have a retirement plan, but everyone says it's too late. As you approach fifty, it's too late.

ALEXANDRA R., 28, is an artist's assistant.

I can't even think about it. Sometimes I try to, but it's either just sort of a vague thing at the center of a big dense cloud, so I can't get to it, or otherwise—for instance when I think about my father dying—it's so painful and sharp that I have to move it away.

So death doesn't figure that large in my fears. Old age is more frightening because there's so much more known about that. I put myself through graduate school working in a nursing home. I liked the job, actually. But when I think back on what it was like there and how older people are compartmentalized, it gives me a very creepy feeling. And thinking about it in the context of single women really takes it all the way out. My thought is that the elderly are already a "fringe" group, already marginalized. So what happens to the status of single women in this? How do the two marginalizations collude? Maybe there's already a more acceptable place in the culture for single elderly women, but it is one that's completely stripped of power. I think of the term "remaindered" as it applies to books or fabric scraps. The vacuum of desire stops being produced, and so they sit there until someone decides how to get rid of them.

Do I think it could change? Well, yes, it could. Already I'm sure at least some, or many, elderly women live differently. And, of course, I'm talking about popular construction and not individual lives. When I think of individuals I knew when I was working there, it strikes me very differently because each one was so dense with personality, even the ones who were bedridden. Or maybe especially.

ANTONIA O., secretary, reserves the backup plan of building herself a log cabin on a piece of land her family owns.

I guess I don't have a specific image of myself when I'm old. I think of myself just as the way I am now but with white hair. Making watercolors and working on stained glass and playing my banjo. . . . I've thought, over a period of years, about how to change things. But I guess I'm just not very good at figuring out how to make money in a way that won't be really awful—I mean, this is dull enough—but I can't imagine what else to do. I got a job at the phone company once, but I only lasted for a few weeks of training because I started imagining myself sitting at a desk taking these phone calls for the rest of my life. Perhaps it was foolish—there are lots of other things you can do at the phone company—but that was the image I got, the awful image of the rest of my life. So I quit and drove home thinking, *I've got to get out of there!* But that was pretty foolish.

So when I think of myself with white hair, I do worry because I don't make much money. I thought of calling the retirement fund office to see how much I'll get a month based on what I m putting in now. I'm afraid to call! I know that's funny, but there you are. They give you a toll-free number to call, and tell you at what hours you can get an operator. I could get the figures for you, but I've yet to call. I mean, suppose I only get two hundred dollars a month. How could I live?

BLANCHE W. has told me she felt she had betrayed herself when she got married.

I do recall that when I was married, my husband used to have fantasies about us growing old together, and I used to shudder in horror. I remember thinking, *Every day for the rest of my life, I have to share this bed with him? When do I get time alone?!*

I don't have many fantasies of old age. Well, sometimes I think I'll die early. Are you going to want all this? It's all my depression. Sometimes I think about a feminist old-age home, that we're all going to have a great time, and I'll have a bunch of my friends and . . . This weekend when my friend Mary saw my new house she said, "Oh, I know what's going to happen. You're going to retire here when you're seventy-five, and you'll spend the next ten years fixing it up." And I was thinking, *Oh, really?* Because I didn't have any connection with that.

I'm not really able to imagine myself as an old lady. I wonder if I can still have my hair long. Will it get really thin? It's not going to get gray—I'm still going to streak it. But at what point will it be inappropriate?

Aside from that, I imagine working pretty much until the day I die. There are many women like that now in my field, and they're good models. Maybe I'd travel a little extra because my mortgage would be paid up.

The other good thing about being old is that I can take acid. I won't have to worry about being really on and pushing and being ambitious and so forth. There will be a time when I can get high and not worry about being hung over. Of course, the big question is, if I ran out of money, or if I couldn't work, would I leave the city? I used to think I wanted to go to the rice fields in Bali.

JENNIFER B., 32, New Jersey.

I do know what I would want in old age. I'd like to be a dignified person.

PHILLIPA C., on her way to a fourth marriage.

Yeah. I do have a fantasy of old age. I'm living—alone, of course—in a large eighth-floor studio apartment on Park Avenue. Maybe at 1199 or maybe in an older building, but it has to be a corner studio with lots of light. It could be on Fifth, but it's a silk-stocking studio. A sunlit silk-stocking studio that's lined with books, or else the New York Society Library is near, because what I do is read. For the last twenty years of my life I've read. . . . Sometimes I read Greek—you know, the Greek myths—And sometimes I read Thackeray. I just read. In the sunlight. It's heaven. And my children are grown and successful and off somewhere. And it's like—you know how I said my perspective changed when I turned fifty? Now I feel like I'm looking backward so I don't do it again. I feel like when I'm seventy I can say, "That's good. I did it. It's over. I had a life. And now I can do what I want." And of course I have a fixed income, but it doesn't have to be a lot. Just enough for books . . . and the occasional movie. But seniors get a special rate. I know that. It would be nice to go to the movies.

That's my fantasy. I've had it for a long time.

MARY ANN B. Among the women I spoke to, money was definitely one of the all-time scariest aspect of daydreams about old age.

The poverty issue I think is the biggest—knowing how to create an old age for ourselves that we could live with—but it's going to take money and lots of it, and we don't have it. There's no way we're going to go back and live with our kids. And women who have been this independent are not going to be good nursing-home patients either. It's going to be like, "You want me to do *what?!*"

Oh, I'm always daydreaming about my future. How do I plan it? How am I going to make my life easier? That's the main theme. But my daydreams are never pushing me in the direction of getting back in a relationship again. I don't know whether I consider myself as unmarriageable or not. But in my daydreams I always see myself as single.

The terrors are about not being independent or not being able to take care of yourself—or running out of money, which is my main thing now because I work so hard, so how am I going to keep doing it? How am I going to support myself as an old person? And I do think I am going to have to keep working. But because none of my long-term relationships were relationships that took care of me, I don't see that option as the solution anymore. I mean, I used to. And I think all of us have a thing about having somebody come and say, "Let *me* take care of you"—and that's just not the reality anymore. Except for the very wealthy men, and most of them are not even in the position of being able to offer that anymore. So I suppose as a single woman I've expanded rather than contracted the number of people I expect to have take care of me when I'm old. I think the habit of independence is going to serve us well in old age. It's not something we're going to give up; it's something we're going to teach everybody else how to do.

POST-OEDIPAL FEMALES
AND BRIDES OF
THE UNIVERSE

Good-bye, Penis Envy

They want to be like men. This is the insult often leveled at women perceived to be powerful. We may say that we admire strength in women, but we give strength a very narrow definition, consisting mostly, I think, of endurance. Single women (and many married women), deemed strong merely by sheer virtue of surviving, are therefore often said to be hard, unsexy, too cranky, too demanding, too—in a word—male. *They are men!* people will exclaim, in a not very friendly fashion. However, there are men and there are men—even among women. If a woman is good-looking and successful, her male friends or colleagues are more likely to say, as an affectionate compliment, that she *thinks* like a man—an important distinction since the woman who "is" a man is not someone widely thought to have sex appeal, whereas a woman can get away with a great deal more if she is merely gifted with male-type cognition. So far as I can tell, what is meant by the latter is a capacity for thinking that is logical rather than associative and directly expressed rather than obliquely referred to. Or it means that this is someone who Gets Things Done. Her way. Or perhaps it means that she expresses frank aggression toward her enemies. Or that she occasionally tells dirty jokes and displays sexual attraction for more than one other person. Something like that.

But, essentially, I think what is meant about a woman who either is or thinks like a man is that she is *tough,* that she is not submissive, sentimental, or unclear in her desire or in her anger. This is where it starts to get weird. The truth is, many single women are quite submissive, sentimental, and very unclear indeed, at least some of the time. But taking the "tough" model as apt on its own terms for the sake of argument, you will notice that there is a good deal of overlap with what we also consider to be good mental health. Autonomy and good ego boundaries are the nearly universal goals of therapy these days, while entreaties to acquire self-esteem and to set limits have become ubiquitous saws. However, there is now general popular agreement that these are essentially male traits. Therefore, if you follow this argument, there is something wrong with single women because they have the same kind of good mental health men have and all women should aspire to.

To add to the confusion, many theorists and psychologists differ and are spending quite a lot of energy lately arguing in books and journals as to whether or not there is such a thing as innate gender to begin with. Is there such a thing as core masculinity or femininity? Feminist analysts, for their part, are divided among those with an "alpha" bias (emphasizing differences between men and women) and those with a "beta" bias (emphasizing similarities), disagreeing about which one is the better belief system and which one is better for women.

It is one of the bitter ironies of this gender-puzzle era that the insult "She thinks like a man" turns into a compliment as soon as you switch contexts, then turns back into an insult at a moment's notice, and that it is good *or* bad for you to "think like a woman"— depending on whom you are speaking to.

There are probably more and more theorists casting their final ballot for nurture over nature, but that doesn't mean that the great Gender Theory bandwagon will slow down. On the contrary, if gender is generally agreed upon to be almost entirely a result of socialization, then everything is up for grabs. If both the alpha bias and the beta bias are out, we're heading for a gender free-for-all that will provide miles and miles of text for decades to come. If we become suspicious of the obvious, the fun will begin. "Core gender identity [is] a dynamic, evolving phenomenon," writes Dr. Michael Tobbins in a paper on the neurobiology of gender differences which appeared in a recent supplement on women in the *Journal of the American Psychoanalytic Association*. (Just think about this: *Core gender identity is a dynamic, evolving phenomenon!*) The reason, according to Tobbins, is that "it is more than likely that the brain, affected by the endocrine secretions, and not the genitalia, is the major sex-and-gender differentiating body part." In other words, in the past anatomy may have been destiny, but these days, apparently, it's all in your mind. . . . (Another score for cybersex.)

"I've come to the conclusion that there is no such thing as gender," one specialist in the field recently told me with a sigh. Well, one would never know it. But unfortunately the current fascination with gender has yet to benefit single women. What they are missing more than anything is a cultural context that provides the possibility of having one's best efforts rewarded rather than viewed with suspicion or exploited and discarded if they overlap with the traits we have assigned to the masculine.

"As single women, our solitude makes us stronger and tougher," I was told by the head of an African-American women's forum. "And that's why we're less attractive, because being vulnerable is attractive."

As it happens, this woman was extremely attractive. Why is being strong "less attractive"? Less than what—or whom? And according to whom? There are sharp, cutting messages encoded in the adjective "strong" when it's applied to women, even by themselves.

Conservatives talk about women having brought all their current troubles on themselves when they began to want to "become men." They say men—real men—are afraid of the new women (or, in current fashion wo/men, or womyn, or whatever). But men have always been afraid and the old woman was at least as scary as the new woman is. What were they afraid of? Well, take your pick: Economic, social, or psychological, you come back to the deep terror men have (and, one might point out, many women have too) of being engulfed by voracious women or penetrated by phallic mothers or their equivalent. The phallic woman is seen as aggressive and masculine, and the fear she inspires also serves as a defense against wishes that stir up castration anxiety. Under the old system, all fears of strong women were converted into the imposition of ritualized power relationships, and women kept their image of sweetness, innocence, and vulnerability. Under the new system you get Demi Moore in her underwear, as a terrifying corporate whiz who will destroy Michael Douglas's career and family in *Disclosure*.

As soon as women went out to work in any significant numbers, the problem of masking "male" ambitions arose. By 1929, Joan Riviere published her famous paper, "Womanliness as a Masquerade" in which she demonstrated that women who are accomplished in the workplace must redouble their femininity when around men so as not to frighten them. Of course, there was nothing all that new about this kind of thing even then. What is remarkable about the paper is not the subject's sensibility, it is that Riviere isolated the masquerade and published the description of that behavior.

It is around this time that the wife-model began to unravel. Femininity and, inevitably, marriage itself became targets, coming under fire as soon as women scientists began to gain more power and credibility. "Why are good marriages so rare—marriages that do not stifle the developmental potential of the partners?" asked psychoanalyst Karen Horney in 1932 in *Feminine Psychology*. "Is marriage perhaps only an illusion, about to disappear, or is modern man particularly incapable of giving it substance? Are we admitting to its failure or to our own, when we condemn it? Why is marriage so often the death of love?"

By 1976, when Dorothy Dinnerstein wrote the seminal *The Mermaid and the Minotaur*, what Horney had thought of as a failure could be recast as "the human project of sexual liberty." Wrote Dinnerstein, "The gathering impulse to break loose from our existing gender arrangements . . . is part of the central thrust of our species' life toward more viable forms." It was a very bold suggestion in 1976, to say nothing of a big order, but Dinnerstein's "human project of sexual liberty" is in fact beginning to take shape after all, ironically enough when AIDS, like the Gay Power movement and feminism itself, has overturned all of our notions about what sexual liberty might mean.

Now, more and more women have stopped masking their ambition with elaborate displays of submission (not that a lot of them aren't still submissive, but it has become unfashionable to display it without also disclaiming it). It is the combination of feminine and the de-femmed sensibility that gives today's woman such an original profile: In a word, she can be womanly and strong—not just strong enough to endure pain, but also strong enough to enjoy freedom.

In no small part, the problem with women's strength also arises because we associate strength with anger. But while it's obvious that some women are indeed very mad at men, the raging, awesome, desexualized, and desexualizing fury invoked by the term "man-hater" is a type that is difficult to locate in real life. The anger seems at least sometimes to reside in the beholder's gaze more tenaciously than in the beheld's awareness or heart. It's true that at one end of the spectrum of political thought there are women who are against intercourse. But why their influence on the female population seems more threatening than that of, say, the scores of eager gig-glers, or cropped-T-shirted waitresses from Hooters, or phone-sex operators walking around out there is hard to imagine. (Though, from what one hears about the personal predilections of female workers in the sex trades, it may be that they oppose intercourse, too, but that's another matter.)

Nevertheless, the term "male bashing" seems to be an equally long-lived cliché. In all these interviews I saw a lot of teasing, groan-ing, anger, yearning, disgust, and desire, but not very much male bashing. Most women seemed less bitter than bewildered and tired—a state that, in my guess, probably closely mirrors that of their married friends. While genuine male bashing certainly does occur in private, in the monologues of female comedians, and in copious quantities in many a woman's novel, the bashing one hears lately in the normal course of conversation tends to be—at most—wry, ironic, and resignedly droll. The more earnest the bashing, the more likely it is that it *accompanies* submissiveness in a woman.

Single women, no less than their married friends—female and male—sometimes wish there was someone to protect them, some-one they could just collapse with. "I get irritated when someone tells me for the umpteenth time how strong I am," I was told recently by precisely the sort of woman people like to think of as strong, endur-ing. In private, what these women often say about strength is that their lives don't permit them to be anything else. "Married women get to break down," one woman said to me. "I'm not allowed to break down."

"It's so hard," one woman kept saying when she cried in the mid-dle of what had seemed like an extremely pleasant roundtable dis-cussion of the single life. But she had just brought up the problems she was having with a man she had decided she did want to marry.

She was forty-two years old. She wanted a child. She wanted, she said, a life. The other women looked on, with considerable compassion. "It's hard," agreed first one and then another. There wasn't any disagreement as to whether it was hard—only as to what constitutes a life.

Laws, values, limits have been tested and defeated and yet haven't really been swept away by any new order. We just got used to living with the detritus of the old. At first there was much talk of a "malaise," but then everyone was working too hard to worry about malaise, fragmentation, or anomie. Somehow, we got used to living in states of bafflement alternating with more pointed escape. Now, the rules of the game are so confused that self-help books propose to provide them. We are always reading lists of "rules" that are supposed to finally give us a structure to become happy. Unfortunately, most of these read pretty much like those of yesterday's woman even while they admonish today's woman to try to have it all/not have it all, whatever, but get a husband. "We understand why modern, career-oriented women have sometimes scoffed at our suggestions," the authors of a book actually called *The Rules* tell us. "They've been MBA-trained to 'make things happen' and to take charge of their careers. However, a relationship with a man is different from a job. In a relationship, the man must take charge. He must propose. We are not making this up—biologically, he's the aggressor." Even if the authors aren't "making it up," man's aggression may or may not lead to a proposal, which may or may not be what a woman wants from him, anyway. Lately, *The Rules* has been joined on the already crowded shelf by *The Real Rules*, by Barbara De Angelis, Ph.D., a mass-market paperback book subtitled: "How to find the *right* man for the *real* you." (The double emphasis leads one to wonder whether the author believes the *real* woman reader had previously found the *wrong* man for her *real* self, the *right* man for her *false* self, or the *wrong* man for her *false* self. At the very least, by my count, it still works out to two guys for every woman once the reader is able to integrate the various components of her own self.)

To further perplex us, nowadays very few women are still willing to be consistently tough or sentimental, aggressive or compliant, penetrating or receptive. One could make the argument, however, that this has always been true of women, and it is only the classification that has become more flexible, as has so much else at the turn of the century. And some even make the argument that this would be true of men, were they given the chance. So many of the old stereotypes are sliding away. Even age-old definitive categories like "rich" and "poor" have become somewhat abstract in our credit-crazed service economy. Both "bossy" and "nice" have become meaningless, since you can now substitute "empowered" and "sensitive." "Pretty" and "ugly" have become fluid, now that so many women would like the advantages of good looks but not the maintenance, and at least a dozen large categories of style (all of which are deemed beautiful by some and ugly by the rest) inform fashion. Seducer and seduced, leader and follower, provider and provided for, tough and weak, together and freaked are seen as more interchangeable now than could ever have been imagined. Since we've gotten through the worst of it, there seems no point in returning to the rigid gender stereotypes. Too many women, satisfied with neither yin nor yang, find themselves sometimes expressing one, sometimes the other, sometimes both at once. "I think of myself as feminine but not as a femme," says one woman I know. She told me that there is now a formulation that lesbians use to distinguish gender stereotypes in women: top and bottom. "So you can be a butch top or a butch bottom," she explained. Well, at least it's an attempt to put some contradictions togther. . . .

It's much easier to refer to women as having "become men" than to assimilate changes in our definition of womanhood. The crux of the matter is that women may not need men to survive, either economically or psychologically, and that is how we used to, at least in part, define being a woman. It is certainly integral to how we have traditionally defined romance. But why isn't it *more* romantic to think that a woman will need a man for many things beyond the granting of identity?

The idea of reforming what women need from men is so incendiary that it generates derision and hostility any time it is invoked. It is, for all practical purposes, forbidden, which leads one to wonder, *what is so taboo here?*

Which horrible taboo are we talking about? I would like to propose, as the only candidate up to the task, the one and only, the Oedipus complex. Except for penis envy, probably no famous

Freudian idea is less in fashion among Americans than the Oedipus complex, not so much because its veracity is in question (the original myth still has enough prestige to take care of that) but, on the contrary, because it has been so overexposed. Even psychoanalysts, in very large numbers, have come to prefer concentrating on issues of separation and individuation in the early, so called pre-oedipal phase. But still, I think that some of the old-time neuroses survive. If they no longer have a starring role, it is not because we repress them in a classical sort of way but because, in our therapy-obsessed age, we have grown so jaded that we feel entitled to ignore them. It seems more urgently needed to access, say, our chic newfangled sense of cyberfragmentation, our much-noted attempts to obviate our spiritual aimlessness and tend to our narcissistic deficiencies, a.k.a. self-esteem problems. Now, self-esteem—there's our kind of issue. And yet it seems to me that much of the family-values brouhaha results from the idea that, at least symbolically, the contemporary unmarried woman violates every rule governing the indispensable sublimation of the oedipal taboo.

Skipping over the basic plot, with which I assume everyone to be familiar, let us recall that the little boy's fantasized oedipal resolution is straightforward. When we come to girls, however, the plot thickens. To begin with, a little girl's oedipal-stage crisis is actually her second experience of rejection: The girl's first overwhelming yearning to merge is not directed toward her father but, like the boy's, toward her mother—thereby condemning her to not one but two major erotic rebuffs before she even hits primary school. But at oedipal-crisis time, while little boys start out by fantasizing that they will defeat Dad and then end up striving to become big strong men like Dad, the girl-child idolizes her father and is malignantly jealous of her mother. Her principal task then, in her resolution of the oedipal crisis, has traditionally been deemed to be entering into an identification with the mother. This was infinitely more problematic than the little boy's assignment. After all, he had a clear separation from his mother. (And for good reason: He fears he will be castrated if he continues to harbor even the fantasy of being so close to Mom.) Plus by separating, he got to emulate the most powerful, "complete" person in the house. It was this, arguably, that inclined the little girl toward the vulnerability and masochism that was the traditional woman's legacy to her daughter. The only way to emulate her mother was to accept the idea of replacing her as someone always lacking the means of independence, always remaining incomplete. The ensuing conclusion was that only by sharing a man's power would one acquire power—traditionally symbolized by the phallus.

Here, just to avoid any old controversies, let me hasten to add that I am referring not to an actual penis (which girls may or may not envy) but to the phallus—the possession of which, in our culture, endows power, autonomy, mastery, triumph, and grandeur, and which, according to fact or legend, we all, men and women, envy, fear, and admire. Indeed, these days girls and women are thought by many theorists to possess no more or less penis envy than boys do. And rather than speak of girls' "castration anxiety" psychologists are careful to refer to "female genital anxiety."

According to Freud, when little girls realize they don't have a penis, it causes them to turn away from their mothers and toward their fathers. Initially, what they want—like little boys—is to have Dad's penis. When they discover that that isn't possible, they substitute the desire for a baby—that is, they move from desiring the father's penis to desiring the father's baby. Eventually, the insistence on the father is sublimated by marrying a Daddy doppelganger, at which point the little girl finally gets the role she has always wanted: that of her mother.

However, if the little girl suffers not from penis envy/castration anxiety but from female genital anxiety, which analysts often attribute to the child's discomfort and guilt at the pleasure she may derive from her own body, then she is not "incomplete." And neither was her mother. And neither must she be in the future, whether or not she becomes a mother.

The modern single woman's most profound transgression is that she refuses to replace her mother, and even worse, she refuses to adopt as her own her mother's stated ideal. Her fate is to not end up (at least not permanently) with the Daddy doppelganger. She is not "missing" a part of the body that can only be replaced by a baby. She doesn't share (or she survives losing a share in) a man's phallus or even his penis. And here, depending on your politics, you have a choice between conjecturing that part of what women have accomplished in this century is to at least be allowed to struggle to have their own phallic power (the job, the money, the independence, the belief in oneself, the clout, such as it is), or conjecturing that twentieth-century women's greatest accomplishment is to manage very well in less aggressive, more womanly modes. Because what has really happened is that women now can indeed have it all: the phallus, the womb, the sperm, the baby, the job, the home, the works. Or none of it, and still be a woman.

I would like to propose that today's single woman is, in fact, not abandoning her mother's goals, but on the contrary fulfilling her mother's fantasies—though these may have been unstated or even unconscious. These are not fantasies to be a man, they are fantasies to be a different kind of woman. In other words, in the parlance of the times, you might term them *Beyond Penis Envy*.

But it turns out not to be so easy to lose faithful old baggage like the concept of penis envy. Not so fast! More than sixty years since Karen Horney suggested that it would be more accurate to speak of female genital anxiety, penis envy is still invoked to explain the single woman's psychology! In a 1991 paper on depression, Dr. Charles Brenner, one of the most prominent and respected American analysts, former president of the American Psychoanalytic Association and of the New York Psychoanalytical Institute, describes a case involving a thirty-three-year-old unmarried woman who sought treatment for "unhappiness and lack of career direction." The patient, it is noted, had been bypassed in the family business on behalf of her brother. Dr. Brenner writes as follows:

> The patient's envy of men and her unconscious anger at every man for having the penis she so envies and wished for did not prevent her from enjoying sexual relations with men. It did, however, make it impossible for her to be happy with a man or to marry one. Marriage had the same significance for her as did her menarche. It meant being irrevocably a woman. To remain unmarried meant, unconsciously, to be a man, a gay blade with a stable of sexual partners to pick from and to exploit for her pleasure. To marry meant to be castrated, as numerous dreams and associations made clear.

And if women become "like" men, what could the men become? To be fair, everyone was freaked out by the masculinity problem, including women, who had made the same erroneous assumption as everyone else: that men are strong. When women admired and sought to emulate certain male traits, *the fantasies women had of the men they would have have been were the very same fantasies men had!* The final fake out is that the kind of men everyone dreamed either of having or being, never existed at all. Honor, discretion, restraint, strength, emotional freedom. They were qualities that in the end were not all that accessible to anyone, at least not in that idealized form we fantasized. Or, on the contrary, both men and women have a right to them. We don't have to lose the male ideal. We can share it.

But that would entail giving up the woman-image we love. We're all afraid, men and women, of losing the woman ideal we've been raised to desire, and we may uncounsciously fear that freeing women from their pain—indeed freeing them from their masochism—will cause the vision of femme loveliness to flee forever from our contemporary lives. Why do we see pain and womanliness as inseparable? "Some women consciously set out to wound their bodies," writes Louise Kaplan in *Female Perversions* in a passage about the "innocent-sounding diagnostic label *delicate self-cutting*." She goes one, "These exceptional cases of deliberate self-inflicted mutilation give us a clue to what *might* be going on beneath the surface of our everyday acts of beautification, *when* and *if* those behaviors are aspects of a perverse strategy designed to keep unconscious the anxieties of abandonment, separation, and castration that might otherwise become conscious and unbearable."

We needn't worry. Getting rid of castration anxiety and altering what we mean by male and female doesn't imply that we'll get rid of women's masochism all together. Unisexual piercing, tatooing, and scarification, so much in vogue lately, is sufficient evidence that any and all genders can provide these dynamics. Perhaps nothing ever really disappears; it's just that the categories get reshuffled: good-bye penis envy, good-bye castration anxiety, hello female genital envy.

In an essay entitled "Beyond the He and the She: Toward the Representation of Masculinity and Femininity in the Post-oedipal Female Mind," Dr. Donna Bassin argues that, on the contrary, the post-oedipal female allows herself to "play out masculine aspects without there being a threat to her core, primary feminine identity, and has linking rather than prohibiting cross-gender representation. . . ." Hence, women will behave in ways that will cause some people to say that they "are" men. But, says Bassin, "This state does not reflect a denial of difference; rather it reflects a psychic organization that uses symbolization to play with difference."

"Play[ing] with difference" can refer to the clothes you wear or the way you talk; it can mean getting the partnership at the law firm *and* keeping a sense of humor. Already, many young women have grown up taking this particular integration for granted. In school, they play the same sports as boys, they're urged to develop an interest in mathematics. And if they can "play with difference," cheating prohibition, they don't have to project all "masculine" traits onto their boyfriends, keeping only the feminine as their lot. Therefore, they hope to fall in love, but they don't expect to be treated badly.

This is the very relationship that adult women would like to have. When I asked, "What is your ideal relationship?" no one—not one single person—mentioned a conventional marriage. Whether or not some had in mind fantasies that they would not articulate is not excluded as a possibility here, but the way in which they answered shows at the very least what they want to appear to be thinking. There was a good deal of unacknowledged fantasizing at the other end of the spectrum, I daresay, the sort of material bobbing around in every woman's psyche that remains inadmissible even in these putatively liberated times, except occasionally as a joke. Even a joke, of course, is an audacious departure if your fantasies are what some prefer to think of as "male"; for example, sex—or a lot of sex—with someone you don't necessarily wish to see in another setting, or spending a night with a lifeguard or, needless to say, all manner of one-night stands. But whether these things are mentioned or not, I suggest we take them for granted; every woman can imagine herself in a wedding gown, and no woman hasn't wanted to make love with the lifeguard. But then what?

One particular fantasy was often expressed: an affair or a marriage that does not necessarily include day-to-day life. Instead, you spend some moments together, a few nights a week or a few nights a month or a year. The idea is to enjoy the relationship but not be oppressed by it. In other words, it is a fantasy in which men and women are free to keep one another company, have sex, have fun, have friendship, consistency, loyalty, and also keep their freedom. Perhaps *this* is Free Love—the real thing—not safety, not money, not "permanences," only companionship and love and, ideally, charm in one's life.

The novelty of our situation has not diminished love's power to transform us. On the contrary, we are if anything more malleable, more subject to change, better able to pass through the metamorphosis it offers. And therein lies a future for women we find hard to imagine in all its splendid voluptuousness: a romantic life that truly expresses the architecture of a woman's emotions. How would it look, such a relationship? It would be a marriage to the world rather than a compact with one person. One can't even conceptualize it. One has to change enough to imagine it. Perhaps that's what all this change is leading us to: more change. Perhaps the noisy and disquieting uncertainty of this era is precisely designed to prepare us to withstand mutation, perhaps the transition is *about* change. And for all that we may be sentimentally attached to the past, we have no choice but to change if we value life even if the confusion gets worse instead of better as our twentieth-century gender categories melt, stream, and flow into the future.

I realize that many people would say that they don't believe in the oedipal, neo-oedipal, or even post-oedipal constructs, but I believe that you could take these themes up again and perform your own analysis from any number of other points of view—object relations, interpersonal or self-psychology, Jungian and neo-Jungian, cognitive psychology, eastern formats, mystico-poetic constructs, and even Christianity or Marxism. The motif stays the same: change and adaptation, death and renewal.

I am aware that many, many women would read these words and be totally outraged. "All fine and good," such a woman might say, "but I'd rather have a boyfriend." I would like to posit that a woman can be married to the world even if she has a boyfriend. Indeed, eventually, a woman could be a bride of the universe even if she already has a mortal man as a husband. After all, men have had these double lives for centuries, so why shouldn't we, if we care to, if we must?

This is the exact opposite of what marriage has provided for

women: protection from the world. Historically, a woman's relationship to the world depended upon a man for access, definition, and
legitimation. So there is, in this unmediated closeness to the Everything Else, a certain romance, and also an intimation of wholeness
much needed to counterbalance the stereotypes of oddness, one-
ness, of isolation or exclusion. Rather than think of the single
woman as quarantined from the normal and desirable world, we can
envision her as, on the contrary, more integrated, more securely connected to her environment. And when we talk about liberty and
autonomy in the context of women's lives, what we are really talking
about is the enlarged psychic space that belongs to those women
who can make use of it. This explains the wide gamut of judgments
on the single woman. From one extreme point of view, she is merely yet another oedipal loser. From the other, she is bold and impressive, gifted with a stout heart, a strong spine, and an artist's
spirituality.

There are those who would vehemently protest that the stout
heart and spirituality of the single life are very laudable, and thanks
but no thanks, they would rather have the marriage, the home, the
sex, the security. But this choice, if it is one, expresses not just judgment but also character. "I prefer this," is what the single woman is
saying. However frustrated the women I talked to may sometimes
feel, I noticed that many were, as a matter of course, engaged in an
extraordinarily creative solitude. Beyond loneliness there's the possibility of a rich interior life. It seems to me that single women have
a possibility of being ultimately less literal, more transcendent. "I
think that it's hard work, and you might be more inclined to try it if
you're single, if you're by yourself," one woman said to me about the
very idea of a spiritual journey. You might say that single women
have become reluctant mystics. Unwilling though they may be to
relinquish the worldly, many find themselves taking introspection
and even meditation, official and unofficial, for granted. They have
the advantage of being, as one woman put it, "most available to what
you see and hear."

It's not only women who are oppressed and tormented by their
own expectations of relationships, it's men, as well. To be single
means to break the pattern—that started somewhere in the beginning of time and seemed until recently to have no end. All you have

to do is listen to a fight between man and wife, between parent and child, and you hear what Selma Fraiberg called "the ghosts in the nursery"—the parents' parents and *their* parents' parents. While all about us, experts of every stripe decry the weakening of the marriage bond, very little praise is heard of the coincident weakening of the once inevitable cycle of dominance and submission.

True, once the dominance and submission judo hold of the classical couple was somewhat loosened, men and women stopped evolving in tight formation. They once had been totally in sync—or so it felt when people fell in love—keeping perfect pace in their social and psychological evolution. This served the purpose of the couple, which, it is fair to say, was principally the purpose of the man as head of the family (and included the support and protection of wife and children). Was the unity worth it?

Once women felt entitled to act in what they saw as their own best interest, the paths began to diverge at a wider and wider angle. Late-twentieth century rate of change being what it is, everybody went into Mach III speed, trying to adjust to the (supersonic? electronic? quantum?) speed of the new environment. Women moved fastest, making up for lost time, perhaps. In some areas, men and women lost track of one another entirely. If we ever had the time, there might be some interesting work to be done in consciously attempting to resynchronize. Already there are attempts here and there in the culture at large, like *You Just Don't Understand,* a work on gender and language by Deborah Tannen, or the popular Dr. John Gray's *Men Are From Mars, Women Are From Venus.* Of all the scenarios that might send the pendulum back, reversing some of the forces that have led to the demographic phenomenon of the single woman in this country, the most promising possibility is of resynchronizing. But perhaps it's too old a metaphor, for the mechanical age is far, far behind us. Perhaps we should hope and strive instead for improved parallel processing. Who knows what the possibilities are or how far-fetched?

Most mysterious of all, perhaps, is the fate of single women with no children. In many instances, their relationships with their family of origin, their lovers, their friends, and their friends' children are marvels of originality and adaptation. It is a group that is impossible to characterize: Some see themselves as having a mission, while others lead frivolous lives, while yet others bemoan their fate. But it's not just other *people* they have unique relationships with; it's also, potentially, to beauty, art, love, and the possibility of living a compassionate life. A woman who remains unmarried and childless by choice must go through a psychological rite of passage to a different consciousness. The kind of spiritual retooling, such a woman undergoes cannot but turn out to be of some interesting benefit to society in some other manner, as well. Already, many of them are artists, doctors, legal-aid attorneys, psychotherapists. Though perhaps, as Louise Kaplan suggests in *Female Perversions* in her discussion of Joan Riviere's "Femininity as Masquerade," they need to sacrifice themselves to prove their femininity. Perhaps, indeed, women will only find new ways to be "incomplete" in this incompletely perfect world. But even so . . .

Whether they are completely solitary, they have families, they are in between marriages, or they are convinced that they will never marry, it seems clear at least that, for some, there are great adventures ahead. For all of our problems, it is beginning to seem likely that there will be more and more women who are able to feel both autonomous and complete. It won't occur to them not to be strong. They will need love, of course, and most will want warm connections, but it is becoming evident that the closeness and communication and love one has with one's friends or one's children or even one's causes are fulfilling in a particularly intense manner when you don't have to provide the immense absorption required by a traditional relationship. There are other meanings to be found, and they are no less moral, worthy, idealistic, or even romantic, if it is meaning that we need. As for the rest, they'll have to improvise. When it comes to love, sex, and status, nothing's ever all said or all done. Once we've noted the big themes, it's the specificity of each place, each time, the ambience, the detours, the details, that glimmer with undiscovered meanings and possibilities.

AN IDEAL RELATIONSHIP

I said I wanted to hear either realistic possibilities or sci-fi inventions. For once everyone had a similar fantasy—what one woman called "a sexy friend."

BLANCHE W., who told us that her cats required too much intimacy.

My ideal relationship? *Oy.*

Weekends only. OK. Maybe one or two nights during the week to just collapse together. Speaking optional. We have separate rooms, so there's no complaint, or maybe separate apartments, adjoining apartments, so there can't be any complaints about my mess. We both can initiate sex and respect each other's yesses and nos. Much as I would get terribly jealous, I still would want us both to be committed to our individual growth as well as to our connection. I would want both of us to be able to have adventures while remaining somehow magically secure in each other's love and respect.

I'll be single forever.

ELLEN P., the textiles curator, often finds herself at lunches and parties surrounded by people she'll never see again.

It certainly wouldn't be sci-fi. It would be like any good relationship you've ever seen, except they're few and far between. I guess it would involve quite a lot of freedom and quite a bit of independence. Either a large piece of real estate or separate houses. I don't think I could live with anyone in the same house anymore, cooped up. I was always impressed with friends of my parents who have two separate bedrooms. And when I was old enough to get it, I thought, *Of course they did; they could afford it.* It might be utopian, but it doesn't involve any kind of futurism in terms of technology. It would involve a lot of money, which may be sci-fi for me to think about at this point.

But that's my fantasy. I imagine somebody who I'm sitting around with, and I'm reading a book and he's reading a book, and we don't have to talk to one another. I know there are marriages like that, but I've never met the person I could do that with.

MARY ANN B., who took her vacation in Mexico this year, with her former husband of nine years ago.

My ideal relationship would definitely be that I'd still be in my own house and so would he, and we would spend weekends or nights together when we felt like it, but I'd always have my own nest to return to. I absolutely love living in a place that reflects my preferences. Like how it looks. When I'm conscious, that is. And I also love having my own sleep-wake cycles. Which is interesting because I found that being in a couple the question of "When are you going to bed?" had lots less to do with sex than behaving like what we both felt would be a normal person: you sleep at night, you get up in the morning. I mean, the great part of divorcing, I discovered, was making all your own decisions about what to eat, when to go to bed, how you should behave with the kids. And once I started making my own decisions in all those areas, that's when I discovered really what kind of person I am. And it's different than the married one. . . . I prefer the single person.

I find that since I became single, the workload has increased, but the level of comfort has also increased—I mean the level of comfort with these decisions.

CALLIE S., 57. She was at times tempted to remarry but "never came close." She shrugs now as if the answer to my question is easy.

Some nice, smart guy with a funny mouth. Interested in some of the things I'm interested in, me interested in some of his things. A little travel together, a movie—"You want to see this? I want to see that. You don't want to see this? Okay, I'll go with my friend instead."

Heterosexual, please God. There hasn't been one of those in my life in I can't tell you how long. I don't want to be married in the married sense. I carry this fantasy along—that sometimes I sleep at his house, sometimes he sleeps at mine, but we don't live together, not a twenty-four-hour relationship. I couldn't do that anymore. I don't think.

Listen, though, if the next time my door bell rings it's Sean Connery, you can cancel this whole conversation. I'm flexible—nothing if not flexible.

ALEXANDRA R., 28, says she'd like company, but doesn't have time for a full-time affair.

It's called a Boston marriage. You live together, but that's it. I think there have always been these relationships that weren't sexual. . . .

Well, the sort of relationship I wouldn't mind at all having with a man is where you're living together and have the intimacy of living together, but you get your own bed! And can sleep together some of the time. . . . As I'm saying all this I'm realizing . . . I was really, really in love with somebody last year who I never got to sleep with. Sort of what I'd think about as I'd be sitting up in bed, reading before going to sleep is how nice it would be to have him lying there on his side reading. So there it was. I did fantasize about having sex, too, but it was the companionship that I really wanted. Not that I don't think about sex or miss it, but that kind of companionship I do really miss. I don't know how I would feel about dealing with all the stuff that comes with it. But I would very much like to have that helpmate. I just feel the buck stops here for everything—the car has to be taken in, the taxes have to be done, the bathroom, all that stuff.

PHILLIPA C. is seeing someone, and I notice that she is talking about a real-life lover rather than a fantasy. She recently turned 50.

It's clear to me that what I am really looking for in a relationship is someone who loves me so much that it heals all my childhood wounds, and the fact that a relationship like this doesn't exist does not deter me to continue to look for it. Through three marriages.

I picture "fear of intimacy" as a code word for "fear of lowered expectations." A real relationship is very different from an ideal relationship, so I don't even know what I'd settle for. Nothing that I've found so far.

What I'm thinking about in middle age is that all my life I thought of men as providers of certain things—money, social status, marriage certificates, children. As a very young child I was aimed to get what I needed socially from men, and for a long time I did that and it worked. I mean, men do provide those things. But now, in middle age all the things I thought I was going to get from men, I have. So I kind of have to reinvent the idea of an ideal relationship, and as far as I've gotten—which is not far—is that I want somebody who . . . I want a companion. That sounds so horrible, doesn't it? It sounds like I'm an old person. I want a friend. I want a sexy friend. And for me the struggle of relationships—maybe you could think of a phrase for this: a postmarital relationship, a relationship without any of the old ideals or the old structures—where there is no reason to have the relationship except the other person, your feelings for the other person. And it may sound incredibly stupid, but I would like to say that all my previous relationships with men have been influenced if not determined by these other things—this desire to be Mrs. Someone or the girlfriend of someone or the desire to have another child or the desire to be married. So it's very hard to have a relationship without any of the old reasons. But I think if you can do it, it's great because it's really just about two people instead of being about society.

You know, when I got married for the first time the minister convinced me to get married by saying that marriage is a public affirmation of a private feeling. And the minister said to me, "Don't you want to join society? Don't you want to take this public? Don't you want to become a citizen, so to speak?" and I said, "Yeah!" And that was what it was about. And now I'm going the other way; I'm in a relationship that goes from public to private because, socially, I'm done.

My ideal lover . . . Let's see. He makes me laugh. He's a good friend. Incredible sex. Oh! I mean! I have to say that for me, discovering sex outside the structure of what society expects from a man and a woman has just been a revolution. What are we going to call it? It's like starting from scratch. There's a lot of sex, a lot of companionship, and I guess what I'm looking for also is being with someone who allows me to see myself in new ways. The Twilight Zone, when women do all the things they're supposed to do, you know?

IN AND OUT OF SYNC, ON AND OFF THE CHART

Marginality and difference.

SUSANNAH W., now in her late 40s, was punished as a child for spending too much time in what her father called "fantasyland." She said she figured out she doesn't need a man's permission to get on with her life.

I always tried as hard as I could to be normal, to be part of a couple. That's why I got married twice. Instead of ambition, I tried to
go for normality. Now I don't. I feel independent of that. I think
maybe it's because being single is an experience that's happening at
the right time in my life. The previous times I've been single, it was-
n't the right time. There was something off, you know, the way
sometimes people say they were born too early or too late. I feel I'm
in sync now.

PAULINE M., 33, the art director, seems anxious.

I do feel optimistic about my future. Or it depends on the day,
maybe. If I'm feeling depressed and low . . . I half expected to get
less vulnerable as I got older. And I feel the opposite happening. I'm
more vulnerable, more frightened, more worried about things: burn-
ing houses, airplanes. . . . I want to become less frightened. I get this
feeling that my fears become this cross to men. I feel like I can hear
them say, "I admire her, but she's so fucking neurotic, I can't touch
her with a pole." That worries me.

**ROSA M., like the other women in the office, wears faux leop-
ard, plenty of eye shadow, lots of blond hair. But there the
resemblance ends.**

I don't have that much in common with my co-workers. I'm the
oddball over there. I don't know exactly what it is, but I can see how
it manifests itself. Starting out the day, eight o'clock in the morning,
they all go in the coffee room, and they talk about what was on TV
last night—they watch the sitcoms—so it's "Oh, did you see so and
so . . . ?" and on and on. Or there's a lot of men bashing, that's another favorite. Like, "He makes me so sick; he sat in front of the TV and
let me do all the work." There's one girl . . . all she talks about is sex;
she talks about it to the degree that there is no limit. And that gets
all the other girls going. I mean, if you think there's something that
you couldn't say, she will push it even further than that. And the rest
just love it, they encourage her, and these girls . . . over the lunch
table they tell everything that they do.

They're all either married or they're living with someone. So they're
in there for an hour in the morning talking about things that I'm not
interested in. Not that I'm not interested in sex, but not like that.

Yes, I do think they're angrier at men than I am. Sure. And then they tease me because, I'm like a nerd, or they'll say, "You know it's the quiet ones who are the more adventurous. She's probably got more stories than we do. Come on, you can tell us." And, "Mum's the word." Or, "Are you going to be in our club?" Because when they went to Cancun they had T-shirts made that said Men Are Pigs. I still have mine. It was abbreviated "MAP." And then it had a picture of a pig with a circle around and a line through it. So everywhere we went, people would come up and say, "What does that mean?" And no matter if it was a man or a woman, they'd say, "Men are pigs." And if it was a man, he would just kind of back off.

Anyway, they try to get me to say if men are pigs or not. And I say, "Well, first of all, I don't have one." And then I say, "To tell you the truth I love men." And then they say, "Oh, get out of here," and that I'm just saying that to blow their minds.

Are men pigs? Well, I've seen a thousand instances where they were. But I still don't want to say that all men are pigs.

BERNICE D., a teacher and writer, has recently found herself asked to appear on panels and contribute to roundtables, with incongruous frequency, on the subject of homosexuality, which bears no relationship to her specialty.

Why haven't they figured out I'm heterosexual? Because I don't have any of the insignia. I don't have a husband, or a boyfriend, or a beau. I don't have children. I'm a feminist. I'm an intellectual. So I'm queer.

Would you like me to tell you my poem? I thought of it the other morning as I was lying awake at five A.M. It's very simple: Heterosexuals think I'm homosexual / Gays think I'm straight. / Queers think I'm omnisexual. / No wonder I can't get a date.

I looked up "queer" in the recent queer theory of writing, to try to explain to my class what it means, because queer has traditionally been a term of opprobrium that many activists, writers, and thinkers have reappropriated as a term of liberation, turning prejudice back on itself. So I've been thinking about the many meanings of queer. I privilege marginality and difference. Queer is the new bohemian. It really is. And that's actually why they think I'm gay.

FEMME TOPS, BUTCH BOTTOMS

The mix-and-match aesthetic.

CLAUDETTE M. introduced me to this terminology.

I don't think of myself as masculine at all. There's a whole discussion in lesbian circles now that's very interesting about the whole idea of butch and femme and so on. And I always felt very alienated by this discussion. I'm not an expert on this but my notion is that the butch is butch and the femme is very feminine. And I think of myself as feminine but not as a femme. And, also, now there's a new thing which is called top and bottom. So you can be a butch top or a butch bottom. So I would kind of say that I'm a femme top. Of course, then I get confused because I get attracted to men. But I'm definitely irritated by people wanting to classify me. Of course, I haven't slept with a man in twenty years, but I do get attracted. It's not from not wanting to, it just doesn't work out.

MARGUERITE M., the Florida widow in her late 60s, is exasperated by the clichés.

Masculine? I don't think so. I know a lot of single women, and I don't think they're masculine. In fact, several come to mind who are excessively feminine. They just reek of it. And that cliché about having to be both mother and father to your kids? I hate that cliché. Because I don't think you can be both. I know I couldn't be a father.

JOCELYN H., whose marriage was fine until she got pregnant.

I've heard people say I'm overwhelming, I'm powerful, I'm intimidating. I really don't see myself that way. I don't know what it is that's intimidating. I don't see it in myself. Maybe I am, but I don't see it. I don't know what I do. I'm very up front with people, I say what I have to say, I speak my mind. I feel that's the way it should be. I think that's what some people say is very overpowering. But what am I going to do, stand there and lie to them?

CHRISTINE L., the Washington lobbyist, who reminded us that

most of the men in powerful positions have wives and children.

It is interesting, as a woman in a sort of high-powered professional situation one of the difficulties is that you cannot behave in a way that is eroticized in any way, and yet in the rest of your life you might want to do that. This is, you know, what we are; we're men and women, but because of the power difference with men, if you act "like a woman," . . . it's not good. You lose power, you lose position in your interactions—with men, that is—so you can't do it. And yet in the rest of your life you might be perfectly willing or desiring to be seen that way.

The fact that you're charming and entertaining and pretty, that should be something you can use in life, not something that's bad.

You're much more likely to find the support to do that as a man than as a woman. The breadwinner role supported by the non-breadwinner role is a societally more comfortable position for everyone involved. I'm not saying I want to be the man in the relationship as we view these relationships. I'm saying I wish there was a man who would do that for me.

BLANCHE W., whose mother's career was stunted by marriage.
I think it was very clear to me growing up that I didn't want to be a girly girl. I didn't want to be a housewife. I wanted to be one of the people I found interesting at my parents' parties. And for the most part the conversations that were interesting were the conversations men had. But when I was a little older and my mother got her Ph.D., she started having couples over in which there were these really cool women. The women might have been sixty-five . . . classics professors who'd written loads of books or doctors who were tops in their specialities, and they weren't talking about diapers or what so and so wore to shul. You know, they were alive, and their eyes were alive.

I had known that I would have to work and support myself because I knew I didn't want to be supported by a man and let them have the kind of power that I saw my father had over my mother. But I really also didn't like that whole decorative female thing. And yet from a very early age I was always worried about other people's feelings. And this is what would be traditionally considered a female character trait—though of course the reductionistic male/female model makes me want to throw up.

The other thing about male/female is it took me a long time to figure out that one of the reasons I didn't have recognizable sexual fantasies is I couldn't get into being the object of people's attention. Yet I can imagine doing things to the other person, and I get turned on by the idea of being active. That's why I can only watch male gay porn. I mean, I haven't seen much female gay porn that's well done. But the male gay porn thing that's great is that they both can be active agents of desire. They can have sex without either of them being denigrated by it. Obviously there are some scenes that aren't that way, that are power plays, but at least some of the time they're both having sex, they're both having fun, and no one seems to be getting badly abused or debased. The other thing is that then I don't have to worry about the porn star, the female porn star, and how badly she's being abused. For whatever reason, *The Story of O* and . . . all that doesn't turn me on. I'm much more likely to be turned on slightly at least by being a dominatrix.

It's a real struggle to figure out how can I say yes without saying no. Just like for a two-year-old, the only way to claim themselves is to say no, I can only have a good time in sex if I'm saying yes, like I'm initiating. It's very easy for me to lose that feeling of agency. It's partially power, but it's also being centered. And that scares a lot of guys.

ELLEN P. refers to herself as being "of a certain age" but looks younger.

I think women are much more porous than men. And I do think my boundaries and sense of self . . . are stronger in that sense, and that I'm more . . . "masculine" in that sense. But I don't feel this makes me very happy, even though I might be more confident than I was. I am more confident than I was. But I wish that confidence wasn't translated again into some idea that . . . I want to be in control, or that I want to have authority. I just have it because I had to have it. And I think there's part of me that always wants it gone, you know? *Please, take it away, take it back!*

I think I would love it if I were with somebody whose life were as complex and fluid as mine is, and wanted to have a relationship that was based on common explorations but not on domesticity. I never thought domesticity was an interesting thing. I thought of it as the enemy. I still think it's an enemy. It's part of our being continuously confined to the most sentimental side. This has never interested me as a topic, or subject. It's one of my fights to have to make up a way of being that has a full or erotic expression, a sense of myself as less the mother, the wife, but more the lover, really. It's almost as if you say that your desiring is as important as your being desired. And women should be allowed to do this without feeling that they are being subversive. And that's not allowed because women have to be in the object state.

LAUREN R. talked about a new resident at her hospital. He's 25.

He came over Tuesday night to talk about these new drugs that are about to be released. I keep thinking, *Will I be able to make a pass at him?* But it feels so grotesque, and God forbid I do this thing that would be violating him, and I like him but I'm aware of this ulterior motive. He doesn't even know. . . . I feel like a dirty old man.

PAULINE M. is one of the many women who mentioned that her life had been tremendously affected by how many men were "taken out of circulation" because they turned out to be gay.

They didn't use to think of themselves as gay . . . especially the men that we found appealing because they were interested in music and literature and not just watching sports on TV. They didn't feel like men-men. In our generation, those are the ones who decided over time that they were gay. What's interesting is that the youngest generation accepts bisexuality again. Among people in their twenties there's much more experimentation and fluidity in terms of sexual orientation. But for our generation, it was liberating to suddenly be gay. And then that all got coded as just being afraid of coming out of the closet. So the irony is that Harvey Fierstein, who wrote *Torch Song Trilogy,* says, "Yeah, I'll believe in bisexuality when I see a gay man hiding an affair with a woman." And that's exactly what happened to me. I had an affair with someone who was living with another man, and he kept our relationship hidden. It was the heterosexuality that became illicit. In a different day and age . . . certainly in the 1920s or something . . . we would have been married.

We might have stopped having sex, but so many married couples don't have sex anyway that what difference does it make?

GINGER G., 34, a landscaper, becomes very exercised when asked about whether she is ever told she is intimidating to men.

And sometimes I look at my friends like that and see how they don't say things because they occasionally appear smarter than their husbands or they pander to them all the time. And I won't do that. For the moment I just don't feel like I need to make those compromises. I mean, if someone said to me, "You know I like you, but if you would just do this thing or that thing . . . " I mean if it was something completely reasonable, all right, but . . .

I asked someone recently, "Do you think that I give the message to men that I'm not available? Do I turn them away somehow?" And this one guy who was married, he said, "Well, I think that you're intimidating to men."

And in sort of a soft, demure voice, I said, "Why?" And he said something about how I always say what I want to say. I can't be with someone I have to watch my mouth with. Or anything like that. Not be me. I can never . . . it always ends up leaking out of me sideways.

RAFAELA'S SUMMER

An entirely different experience of love.

RAFAELA Z. fell in love last spring. And although she doesn't feel the romance has a future, she finds her interest in men renewed.

And I think it's permanent, in so far as anything can be permanent. But that's a whole other story. I'm fifty-two years old. I just said to my shrink this morning, "It's the height of arrogance that I want to meet a man now."

I had an entirely different experience of love. I would ultimately say I felt sixteen or twenty-two. But also I should say that we didn't actually become lovers. Which was fine. I mean, it wouldn't have been permanently fine, but it felt like the right process. And so, the desire I felt . . . ! I kept imagining what it would be like to make love with someone whom I had gotten to know. But also when I would know that I was going to see him, I had this kind of . . . I'd be laughing inside. . . . I just had this kind of delighted anticipation. Which I'm sure also had something to do with being at this time of life, having turned fifty, and here is this man halfway through his fifties, and we've each had a great deal of life. I mean, he said that once. We had a conversation sort of at the beginning, and he said, "Well, we're both rebuilding our lives." There was this sense of both of us having gone through all this pain and agony and now we can have some other kind of relationship. But I think that's very hard to do. It's very hard not to be defeated by the old projections.

I was so scared, too. I was scared of . . . Well, I now think I was just scared. At the time I had a million different things. . . . I was scared because it was a man. I was scared because his marriage didn't seem quite over. I was scared because he was someone who had so many things I wanted, and I was scared I wasn't as interesting to him as he was to me. And it was so tender it just completely broke my heart. And now I feel kind of insane because I don't feel it will really happen.

I do feel we were defeated by projections from the past, the fears, the old paradigms closing in. And then sometimes I think, well, that even if it were over, it would have been worth it. But also that it's either over or this is the crisis. . . . like in *Persuasion*; you know, it's the eight years when Anne Elliot is suffering away and Captain Wentworth is totally gone and . . .

It's strange how immediate it seems to me. I had this feeling for quite a while at the beginning that I was making it up, but then it became clear that I was not. Now several months have gone by.

How did solitude seem afterward? I had a great summer, even though I was grieving. When I figured out that the marriage wasn't quite over, his marriage, and that his wife was around, and there was all this gossip, I made the decision not to see him, and I made the decision not to see a lot of people. I simply stopped answering my telephone and made my movements erratic and saw very few people and confided in very few people and found out that I had a self and a life. And I was also in grief but I was able to . . . move on, you know. In a funny way it's because I allowed myself to have those feelings for him, I allowed myself really to feel it and say yes, I was in love with him; yes, I am in love with him; yes, this moved me very much; and yes, I'm very sad and isn't it a glorious summer? And then I had to do a good deal of traveling for my work, and I relinquished myself to that. So that by the time the fourth month came around I really felt free.

And then I went to a party and I saw him. And he was so funny. He said—it was a big party, a big space, a lot of people there, and people who knew what was going on were trying to either keep us apart or observe what we really did, and I tried to walk through a door where I knew he'd be, and he just played the scene perfectly. He said, "Oh, it's been a long time. Where have you been?" And I said, "Prague, Montana, here . . . " So that was kind of flirtatious and decorous. And at the end of the evening I went over and said, "I've just come to say good night." And he said, "How are you?" And that was a different kind of conversation. And then I just left, and I just knew that I wasn't . . . well, that we weren't finished in some way. So then I had to recapitulate the grief. All in one evening, I had the honeymoon and then I had the grief.

But I decided that I could call him, and we could talk, and I felt sad but I didn't feel angry or blame him. In other words, I felt equal, or separate. So that's the state it's at. I sort of left him a message saying I would call again because I didn't want to have to wait for his call.

I've never been so happy as I was in those weeks. It's really true. It's so pathetic. It's just who I am, you know? I'm just not able to be kind of cynical and half way. So I always get hurt. People say, "Oh, I don't want you to get hurt." And I say, "Well, how else do you do it? Love hurts. I mean, it doesn't always, but I don't know how you do it without that risk?"

Oh, no, I haven't done anything self-destructive. I've done that so much that I couldn't do that again. But I'm quite heartbroken. I just think it will mend, and I'll go on to the next part.

Therapy? Oh, yes, I've been doing major surgery in the therapy department. Major surgery, really. Organ transplants and liposuction. You know . . . Bones reset. Cracked and reset. Repositioned. No, no brain surgery—no, not lobotomy.

The important thing is that I had an entirely different experience of love. I couldn't believe it. Let me try to describe what it felt like.

It felt like . . . like a kind of layer between my skin and my spirit. That sounds abstract, but it was very concrete. It was just this kind of little sneaking-in heat or . . . it also could have been some kind of little opening. And I was . . . I kept thinking, *Can this really be happening?* because I did feel, *If this doesn't work, I'm just going to be dead.* And it was a real transaction because I still have the feeling it left me with.

And when I saw him, I just felt everything again. Not in the movie scene but in the second scene when he said, "How are you?" He said . . . "How *are* you?" He always had this particular way of saying "How are you?" which was this particular signaling of the deeper level, and I had a way of saying, "Fine," which also communicated all my layers, too, and then I had this tremendous feeling because I was with him and I had been missing him so hideously. But it wasn't that feeling of an amputated limb had been missing, which is the feeling I'd had in the past with lovers.

So you can imagine I have this tremendously vulnerable feeling about it because I opened myself up in a way that I can't shut down except without hideous cost to myself—which I am not willing to do because that's the whole change in me. And I saw it as a kind of restoring of some essential part of my femaleness that was long lost. Really long lost. And hope. A kind of feeling of hope that was also long lost. And if I shut it down, the cost would be too great. But walking around feeling like this . . . Anything I do now is a kind of risk.

THE LAST WORD ON SOLITUDE

Losses and unexpected pleasures.

LISA C., 33, who has such painful family memories, says she finds that she's been feeling all right lately. About the rest she'll see.

Well, what happens when you get to the certain point inside you that is really the right place to make those decision from . . . something happens, and you . . . The right person comes along, who says the right things to you, something happens, and slowly but surely you do make up your mind and it feels right. But I think that in order to get there, you have to have a certain kind of clarity.

FELICIA C. When I asked her if she thinks it's true that women living alone have greater access to a spiritual life, she laughed.
    Well, or a pet . . .
    Yes, I do believe women are able to do it, but it's so difficult to connect with that part of yourself. I think that it's hard work, and you might be more inclined to try it if you're single, if you're by yourself. And it also requires some hope. So if you get the inclination to work and the hope at the same time, then it can be extremely successful.

RENNIE N., the composer and piano teacher in Cape May.
    These very powerful issues of solitude are not particularly identified with women. They're kind of religious-ascetic issues. A certain sense of sacrifice of some things, like in regard to children. My worry about being with a man is that I'll lose a certain kind of concentration. When I think of traveling alone, it's always very lonely and very bleak, but it's also an extremely rich situation. There's something about being stripped down that makes you also the most available to what you see and hear.

AMELIA J. was reluctant to answer my questions about her spiritual life. I said, "All right then, but can you speak of hopes and dreams?"
    Well, of course, having come from this secular Jewish family, I would be kind of embarrassed to talk about spirituality. Someone might say to you that I am a very spiritual person, but I don't really know what it is. I do like sitting, doing Zazen. For twenty minutes you sit with your eyes closed, and you follow your breath. And when it's done, you can still feel terrible, but you feel very clear. It's like psychoanalysis—basically what happens is that it opens you up to yourself. It opens your defenses to your feelings, and you feel much better even if nothing much happens. You feel clear; it's a wonderful thing.
    Hopes scare me, or at least saying them out loud does; they feel very secret and private. I think you'll have to ask someone else about

hopes. As for dreams . . . I must say I wish I had happier dreams, but in fact most are at best enigmatic, if not disturbing.

Maybe single women can get more spiritual because they don't need to distort their personalities in order to stay in a relationship. But there is another distortion or something in the personality due to the absence of a relationship. There's a place in myself that I don't inhabit, which doesn't develop, and that is the place of . . . shall we call it "intimacy"?

SALLY H., now in her early 40s, founded and runs an on-line server.

You know how, if you make yourself do it, you work really well when you haven't had sex in a while and you absolutely must have it? It's like that. I have definitely begun a transfer of feelings about romance from men to life. It's relatively recent or, rather, my awareness of it is new, so I am not sure how well I understand it yet. I really would rather have a husband but I don't, so I have to live instead. Wait, that's not quite right. . . . Let's say it this way: that longing and energy have to go somewhere, so they go into a romance with life.

BILLIANA M., 52. She's finally settled in her new home—a small apartment, but she says it really feels like her own place.

Would I marry again? I would. It's a possibility, put it that way. I've sworn nothing off. But it would have to offer me something that's far better than this, and this is so damn good—the sense of self-possession, the sense of intactness.

I feel as if I have had a very satisfying long-term relationship. I've had a family and still do. I've had a full-blown, overt, active sexuality. And if none of those things are part of my future, so be it. I adore solitude on a regular basis; I need a dose every single day. What I have now that I've never had as far back as I can remember is that I don't feel I'm in basic life-and-death survival mode. It's just so much more mellow.

Sometimes we're on the light side, and sometimes we're on the dark side. I've finally cut myself a break. I am entitled to a space just because I'm here.

EPILOGUE

As I was ending work on this book, and until the very last possible moment, I continued to interview single women. While I concluded the final tasks of readying the manuscript, proofreading, checking statistics, I was still working my way down a list of people who had promised to be available around deadline time, in case of gaps that had to be filled in. For instance, it's just in the last few days that I spoke by phone to Annette F.—who had originally described herself as a wife and mother "fallen off the grid" in the two years since her marriage broke up—and she announced, "I'm involved with someone!!!" And, only yesterday, I learned that Billiana M.'s mother had a stroke and will be coming to live with her. (You may remember, she used to give Billiana, fourteen and pregnant, icy stares when she was living at home and finishing ninth grade.) Marina T.'s husband has now been dead two years, and though she did not mention him when we last talked a couple of weeks ago, she described fall in northern Massachusetts, how beautiful and painful it is. Susannah W., who rewrote *Little Women,* before her father took her desk away, has recently won her field's equivalent of a Pulitzer prize. She says it's too late for her to have children now, "but I'll be a fantastic aunt." The other day, Reah S. showed me of a photograph of herself holding her sister's baby, smiling broadly—she, not the tiny baby—so I guess that she, too, may turn out to be a fantastic aunt.

Anita S. went to Romania and brought back a little girl, whom she named after her grandmother (the one in the dream, who always wore wonderful colors). Anita just recently went back to work and could only communicate with me by answering-machine messages—all of hers left in the characteristic hushed voice of a woman desperate not to rouse a toddler in repose. And just a few hours ago, I got a call from Cathy D. Her baby-sitter was sick, and she was in the midst of an important meeting—did I know of anyone available for two hours starting in twenty minutes?

As for myself, I am hastening, for the preschool day ends any moment. I can imagine how much hasty work is done between mid- and late afternoon on weekdays by mothers whose young children will soon be released, shouting with the pleasure of liberty, ready for kisses and hugs and snacks and the playground, their metabolism revved up to go, go, go. The egregious haste characterizes just about all mothers these days, but the single mothers I know are breaking all the normal human speed limits.

Early one recent morning, I bumped into Phillipa C. on the street. I almost didn't see her, as I was rushing back home from taking my son to school. I was wearing a raincoat over my nightgown. "I feel like an escapee from *Diary of a Mad Housewife*," I said. She had on an extremely natty black double-breasted suit and seemed more in line with the cast of women executives in *Network*. "I'm rushing to a meeting," she said, "but then I'll be switching costumes and doing your part." Phillipa who—you may recall—had fallen in love with someone she met in AA and kept saying, "This can't be happening; it's too good to be true," is no longer in the relationship. "It *was* too good to be true," she said. What's more, one of her three ex-husbands is suing her, she told me. Before I had fully expressed sympathy, she had dashed off into the drizzly morning.

Just this week, I've spoken with Amelia, Andrea, Jane, and Martha, among others. Molly's mother, Jean, told me yesterday that she was upset because Molly was having trouble adjusting to a new teacher this year. On the other hand, Jean has got a new job she likes much better than the last (the last time I talked to her, she told me, "I'm so depressed about my work situation, I can't think straight") and the top person at the company is a woman, who undoubtedly has a different view of child care issues that Jean's previous employer.

There are several women I haven't spoken to since the interviews, and I wonder about them. Is Megan L. more cheerful? Is Evelyn B.

still working behind the screen in the dining room? I ran into Monica V. once, and she clearly was a bit surprised at how warmly I greeted her: Our talk was already in the past for her, while I still "saw" her every day, in these pages.

The problem is: I hate to say good-bye to the characters who have been my companions on this journey. There are so many of them, and the project has lasted so long that sometimes I imagine them as fellow guests on a big cruise ship. When I need an answer to a question, I go to their staterooms to ask it. Lately, I keep picturing them all together, as if in a chorus. I think it should be a chorus in an opera, since that was my initial image for relationships: grand opera, filled with passion, lust, intrigue, artful dominance and submission, and painful third-act curtains.

Perhaps the metaphor comes to mind because my mother was once an opera singer. She will soon be celebrating her ninety-second birthday—she was merely in her early eighties when the Belgian professor you read of wooed her with untoward alacrity, and she suggested he take a Valium. Lately, though she is less besieged by official suitors, her physical therapist told me he has come to rely on her for inspiration. He has her walking on a treadmill now, for a minute or two at a time. In the two and a half years that have followed an operation, she has gone from wheelchair to walker to cane and soon expects to walk unassisted. "I am nearing my liberation," she says. I overheard my son asking her if he could keep the cane, and she agreed. Luc took some of his very first steps holding on to the cane, and he's not quite taller than it yet.

There were several friends of my mother's who were interviewed for this book, and they have been among my favorite subjects. I have taken to inviting them to my home for family celebrations, however, so I see them from time to time, and therefore I am fortunately in a position to remain a sometime confidante in matters of gender relations. My favorite model for December romances is Mrs. Valentine J., whose lover, you may recall, came to see her every weekend for many years and seemed to have the patience of an angel. Alas, not long after our interview, I heard that Valentine's lover had become ill and died, and she was going through a very bad period. I spoke with her on the phone. "Yes," she said, "it's hit me quite hard," her voice emptied of the play and vitality I had become accustomed to. "Quite hard." I didn't know what to say. What can you say at the end of such an affair—no doubt her last affair? I thought of how much trouble we go to, how much work and pain and planning in relationships between men and women, and then one day, one of you dies, anyway, and, as Pagliacci would say when the final curtain descends, *La comedia e fini.*

But some time afterward, I had the pleasure of seeing Valentine again, at my mother's birthday party, where a number of octo- and nonagenarian friends were in attendance. Two years after our interview, still perfectly coifed, still showing great legs and wearing exquisite shoes, Valentine had recently celebrated her own birthday—her ninety-fourth. "Yes, I've gotten myself back," she told me when I complimented her appearance. Later, she drank a little champagne. "And if you meet any men," she told her friends, "let me know if one of them is looking for a girlfriend."

The young woman who told me that she thought her mother's single-women friends were "pariahs" was recently married. So was Sabrina F., the producer, for the fourth time. Amelia J. is no longer seeing the European friend whom she so enjoyed kissing in the taxicab. Eileen Y., the watercolorist who couldn't get herself to tell her brother-in-law he was clueless, has won a number of other prizes and awards, and as I write, an exhibit of her work is going up at a major museum.

Jocelyn H.'s son almost joined the navy, but he's decided instead to go to college after all. In any event, he's leaving home, soon. Lucy L., who told us that she could never live without a cat again, is moving soon to a smaller apartment: Her oldest son moved out with his girlfriend (they just had a baby), but she's in a bit of a jam because her youngest son, who had moved out, has now moved back in. Of her cat, Lucy says, "It's amazing; he's now an old gentleman and has to be taken care of all the time." On the animal front, there was a great deal of activity: Old cats and dogs died, new cats and dogs were born and adopted. Psychotherapists came and went. Some of the women got off of antidepressants, others got on. Pauline M. (who had told us she worried that she was becoming more vulnerable), went into a psychiatric hospital for a while, but she is now out. Martha H., when I called for an update, had just learned from her gynecologist that she was parimenopausal. ("How am I? I'd like to get hit by a bus so I could lie down for two months. How's that?") A number of women went on hormone replacements, and no one that I know of went off. How many other women have gone on or off of diets, I don't even want to think. Notwithstanding the statistics for good health among single and divorced women, there has been illness and quite a bit of surgery. The endocrinologist, Blanche W., she of the lamas and the Tantric cybersex, recently underwent a hysterectomy, and then while not yet recovered she broke her arm. She's spending time at home reading and dreaming, and says, "I feel I'm at the beginning of a new phase." Amazingly enough, as far as I've heard, none of my interview subjects for this book has died, I'm glad to report.

So it's unreasonable, I know, that I should feel so heavy-hearted at parting from them in the frozen form that they will soon assume on the printed pages of this book. But I have found them so *interesting*. There were only a couple of nasty moments (Evelyn B. telling me she felt no kinship to childless women, the aforementioned young woman informing me that single women are revolting pariahs). But for the most part—and this is one of the discoveries, for me—these "tough" and "strong" women are remarkably tender, for all that they are also so often funny and quick.

What's more, their stories continue to fascinate me. That's at the root of the problem, I think: It's impossible to get any closure here because the stories go on, playing off of the old and new stuff of life. And as for the others, even though I must relinquish adding their voices to this book's chorus, some of the untapped prospects have stayed as clearly in my mind as if I already knew them and had written down their stories. I didn't get to call the television-news producer I was introduced to at a party, one of the most beautiful women I've met, whose passing remark appears in the first chapter of this book: "I don't even put down 'divorced' when I'm filling out forms," she said while she was scribbling her phone number down for me. She would love to talk, she told me. There were dozens of women whose names I had been given by someone who knew someone who knew someone, because they had an interesting life or were known to have well-defined opinions on this subject or were deemed to be a good storyteller, whom I haven't had a chance even to call. A number of the women I interviewed at first were already my friends, but I soon felt a real bond even with the ones who came to me via someone who knew someone who knew someone, or those I met by chance at the gym or on line at a movie theater. My very first idea for this book—that single women really could be a constituency if they only saw themselves as having much in common—would come back to me as I spoke to women who were far from my experience and who said many of the same things I had felt or heard from others over this whole decade.

Just today, I spoke to a woman I'll call Katie K., a financial consultant at a large investment firm. Her office is in the Midwest, but she has a southern accent. I didn't ask her where she was born, however, since I was trying to keep our conversation short. She was a Catholic—a devout one who goes to Church and believes in the classical sense—and I thought it would be interesting to get from her some succinct remarks regarding the spiritual life of single women. A paragraph or so was all I wanted, and I had planned to keep our conversation brief. Nevertheless, she began, as many of my subjects did, at the beginning, as though if she was to tell me of her current spiritual state she would have to explain how she got from there to here: "My life has always been kind of chaotic. My mother died when I was twelve, and I had four younger siblings, three brothers and a sister. . . ."

Half an hour later we were still talking, and she had just told me of the last serious relationship she'd had, which ended when she discovered he was lying to her. "Since then, I date, but I've been celibate," she told me.

"How is that?" I asked.

"You know, actually, it isn't too bad. Sometimes it bothers me, but I'm getting used to it. It's been almost eighteen years! I have so much stuff going on in my life, and it's not at the top of the list. One of my priorities is helping other people, and that's more important. And work keeps me busy. Certainly my social life keeps me busy enough."

Eighteen years! What strange lives we women have. "Do you like sex?" I asked.

"Yes," she said. "Oh, yes, very much. But I believe in remaining celibate at this point. I haven't met someone with whom I would care to share that aspect of my life with. Why? I think it's because internally, that is just how my heart feels. It doesn't have to do with logic; I've never really been in love with anyone again to share that with. I've dated a lot, but I haven't had somebody I would love."

I asked her what her ideal relationship would be. "I don't care anymore if he's the best-looking guy in the world," she said, "because I know too many guys who are great looking, but they don't have the personality. So it would be the personality. The ability to laugh and to be laughed at. Someone who would accept me on my own terms and wouldn't try to change me. Because I'm not the changing type. Unless, of course, I *want* to change."

I pointed out many people would say that she is living "like a man" and asked if she agrees.

"No," she said. "No. I feel like myself. My house is very feminine, I think, the way I have it decorated. I mean, it's overly overly . . . It's not sparse by any stretch of the imagination. I would say it's feminine. . . . I don't know how else to put it. Of course, I have so many things lying around everywhere. I'm home for lunch and I'm thinking, *Oh, my God, I have so many books!* I don't know where to put them; I am going to have to go out and buy another bookcase I think.

"Do you have nice sheets?" I couldn't prevent myself from asking.

"Oh, yeah," she said. "Of course! I have really nice sheets, and I buy new sheets once a year whether I need them or not. Usually I go to Penney's, and I buy the Egyptian cotton sheets. I like 'em! I get the two-hundred fifty or the two-hundred eighty count, you know?"

A few days ago, I said good-bye to Janie A., who is moving to Hong Kong next Monday with her formerly married lover. He and his ex-wife came to an agreement. It was she who told us she was afraid she would be bored if she ever got to live with her lover, so I'm curious to know the outcome; perhaps things will get magically easier, once they're away. I wonder if she, too, will turn out to be a fantastic aunt, or if she'll decide, after all, to be a mother.

She's the only one that I know of who went as far as Hong Kong, but there were plenty of other moves. Regina M., who had the dream of finding the bigger room in her house, moved from the country to the city, at least temporarily. Linda P. moved from Seattle to L.A. Tammy F. moved from L.A. to San Francisco. Mary Ann B. moved from Connecticut to New York to Oregon. She, who had remained celibate for six years, confided that "love and sex had made a spontaneous comeback." She was in a wonderful mood. Just before leaving town, she dropped in at my son's third birthday party, bringing a very handsome man with her. I didn't get very much time to talk to him since he was soon in an intense and long conversation with Valentine J. It was a good party, I think, and Luc certainly was thrilled with the Thomas the Tank Engine decorations, the presents, and the festive gathering of his friends. "I'm big, big, big," was his characterization of his present status, and he learned to hold up three fingers to indicate his third birthday.

It's so odd for me to realize that this book was begun long before he was born. The other day he told me that, yes, he did plan to get married some day and wanted six children—half boys, half girls—and he would do "all the work." He didn't get the idea from me; perhaps he learned it at school from one of his teachers or one of his little preschool girlfriends. (*La comedia non e fini.*) Of my mother's other friends, Ida R., who is now blind, couldn't come, because she had a previous engagement (she is still very much in love). But in attendance were Beatrice H., the one who told us she once gave her heart away for good, and Rebecca S., who has taken up the piano again lately and who is still redecorating her apartment.

ACKNOWLEDGMENTS

The heart of this book is the women who talk in it, and although the details that might reveal their identities have been changed, I hope individual voices can be heard here in all their tenacity and humor. From beginning to end I was struck by how magnanimous my subjects were in talking to me about their lives. Very busy women gave me a great deal of time. Very private women confided their ideas and their secrets. They were invariably willing both to laugh at themselves and to speak from the heart. I will always be grateful, moved, and inspired by them.

Some of the essays and articles I have written over the years were the forerunners for this book in content and in tone, and I would like to mention the generous and talented editors who collaborated with me on these pieces. In 1979, I wrote a first-person essay on friendships between gay men and straight women for *The Village Voice* that was published as "Odd Couples"; the idea was Susan Lyne's, then managing editor. In 1980, *New York Magazine* senior editor Nancy McKeon assigned me an article that ran under the title "Mid-Life Maternity Blues." In 1981, I wrote a piece—part prose, part monologues—about a group of women friends for Clay Felker, who was then editing the Manhattan section of the *Daily News*, which turned out to be so long that, even though it was edited down to a fraction of its original size, it was published in daily installments over the course of a week under the umbrella title "Ladies Night." (The full version was published in the mid-eighties in a collection, *The Dog is Us*.) In 1987, "Double Trouble," a humor piece about the problems of pair-bonding organisms, ran as the first in a series of columns I wrote for *New York Woman*, Betsy Carter's magazine. In 1989, I worked with Patricia Towers at *Mirabella* magazine on editing down to an almost manageable length a marathon round-table interview with six single women that was published under the title "Sex in the Age of AIDS." In 1990, Judith Daniels, then at *Glamour* magazine, asked me to write an essay that was published under the title "Childless and Second Class." It's surely a sign of the times that not one of these editors is still with the publications mentioned above. Nevertheless, these memorable companions have stayed with me, at least in spirit.

Jo Bonney, Susan Chace, Marilyn Johnson, Adam Moss, and Caroline Tiné all read parts of this book and made suggestions that were enormously helpful. Marilyn Sides read every chapter two or more times and helped me solve a number of bedeviling structural problems—on one occasion confined in my home as my house guest, for which she should be given a Martyr to Writing medal, at least.

I offer special thanks for aiding and abetting, for conversation and inspiration, for tips, sources, information, and education, to Peter Dunn, Lee Aitken, Mary Kay Blakely, Susan Cheever, Ken Corbett, Michael Cunningham, Muriel Dimen, Lois Draegin, Scott Bedson, Rochelle Feinstein, Nancy Gengler, Ivan Goldberg, Greg Grove, Dalma Heyn, Anat Hoffman, Peter Minichiello, Cathy Nonas, Sue Shapiro, Carolyn Specht, Milton Swaby, and Ofelia Zapata. I have also benefited from the help of a number of institutions and groups. In particular, I would like to express my gratitude to the Corporation at Yaddo, to the members of the Zulu conference on the on-line service echo, and to the members of the group that met throughout the years of the Bush administration under the name of New York Women Against Right-Wing Scum.

I am grateful for the diligence and intelligence of the transcribers and researchers who worked with me: Chris Bagley, Pat Braus, Leesa Chalk, Ephen Glenn Colter, Lisa Feder, Maya Gottfriend, Sabrina Meah, Amanda Murray, Victoria Robinson, Lisa Specht, Judd Stark, Paige Williams, and, especially, Madeline McIntosh.

As I was ending work on this book, I benefited greatly from the help of several professionals. I would like to thank Amy Finnerty for the tremendous contribution of her research assistance, Dale Evva

Gelfand for her sensitive and precise copy editing, and jacket designer Carin Goldberg for her dedication and her powers of invention.

Amanda Urban of International Creative Management championed this project from the first mention of it some time in 1990. She urged me on when I stalled trying to write the proposal for it, and nearly a decade later still sustained and voiced her enthusiasm. I am most grateful for her loyalty to it and me.

Gerald Howard, of W. W. Norton, has been steadfast in his commitment to this book, and every aspect of the final product has been influenced by his passionate engagement with the subject and with these women's ideas, and by his belief in the material's possibilities. I thank Jill Bialosky, Louise Brockett, Eve Grubin, and Cathy Melnicki of W. W. Norton for their generous help and forbearance.

The Improvised Woman and I will always be indebted to the talented Heather Ramsdell, whose assistance, industry, and wit made the completion of the work possible.

The two persons who most eagerly awaited the conclusion of this work and who must be credited with urging me most eloquently to press toward the finish line are my mother, Chaja Kleinwecksler, and my son, Luc Leon Clements.